Narratives of Academics' Personal Journeys in Contested Spaces

Also Available from Bloomsbury

Narratives of Becoming Leaders in Disciplinary and Institutional Contexts,
edited by Anesa Hosein, Namrata Rao and Ian M. Kinchin
Academics' International Teaching Journeys, edited by Anesa Hosein,
Namrata Rao, Chloe Shu-Hua Yeh and Ian M. Kinchin
Early Career Teachers in Higher Education, edited by Jody Crutchley,
Zaki Nahaboo and Namrata Rao
Cosmopolitan Perspectives on Academic Leadership in Higher Education,
edited by Feng Su and Margaret Wood
Dominant Discourses in Higher Education, Ian M. Kinchin and Karen Gravett
Creating the Desire for Change in Higher Education,
edited by Didi M. E. Griffioen
Learning to Lead for Transformation, Emmanuel Ngara
The Educational Leader in a World of Covert Threats, Mike Bottery
Leading Educational Networks, Toby Greany and Annelies Kamp
Strengthening Anti-Racist Educational Leaders, edited by Anjalé D. Welton
and Sarah Diem
Race, Education and Educational Leadership in England, edited by Paul Miller
and Christine Callender

Narratives of Academics' Personal Journeys in Contested Spaces

Leadership Identity in Learning and Teaching in Higher Education

Edited by
Namrata Rao, Anesa Hosein and Ian M. Kinchin

BLOOMSBURY ACADEMIC
LONDON • NEW YORK • OXFORD • NEW DELHI • SYDNEY

BLOOMSBURY ACADEMIC
Bloomsbury Publishing Plc
50 Bedford Square, London, WC1B 3DP, UK
1385 Broadway, New York, NY 10018, USA
29 Earlsfort Terrace, Dublin 2, Ireland

BLOOMSBURY, BLOOMSBURY ACADEMIC and the Diana logo are trademarks of
Bloomsbury Publishing Plc

First published in Great Britain 2023
Paperback edition published 2025

Copyright © Namrata Rao, Anesa Hosein and Ian M. Kinchin and contributors, 2023

Namrata Rao, Anesa Hosein and Ian M. Kinchin and contributors have
asserted their right under the Copyright, Designs and Patents Act, 1988, to be
identified as Authors of this work.

For legal purposes the Acknowledgements on p. xvii constitute an extension
of this copyright page.

Cover design: Grace Ridge
Cover image: © baona/iStock

All rights reserved. No part of this publication may be reproduced or transmitted in
any form or by any means, electronic or mechanical, including photocopying,
recording, or any information storage or retrieval system, without prior
permission in writing from the publishers.

Bloomsbury Publishing Plc does not have any control over, or responsibility for,
any third-party websites referred to or in this book. All internet addresses given in this
book were correct at the time of going to press. The author and publisher regret any
inconvenience caused if addresses have changed or sites have ceased to exist,
but can accept no responsibility for any such changes.

A catalogue record for this book is available from the British Library.

Library of Congress Control Number: 2023939234.

ISBN: HB: 978-1-3501-9695-7
PB: 978-1-3501-9702-2
ePDF: 978-1-3501-9696-4
eBook: 978-1-3501-9697-1

Typeset by Newgen KnowledgeWorks Pvt. Ltd., Chennai, India

To find out more about our authors and books visit www.bloomsbury.com
and sign up for our newsletters.

Contents

List of Figures	vii
List of Tables	viii
List of Contributors	ix
Foreword *Tansy Jessop*	xiii
Acknowledgements	xvii

Introduction to Leadership in Learning and Teaching in Higher
    Education within Contested Spaces   1
    Namrata Rao and Anesa Hosein

Part 1 Navigating Leadership in Marginalized Spaces

1 Growing into Antiracist Leadership in the American Context   17
    Laurie L. Grupp

2 Establishing Leadership Integrity in Learning and Teaching as a
    Professor   33
    Susannah Quinsee

3 Developing Higher Education Pedagogy as a Pioneer   49
    Mari Murtonen

4 A Leadership Journey in Change and Uncertainty   65
    Jeni Fountain

5 Participative Leadership as an Early Career Academic   81
    Andrew Kelly

6 Clarifying the Fuzzy Lines of Programme Leadership   95
    Patrick Baughan

Part 2 Engaging Values, Resilience and Serendipity in Leadership

7 Towards a Community for Teaching Excellence at a Research-Intensive University 113
   Stephanie Laggini Fiore

8 The Need for Time and Space for Leadership Development in Learning and Teaching 129
   Hannah-Louise Holmes

9 An Accidental Journey towards Educational Leadership 147
   Leopold Bayerlein

10 Valuing Collaboration in the Leadership of Learning and Teaching 163
    Sandra Jones

11 Our Journeys through the Scholarship of Leading: What Matters and What Counts? 179
    Wu Siew Mei and Chng Huang Hoon

Part 3 The Future of Learning and Teaching Leadership

12 Towards an Ecological Perspective: Reflections on Leadership Journeys 197
    Ian M. Kinchin

Index 215

Figures

6.1	Core components of programme leadership	99
10.1	Conceptual collaborative *leadship* ecosystem for learning and teaching	173
12.1	The adaptive cycle	199
12.2	The relationship between leaders (●) and team members (○), conceptualized as linear (A), networked (B) and ecosystemic (C) arrangements	206
12.3	A typology of narratives	208

Tables

0.1	Contributors and Their Contested Contexts/Spaces	8
3.1	Development of Finnish University Pedagogical Education and my Personal Career Path since the 1970s	57
9.1	Personal SWOT Analysis	157
12.1	Threshold Concepts in Leadership for Sustainability That Have Consequences for Leadership Roles	202
12.2	Summary of the Themes and Subthemes Relating to How Healthcare Leaders Developed Organizational Resilience during the SARS Crisis in Singapore in 2003	204

Contributors

Patrick Baughan is Head of Education at the University of Law (ULaw) in the UK. He holds affiliate roles for both the Society for Research in Higher Education (SRHE) and the European Educational Research Association (EERA). He has previously held positions at Advance HE (UK), University College London (UCL), City, University of London, and the University of Leicester. He has published widely in areas including sustainability and environmental education, assessment and feedback, educational integrity, and qualitative research approaches. His PhD focuses on sociological perspectives about sustainability in higher education curricula. He has significant leadership experience, having led programmes, institutional initiatives and multi-institution collaboration projects. He is a Senior Fellow of the Higher Education Academy (SFHEA).

Leopold Bayerlein is Associate Professor in Accounting at the University of New England, Australia. He has a PhD in accounting and is a CA, CPA and Senior Fellow of the Higher Education Academy. His research aims to enable future graduates to provide meaningful contributions to global societal challenges through developing frameworks that embed holistic educational principles in the Australian and international university environment. Leopold's teaching focuses on financial accounting for both undergraduate and postgraduate students in a face-to-face and distance learning environment. He has received numerous institutional, national and international awards for his innovative use of technology in teaching.

Jeni Fountain is Faculty Dean of Health, Education and Environment at Toi Ohomai Institute of Technology, New Zealand. She manages a diverse, multi-levelled programme portfolio that delivers to a wide geographical region. Jeni's career started in primary and secondary school education, across both teaching and management roles, before moving into the tertiary sector. She is a beginning researcher with an interest in change leadership that improves staff and student outcomes. Jeni has previously owned and operated hospitality business and is a practising lawyer.

Hannah-Louise Holmes joined Manchester Metropolitan University, UK, in 2005 as Associate Lecturer and progressed to Head of Department in Accounting, Finance and Banking. In this role, held since September 2018, she has responsibility for over 1,300 students and 45 FTE staff. She has oversight of undergraduate, postgraduate and collaborative programmes and leads her academic team, supporting them to develop their teaching and research activities. She also manages department projects to achieve institutional targets, such as greater international student numbers and improved graduate outcomes. At faculty level, she is leading a strategic project to address the awarding gap.

Anesa Hosein is Associate Professor and the Head of Educational Development and Research at the University of Surrey's Institute of Education, UK. Anesa is interested in how marginalized identities affect higher education participation both for students and academics. Her current research revolves around investigating migrant academics as well as student mental health.

Chng Huang Hoon teaches ethnography and leadership at the National University of Singapore (NUS), Singapore. She served as Associate Provost (2012–20) and has directed the Chua Thian Poh Community Leadership Centre in NUS since 2019. She was the co-President of the International Society of the Scholarship of Teaching and Learning (2020–1). Her current interests include thinking about cultural transformation, diversity and inclusion. Her key publication is 'Leading change from different shores: The challenges of contextualizing the scholarship of teaching and learning' (with Katarina Mårtensson and Brenda Leibowitz, *Teaching & Learning Inquiry*, 2020).

Sandra Jones is Professor Emerita at RMIT University, Australia, and Principal Fellow of the Higher Education Academy, UK, now Advance HE. Sandra has thirty-two years of experience in higher education and has been a formal positional and informal leader in learning and teaching at all levels of the university. She has been a leading innovator in learning and teaching design and delivery and is internationally acknowledged for her research into a distributed leadership approach for higher education.

Andrew Kelly is Manager, Learning Support at Edith Cowan University, Australia. In previous positions, he held teaching roles at Charles Darwin University, Australia, and Western Sydney University, Australia, both of which focused on developing academic literacy skills for first-year university students. He has also published papers in several journals related to teaching and learning, including the *Journal of Academic Language and Learning*, the *International Journal of Online Pedagogy and Course Design* and the *Journal for Teaching and Learning in Higher Education*. His current research interests focus on academic integrity and supporting diverse cohorts in transitioning into tertiary studies.

Stephanie Laggini Fiore is Assistant Vice Provost at the Center for the Advancement of Teaching at Temple University in Philadelphia, Pennsylvania, where she leads efforts to support faculty in implementing evidence-based teaching and curricular practices. Her current research examines how academics' role-identity frames their teaching decisions and ability to implement teaching changes. Stephanie has thirty years of teaching experience in Italian language, literature and culture, and pedagogy in higher education. She has previously served as head of the Italian programme and director of the Intensive English Language Program at Temple. Stephanie earned her PhD in Italian from Rutgers University.

Laurie L. Grupp is Dean of the School of Education and Human Development at Fairfield University in Connecticut, United States. Her research interests include bilingual special education, change leadership, educational development and reflective practice. In her faculty and leadership roles, she has engaged in efforts to promote diversity, equity, inclusion and racial justice, while supporting faculty in all aspects of their professional growth.

Ian M. Kinchin is Professor of Higher Education in Surrey Institute of Education at the University of Surrey, UK, where he is engaged in the professional development of university teachers. Ian has published research in the fields of zoology, science education and academic development. He has a PhD in science education and a DLitt in Higher Education.

Mari Murtonen is Professor of Higher Education Pedagogy and Director of the UTUPEDA Centre for University Pedagogy at the University of Turku, Finland. She is Editor-in-Chief of the *Finnish Journal of University Pedagogy*. Her main research domains are teachers' development of pedagogical expertise in traditional and digital environments, students' development of scientific thinking and research skills in university education, and conceptions, beliefs and attitudes on knowledge.

Wu Siew Mei teaches English language and communication skills to both undergraduate and graduate students. She is also Director of the Centre for English Language Communication, where she oversees the academic and professional development paths of a fifty-six strong staff force. Her research interest stems from related English-language classroom issues, including investigations into the nature of academic writing, objective testing in large-scale English language proficiency assessment and the validation of test descriptors. She has also recently published in educational practice and scholarship journals such as the HERDSA journal and the *Asian Journal for the Scholarship of Teaching and Learning*.

Namrata Rao is Principal Lecturer in Education at Liverpool Hope University, UK, where she coordinates the School of Education's postgraduate taught programmes. Her key areas of research and publication include (but are not restricted to) various aspects of learning and teaching in higher education that influence academic identity and academic practice. She is a Senior Fellow of the Higher Education Academy, co-convener of the Learning, Teaching and Assessment Network of the Society for Research in Higher Education, and member of the Research and Development group of the Association for Learning Development in Higher Education. Her recent publications include a coedited book *Early Career Teachers in Higher Education: International Teaching Journeys* (2021), published by Bloomsbury.

Susannah Quinsee is Assistant Vice President (Educational Development) and Director of Learning Development at City, University of London, UK. She leads the Learning Enhancement and Development Directorate, which encompasses educational development, technology-enhanced learning activity and academic skills. Susannah is a National Teaching Fellow (2011), a SEDA Senior Fellow and Advance HE HEA Principal Fellow. In 2017, she was appointed as a Learning and Teaching Excellence Ambassador by Advance HE to promote educational development. She is a Lego Serious Play practitioner and is undertaking research on playful leadership. Susannah has four children, including twins. She is continually reflecting on how to balance life as a working parent.

Foreword

Tansy Jessop

Stories are powerful. They unearth ideas lurking in the hinterland of our hearts and minds, playfully coaxing us to reflect on our own stories and shaping our understanding. Like a child at bedtime, our interest is piqued when someone says the words: 'Let me tell you a story…'. The title of this edited collection is arresting because it invites the reader to reflect on stories about their own and academic leaders' personal journeys. Significantly, the reader is invited to tune in to the personal narratives of leaders in a professional context where things are not simple, predictable or easy. These stories take place in a battle between the forces of competition, the market and metrics, and those of collaboration, participation and playful scholarship. Yet as you read this book, you will find that the battle is much less one between heroes wielding their swords to the death against villains than an epic tale about countering myths and reclaiming truths about the value of higher education as a noble educational endeavour. It is, as Ian Kinchin argues in the final chapter, an ecological challenge to find a sustainable model of higher education which cultivates a garden with seeds of care and resilience, while removing the weeds which threaten to crowd out delicate flowers fighting for air.

A good story weaves threads between the personal and the public; the private and political. In this collection, personal journeys intersect with professional stories, as academic leaders navigate different contexts, roles and dilemmas. Cecil Wright Mills speaks of the need for good sociological research to weave between the personal and the public, to avoid personal stories becoming narcissistic (Wright Mills, 1959). The anthropologist Ruth Behar argues that 'a personal voice, if creatively used, can lead the reader, not into miniature bubbles of navel-gazing, but into an enormous sea of serious social issues' (Behar, 1996, p. 14). This collection is an invitation to readers to engage in serious social issues about the purpose of higher education from the vantage point of eleven emerging and established leaders in learning and teaching in Australia, Finland, New Zealand, Singapore, the UK and the United States of America.

Anyone who has spent time in higher education will know that learning and teaching occupies an ambivalent space in the academy. Indeed, as the title of this book indicates, learning and teaching is contested: on the one hand, it is the bread and butter of universities, providing core funding, a reason for their existence and continuity of a research pipeline through educating generations of scholars; on the other, it is often seen as less prestigious and lower in significance than research. Promotions and university leadership roles have traditionally flowed to those with excellent research profiles rather than those whose eminence is in teaching. The introduction of teaching and research contracts, a move with powerful and even laudable drivers, has fed into the hierarchy and inscribed a perception that looks more like a divorce than a marriage between two complementary and equal partners. However, a fresh wind is blowing, with many institutions, like my own, working to re-balance promotions towards education. Indeed, I owe my own professional story to this zephyr, rippling gently across the UK sector (Denney, 2020).

'Navigating Leadership in Marginalized Spaces' (Part One) sets the tone with an opening chapter from Laurie Grupp at Fairfield University. Laurie's chapter uses a conceptual framework for antiracist leadership to develop a reflective approach to leading in the public academic sphere. She addresses the marginalized spaces of diversity, equity and inclusion and re-centres them at the heart of the educational endeavour. Laurie stresses the importance of authentic engagement, building meaningful relationships, humility, vulnerability and fear throughout her leadership journey. Her chapter underlines that leadership is always unfinished business yet needs the impetus of both intentional and morally grounded action.

Susannah Quinsee from City, University in London, explores her own personal journey as a 'third space' academic leader in educational development, playfully capturing the parity of esteem question in the title of her chapter: 'Establishing Leadership Integrity in Learning and Teaching as a Professor'. She challenges common assumptions about what constitutes a 'real' professor, including its gendered and academic practice aspects. Susannah suggests techniques for building credibility and authenticity as an educational leader, including the growing evidence base about teaching and learning. Shifting to Finland, Mari Murtonen provides a case study which builds on the idea of evidence-based practice. Nationally, Finland has placed an emphasis on research into higher education pedagogies to enhance the quality of education.

Leading in a context of change and uncertainty is the topical subject of Jeni Fountain's chapter about her leadership journey at Toi Ohomai Institute of Technology in New Zealand. Jeni describes having to take deep breaths and hold them in, within the context of externally imposed turbulence in the sector and Covid-19. Her chapter uses the concept of 'freezing' and 'unfreezing' to explore navigating changes. In it, Jeni provides insights from personal experience about how to recognize vulnerabilities and address them in pursuit of self-awareness and well-being.

Vulnerability can take many forms. Andrew Kelly's chapter homes in on his story of leading a large learning and teaching team as an early career academic. Most learning and teaching leaders have plenty of leadership experience and a strong academic profile to enable them to lead. How does a relatively junior academic step up to lead? Andrew argues that participative leadership with a team of professional services and academic staff at Edith Cowan University has enabled him to lead credibly and embrace the wisdom and contributions of his team. Andrew provides a guide to participative leadership and shares his strategies for leading using this approach. Hannah Holmes picks up the theme of early career leadership in learning and teaching later in the book, taking the perspective that interactions with mentors and carving out time and space to develop are important.

Perhaps the most pivotal yet fuzzy academic leadership role of all is that of the programme leader. The thread that holds together all university programmes is in the hands of the programme leader, often a rotating role, sometimes seen as a duty and a diversion from research, and most often a role best prosecuted more through influence than authority. In the final chapter, Patrick Baughan draws on his insights as a programme leader in three different universities to distil what it is that programme leaders do and the challenges they face. Patrick argues that the sector needs to do more to clarify ambiguities and consistencies about the role and provides several recommendations for making the most of programme leadership.

Part Two focuses on engaging values, developing resilience and taking delight in serendipity as part of leading in learning and teaching. Stephanie Laggini Fiore from Temple University makes a case for cultivating an informed teaching community. Its purpose is to bring joy in teaching, where the thought of teaching may otherwise spur feelings of trepidation and ambivalence. Stephanie's chapter encourages leaders to develop collegial networks to share powerful learning and teaching moments, nurture collective wisdom and counter the inattention to teaching perpetuated in some research-intensive university cultures.

In his accidental journey towards leadership, Leopold Bayerlein focuses on personal intentions, identities and personas as powerful devices for emerging leaders. In a complementary chapter, Sandra Jones, also in an Australian context, describes becoming a leader through Scholarship of Teaching and Learning and initially adopting a position-based approach. Through serendipity, Sandra comes to adopt a collaborative and distributed approach to leadership and offers a conceptual framework for distributed leadership in higher education.

Wu Siew Mei and Chng Huang Hoon draw on their experience of leading change towards a more teaching-centred culture at National University of Singapore. Their notion of the 'scholarship of leading' uses ideas about liminality, identity negotiation and networks as frames of reference for their efforts to influence culture change in a research-intensive university. They exemplify how to challenge an institutional culture through their new promotion policy which values education.

Ian Kinchin reflects on the leadership journeys reflected here in the final chapter. He proposes the heuristic of ecological leadership as a way of charting a future for learning and teaching in higher education, as a dynamic and adaptive form of leadership for turbulent times. Ecological leaders can help to cultivate sustainable educational futures, developing care and resilience in the destabilizing environment of higher education. In his chapter, Ian differentiates between a network and an ecosystem and applies ecological theory in the living laboratory of a single academic department.

I commend this book to you. It is a refreshing departure from a 'how to lead' manual for learning and teaching leaders. It calls to our own stories and poses questions about our identities as educational leaders, our influence and the impact of external factors on our approaches to leading. Many of the stories here reinforce the value of the collaborative practices which are at the heart of academic development. This book invites us to reflect on our own practice, to exclaim 'aha' as we recognize elements of our own experience, and to celebrate the joy and serendipity of encounters with leaders in the learning and teaching community.

PVC Education, University of Bristol

References

Behar, R. (1996), *The Vulnerable Observer: Anthropology That Breaks Your Heart*, Boston: Beacon Press.

Denney, F. (2020), 'Understanding the professional identities of PVCs education from academic development backgrounds', *International Journal for Academic Development*. https://doi.org/10.1080/1360144X.2020.1856667.

Wright Mills, C. (1959), *The Sociological Imagination*, New York: Oxford University Press.

Acknowledgements

This book has grown out of the conversations that the editors have had amongst themselves and with others on the challenges of becoming and being leaders in learning and teaching and the contested spaces within which this leadership often exists. Each of the individuals who participated in the casual corridor conversations on how learning and teaching leadership is fraught with challenges and is often seen as a second fiddle to research leadership has contributed implicitly to the conception of this book idea. However, we owe a particular thanks to Alison Baker, Senior Publisher, Education and Linguistics, who helped translate our sketchy ideas into a publishable book. She has been a pillar of support over the process of putting this book together during the challenging time the world was experiencing owing to the pandemic, which led to some inevitable delays. We would also like to record our thanks to Anna Elliss, Editorial Assistant for Education at Bloomsbury.

We are indebted to all our colleagues and friends who, in sharing their learning and teaching leadership journeys and how these have been influenced by their gender, race, position in the hierarchical order and the conceptions of teaching versus research, have disclosed fascinating insights into their experiences across many continents, including Europe, Asia, Australia and North America. We would like to express our collective appreciation to J'annine Jobling for her helpful comments on the final draft of the manuscript. In addition, we are grateful for the funding from Liverpool Hope University that supported the proofreading for the volume. We must each say a special thank you to our families for their patience and support as we pursued our intellectual project.

Introduction to Leadership in Learning and Teaching in Higher Education within Contested Spaces

Namrata Rao and Anesa Hosein

Background

Whilst much has been written about leadership in academia, this literature is often conflated with leaders who excel in research (see, e.g. Bryman, 2007; Dopson et al., 2016). However, less is known and written about leadership specifically in learning and teaching (Hofmeyer et al., 2015; Shaked, 2021). This may be owing to the contested space learning and teaching occupies with few opting to take these leadership position due to the rewards and prestige (or lack of) attached to learning and teaching leadership as opposed to leadership that rewards research. The various research excellence frameworks (such as the Research Excellence Framework in the UK and the Excellence in Research for Australia) have emphasized the importance of research often sidelining teaching. Where there are teaching excellence frameworks, these do not celebrate an individual's endeavour but rather a team delivering the teaching. The university league tables further exacerbate reliance on individual research excellence as opposed to individual teaching excellence, hence diminishing further the importance attached to teaching excellence and consequently the value of leadership in learning and teaching. The combination of these factors has implied that those who become or aspire to become learning leaders often occupy marginalized spaces. However, over the last decade, with the increase in teaching only roles, particularly in the UK, the United States and Australia, (Hosein, 2017; Locke, 2014; Probert, 2013), the likelihood of progression may be only within learning and teaching positions, if any.

Mindful of this growing breed of learning and teaching academic leaders and those with an interest in situating themselves in this field, a book capturing the journeys of those in learning and teaching leadership positions appears timely. Therefore, this book brings together narratives of individual academics working as learning and teaching leaders within their different country contexts, occupying various forms of contested spaces such as that owing to their gender, ethnicity, race and years of experience which creates different kind of challenges for their leadership and helps shape their leadership identity.

Why the Focus on Leadership in Contested Spaces?

Learning and teaching have often been considered second fiddle to research (see, e.g. Chen, 2015), therefore those occupying and aspiring for leadership positions within this marginalized space would struggle to access stories of success in such leadership positions and indeed journeys of those who have occupied such a space. Such stories may be valuable to learn from for those desiring to establish themselves as learning and teaching leaders in spite of all the counter-narratives. These marginalized leadership positions, owing to the unique identities of the leaders who occupy them, such as whether they are females, migrants, early career academics or any other such identities, may further compound the complexities of these learning and teaching leadership roles.

The personal narratives, in this book, provide unique perspectives on the sense-making of academics as they reflect on their learning and teaching leadership journey in different international settings and how these journeys are shaped by their contested identities and the marginalized spaces that they inhabit. Often such identities and spaces are not recognized in higher education which may lead to even more isolating and challenging leadership journeys. The chapters in this book seek to contribute to our understanding of the subjective experiences that academics encounter. Further, the personal narratives capture how these contested identities and marginalized spaces influence the learning and teaching leadership practices in various educational, cultural and national contexts. We now look separately at four marginal spaces that can influence leadership: gendered, colonized, positional and serendipitous. Whilst we adopt a rather simplistic approach in this chapter in considering one space at a time, it is to be acknowledged that these may be intersectional (Crenshaw, 1991).

Gendered Spaces

Whilst leadership itself is a contested space, the gendered identity of a leader may obscure this further. Departmental and university leadership positions are often occupied by individuals considered to require masculine traits and indeed are often occupied by males (Herbst, 2020). These leadership positions are occupied usually by male academics who have a strong research profile (Leišytė and Hosch-Dayican, 2017). The reason for this is that the majority of the teaching load is undertaken by female academics (Locke, 2014; Marchant and Wallace, 2013). For these female academics, the most likely progression route is expected to be within learning and teaching leadership positions. In response to our open call for contributions to this book, most expressions of interest came from female academics as opposed to male academics, which perhaps gives a further sense of the terrain more internationally. Much has been written about the challenges faced by women leaders in academia and their marginalization (see, e.g. Patel, 2018). This thus creates additional layers of tension and challenges experienced by learning and teaching leaders owing to their gendered identities and often becomes the bases for further contestation and marginalization as expressed in the narratives of some of our chapter contributors (see, e.g. Chapter 2 contributed by Susannah Quinsee).

Colonized Spaces

Higher education may reflect 'white privilege' and a colonized space, particularly with respect to ethnic and migrant identities. For example, often an individual's ethnic identity may be related to their migrant status, which, for academics, may have implications for their access to and success in leadership position. Hence, there may be a perception that if you are non-native, non-Western and non-white individual, your leadership and the 'funds of knowledge' you bring to the leadership position may be less valued (see, e.g. Arday, 2018) although this may be less of an issue if the academic has a strong research profile (see, e.g. Nachatar Singh, 2021). This is particularly true for pedagogic leadership as the learning and teaching practices of the Western world are often considered superior to those adopted in the non-Western world (see, e.g. Kinchin et al., 2018; Rao et al., 2019). Consequently, the pedagogic knowledge of migrant academics is sometimes less valued.

Leadership positions are very much 'colonized spaces' where the 'White Privilege' is commonplace (Bhopal and Brown, 2016); if you are a migrant from the non-Western world, your knowledge and indeed your leadership may be less privileged. When we consider the leadership of learning and teaching, this becomes even more complicated where the learning and teaching practices of the non-Western countries may be questioned for their legitimacy. There is an assumption that those coming from the non-Western world have pedagogical practices which are out of tune in the current/Western world. The teacher-centred pedagogy relying on rote learning is often looked down upon, and indeed a learning and teaching leader originating from such spaces is often looked as being someone who does not qualify to be a learning and teaching leader particularly in the Western context. Therefore, to establish oneself as a learning and teaching leader against the backdrop of such views of pedagogic practices of leaders originating from the non-Western world poses further challenges. Indeed, two of the editors of this book identify themselves as migrant Asian females who both occupy leadership positions within learning and teaching – one being an Associate Professor in higher education and the other a Principal Lecturer in education. Both have experienced an unconscious bias (often self-inflicted) which has challenged their learning and teaching leadership, where they have often questioned their pedagogic values and training, and its relevance in the new country context they teach within (Anesa being from the West Indies and Namrata from India, both are currently employed within the UK). A sensitivity to how one's ethnic identity shapes their leadership is explored and elaborated by Laurie Gruppie in her chapter in this book (see Chapter 1).

Positional Spaces

Leadership is often conceptualized and defined by an individual's position and the places of power they occupy. The position one occupies within the leadership food chain in a sense has an impact on the influence one can possibly exercise to enable their leadership. For those academics concentrating on learning and teaching, there has been limited access to positional power. However, additional roles have grown in the more recent decades with universities focusing their attention on learning and teaching focused jobs. These roles are often driven by the neoliberalist agenda and the need to demonstrate a commitment to improving the student experience (Hosein, 2017). The development of the learning and teaching focused academic developer positions (an emerging group of faculty and institutional academic developers, those entrusted in developing the learning and teaching expertise of the institution) coupled with the demands posed by the increasing neoliberalization nonetheless have necessitated that staff focus on their development as teachers alongside demonstrating their competence as researchers. Through these measures, learning and teaching as a source of power and leadership has grown and is increasingly occupying centre stage in institutional strategic plans and other areas of significance. For example, within the UK, the National Student Survey and the Teaching Excellence Framework have been drivers in developing more recognition for learning and teaching with more established pathways for leadership, including positions of Directors of Learning/Teaching (overseeing a department) and Associate Deans of Learning/Teaching (overseeing the faculty). Mari Murtonen (in Chapter 3) shares her journey about how these leadership positions in learning and teaching developed and became available to her within the context of Finland with increased focus on, and attention to, enhancing learning and teaching within the higher education sector in Finland.

There have also been the traditional ill-defined positions such as the programme leader (PL) (the individual managing and leading on the development of a degree) or the Module Leader (an individual managing the leading on the development of a unit of learning). The presence of these individuals in these ill-defined positions with limited positional power has offered these leaders some opportunities to influence the quality of learning and teaching. Often such individuals may lie in the margins of a subject area/faculty occupying positions as a steppingstone to another position, to gain promotion, because of seniority in the system and in some rare cases of nepotism. Such interstitial leadership positions can be uncomfortable and lonely. Patrick Baughan (in his narrative included in Chapter 3) elucidates the challenges posed and opportunities offered in these in-between leadership spaces for learning and teaching, which has been instrumental in his leadership identity as an individual who has not been bound by positional spaces to exercise his leadership in learning and teaching.

Rhizomatic or Serendipitous Spaces

The pathways taken by learning and teaching leaders frequently are unique and can be seen as rhizomatic (Deleuze and Guattari, 1988). Rhizomatic in the sense in that leaders may take journeys in different directions and get to similar or different points but still be seen as leaders. These pathways are often not well thought out, and arrival at the leadership position may involve a certain degree of serendipity (being at the right place at the right time) and luck (Svensson and Wood, 2005), but serendipity may be also gendered (Ottsen, 2019). Serendipity is usually termed as being in the right place at the right time. When we say 'right time', this does not only mean 'clock time' but also refers to the time in a person's life when they are now able to take up opportunities of leadership. By time we also mean the right time for the rhetoric of learning and teaching, that is, the right time for universities, for example, recognizing the need for more learning and teaching through setting up particular centres or jobs, or a vacancy arising. The right time also needs to be twinned with the right place; that is, the university (or even cultural system or country) is probably ready for a change and looking for outlets in growth in learning and teaching and the emerging leader can step in.

These serendipitous activities that lead to leadership are time-space bound and what we refer to here as rhizomatic spaces. For example, Leopold Bayerlein speaks about his rhizomatic space being an 'accidental' journey, a space he did not plan to occupy but became his. Sandra Jones refers to how her journey was serendipitous and that it was influential first and then positional.

Why Personal Narratives?

As the leadership journeys of individuals are unique, influenced by their individual perspectives and their distinctive contested spaces, it was important in the writing of these chapters that the contributors adopted a narrative approach to help capture the differences and diversity of their behaviours (Polkinghorne, 1995) in their leadership journeys. In writing of their narratives, the contributors adopted the three-dimensional space narrative structure (Clandinin and Connelly, 2004), wherein the leaders highlighted their personal experiences, past and present actions and their unique contested spaces (the landscapes which influenced their experiences/journeys) which shaped their leadership identity. The eleven leaders have been included in this book highlight the various aspects which influenced their leadership journeys, such as their gender, ethnicity, position, years of experience and serendipity. The contributors made judgements on what aspects of their lived experiences they considered as salient to contributing to their leadership identity. The purpose of engaging the contributors with the narrative approach was to encourage them to make sense of their leadership journey and organize it into a body of knowledge which offers value to others as well (Gudmundsdottir, 1995). The emphasis was to give voice to their leadership journeys to uncover nuances such that they work as an inspiration and offer guidance for others aspiring to go down this route.

The Narratives of Leadership in Contested Spaces

This book captures the narratives of eleven leaders in learning and teaching who share their leadership journeys within their different contested spaces (refer Table 0.1 for further details). These contested spaces were divided into two parts, the first section focuses on how leaders navigate marginalized spaces and the second section highlights how values, serendipity and resilience play a part in these contested and marginalized spaces within which they emerged as leaders.

Using the conceptual framework of antiracist leadership, Laurie Grupp explores through a reflective approach how the broader context of the diversity, equity and inclusion within her university based in the USA can affect the leadership journey. She suggests that the leadership path can be marked by conflict and resilience, setbacks and deep learning, frustration and renewed commitment. She emphasizes the importance of authentic engagement, building meaningful relationships, humility, vulnerability and fear, throughout an intentional growth journey which she explores in the context of growing into antiracist leadership in learning and teaching.

Susannah Quinsee explores the tensions between teaching and research indicating that learning and teaching is not always held in the same esteem as research in some higher education institutions in the UK. She indicates that if one chooses to pursue a career in educational development, the notion that you are not a 'real' professor is an accusation that one may, unfortunately, frequently encounter. Using the concept of a 'third space' professional and playful leadership, she challenges the assumptions about what a 'real' professor is and highlights the external and internal factors that influence the credibility of a professor.

Mari Murtonen describes her path to becoming a professor and director of the University of Turku Centre for University Pedagogy (UTUPEDA) in her chapter. Whilst Finland strives for quality education at all levels including university education, Mari discusses in her chapter some of the typical problems that many Finnish universities have faced since the 1990s in establishing learning and teaching as a rightful field in universities and having the recognition and need

Table 0.1 Contributors and Their Contested Contexts/Spaces

Author	Country	Contested Spaces
Navigating Marginalized Spaces		
Laurie Grupp	USA	Colonized: Diversity and Inclusivity
Susannah Quinsee	USA	Gendered: Research vs. Teaching
Mari Murtonen	Finland	Positional: Disciplinary Area Recognition
Jenni Fountain	New Zealand	Colonized: Indigenous Diversity and Inclusivity
Andrew Kelly	Australia	Positional: Early Career Academic
Patrick Baughan	UK	Positional: Leadership on the margins/in fuzzy ill-defined spaces
Values, Resilience and Serendipity		
Stephanie Laggini Fiore	USA	Positional: Leading learning and teaching in a research-intensive university
Hannah Holmes	UK	Positional: Early Career Academic
Leopold Bayerlein	Australia	Serendipitous: Educational Leadership
Sandra Jones	Australia	Serendipitous: Collaborative leadership in a competitive space
Wu Siew Mei and Chng Huang Hoon	Singapore	Positional: Leading learning and teaching in a research-intensive university

for leadership in this area and the development of higher education pedagogy over the past two decades.

Jeni Fountain explores through bi-cultural, economic and social lenses, how as a learning and teaching leader in New Zealand, she managed to keep breathing through an era of constant change, including through the Covid-19 pandemic. In her chapter she unpacks these three dimensions, explaining their impact and implications for her leadership and in doing so she shares some of her vulnerabilities indicating alongside how she recognized these and the steps she took towards rectifying them.

Many learning and teaching leaders in higher education work for decades before they develop the necessary experience and scholarly reputation to be appointed to positions that may influence learning and teaching institutionally and beyond. Therefore, the current scholarship on learning and teaching leaders in higher education often overlooks perspectives and experiences of early career academics in learning and teaching leadership roles, largely because these cases are uncommon. Using the concept of participative leadership, Andrew Kelly explores his transition from being an early career academic in an academic teaching role to leading a large learning support team, encompassing a range of professional roles relevant to tertiary learning and teaching within an Australian university. He provides authentic insights to legitimize the learning and teaching leadership early career academics can offer within higher education and elaborates on the value of the participative leadership approach.

Although there is a wealth of literature available on academic leadership, few publications focus on programme leadership (PL) and the role and responsibilities of the PL. Patrick Baughan outlines the role of a PL, based on his experiences of being a PL at three different universities in the UK. He considers the opportunities and challenges associated with the role, makes several recommendations for practice and emphasizes the need for the higher education sector to do more to clarify ambiguities and inconsistencies – what he refers to as 'fuzziness' – associated with the role.

Stephanie Laggini Fiore views a learning and teaching leader as a collaborator, who intentionally cultivates an informed teaching community to maximize student learning and success, despite institutional cultures that may perpetuate inattention to teaching. Using the concept of community, Stephanie, in sharing her leadership journey within a research-intensive university in the USA, explores the value of helping others to realize powerful learning and teaching experiences that create joy. She elaborates on the importance of developing collegial networks whose shared wisdom can extend into seemingly remote and sometimes resistant parts of a research-intensive university.

Hannah Holmes indicates that leadership in learning and teaching is often shaped by experiences during one's early career. She emphasizes that at each level of an individual's career, one has different leadership responsibilities and outlooks. She acknowledges that without support innovation is restricted. Using both, the social interaction and democratic leadership theories, she explores how her leadership as an early career academic evolved owing to the interactions with her mentors. She concludes by providing recommendations on how early career academics can use their early experiences for creating their leadership approach for learning and teaching as senior academics.

Leopold Bayerlein shares his story of a career-long transition from personal teaching success to emerging educational leadership where he identifies three actions and one core skill that he proposes are transferable to other contexts and pathways to leadership in higher education. The three actions that support the development of emerging leaders are (1) an identification of personal intentions that underpin an individuals' work, (2) the use of personas as conceptual vehicles to describe activities and develop identity holistically and (3) a clear communication of personal intentions and personas to others. In addition, Leopold identifies the need for individuals to understand how and why they make decisions as a key career development and leadership skill.

In narrating her journey, Sandra Jones shares her commitment to building leadership through collaboration. She explains that her initial leadership was influence-based, which later translated into position-based. Serendipity enabled her to adopt and promote a distributed leadership approach, focusing on a collaborative approach to leading learning and teaching within an Australian university. Whilst this placed her in a contested space owing to the individualistic and hierarchical approach to HE leadership, she remained committed to a collaborative approach. She shares in her narrative a conceptual collaborative *leadship* ecosystem that acknowledges, not just the six tenets of a distributed leadership approach, but also the energy transformation that occurs when learning and teaching experts interact collaboratively.

Wu Siew Mei and Chng Huang Hoon suggest that the call for effective academic leadership is clarion as good leadership is critical to organizational health. They indicate that an institutional culture change would entail a focus on the assumptions, norms and practices that determine institutional priorities and recognition of such leadership effort. Using concepts of liminality (Meyer and Land, 2005), identity negotiation and networks (Roxå, Mårtensson and Alvertag, 2010) as frames of reference, they share their effort to influence culture at the unit and institutional levels with a Singaporean university and what this meant for their identities as academics and leaders in a research-intensive context.

In the concluding chapter, Ian M. Kinchin explores the concept of ecological leadership and the associated concepts of sustainability, ethics of care and resilience. He views the processes of ecological leadership through the lens offered by the adaptive cycle – a heuristic that summarizes the dynamism between stabilizing and destabilizing environmental factors. By considering the activities of an ecological leader, within an ecology of narratives, Ian highlights that a leader can be reconceptualized as a 'narrative ecologist' who supports team members in their professional development by providing a space to construct their own counter-narratives in an 'ecological garden', protected from the hegemonic 'narrative monoculture' that dominates higher education.

Conclusion

The editors hope that the stories of the eleven emerging and established leaders included in this book will offer valuable insight into how these individuals have navigated to their current learning and teaching leadership roles whilst negotiating their contested identities. We hope these personal narratives from different international contexts will provide unique perspectives on the learning and teaching leadership and how this is shaped by an individual's contested identities and the marginalized spaces they inhabit. Often such identities and spaces are not recognized in higher education which may lead to even more isolating and challenging leadership journeys. The book contributes to our understanding of the subjective experiences that academics encounter in their leadership journeys. Further, the personal narratives included in the book capture how the contested identities and marginalized spaces influence the learning and teaching leadership practices in various educational, cultural and national contexts. We hope the wide geographical coverage will be helpful in capturing the diversity of the journeys.

References

Arday, J. (2018), 'Understanding race and educational leadership in higher education: Exploring the Black and ethnic minority (BME) experience', *Management in Education* 32 (4): 192–200.

Bhopal, K., and Brown, H. (2016), *Black and Minority Ethnic Leaders: Support Networks and Strategies for Success in Higher Education*, London: Leadership Foundation for Higher Education.

Bryman, A. (2007), 'Effective leadership in higher education: A literature review', *Studies in Higher Education* 32 (6): 693–710.

Chen, C. Y. (2015), 'A study showing research has been valued over teaching in higher education', *Journal of the Scholarship of Teaching and Learning* 15 (3): 15–32.

Clandinin, D. J., and Connelly, F. M. (2004), *Narrative Inquiry: Experience and Story in Qualitative Research*, San Francisco, CA: John Wiley & Sons.

Crenshaw, K. (1991), 'Mapping the margins: Intersectionality, identity politics, and violence against women of color', *Stanford Law Review* 43 (6): 1241–99. doi: 10.2307/1229039.

Deleuze, G., and Guattari, F. (1988), *A Thousand Plateaus: Capitalism and Schizophrenia*, London: Bloomsbury.

Dopson, S., Ferlie, E., McGivern, G., Fischer, M., Ledger, J., Behrens, S. and Wilson, S. (2016), *The Impact of Leadership and Leadership Development in Higher Education: A Review of the Literature and Evidence*, Leadership Foundation Research and Development Series, London: Leadership Foundation for Higher Education.

Gudmundsdottir, S. (1995), 'The narrative nature of pedagogical content knowledge', in H. McEwan and K. Egan (eds), *Narrative in Teaching, Learning and Research*, 24–38, New York: Teachers College Press.

Herbst, T. H. (2020), 'Gender differences in self-perception accuracy: The confidence gap and women leaders' underrepresentation in academia', *SA Journal of Industrial Psychology* 46 (1): 1–8.

Hofmeyer, A., Sheingold, B. H., Klopper, H. C. and Warland, J. (2015), 'Leadership in learning and teaching in higher education: Perspectives of academics in non-formal leadership roles', *Contemporary Issues in Education Research* 8 (3): 181–92.

Hosein, A. (2017), Pedagogic frailty and the research-teaching nexus', in *Pedagogic Frailty and Resilience in the University*, 135–49, Rotterdam: Brill.

Kinchin, I., Hosein, A., Rao, N. and Mace, M. W. (2018), *Migrant Academics and Professional Learning Gains: Perspectives of the Native Academic*, London: Society for Research into Higher Education Research Report.

Leišytė, L., and Hosch-Dayican, B. (2017), 'Gender and academic work at a Dutch university', in Eggins, H. (ed.) *The Changing Role of Women in Higher Education*, 95–117, Cham: Springer. https://doi.org/10.1007/978-3-319-42436-1_5.

Locke, W. (2014), *Shifting Academic Careers: Implications for Enhancing Professionalism in Teaching and Supporting Learning*. York: Higher Education Academy. https://www.heacademy.ac.uk/system/file/res ources/shifting_academic_careers_final.pdf.

Marchant, T., and Wallace, M. (2013), 'Sixteen years of change for Australian female academics: progress or segmentation?', *Australian Universities Review* 55 (2): 60–71.

Meyer, J. H. F., and Land, R. (2005), 'Threshold concepts and troublesome knowledge (2): Epistemological considerations and a conceptual framework for teaching and learning', *Higher Education: The International Journal of Higher Education Research* 49: 373–88.

Nachatar Singh, J. K. (2021), 'International academics' lived experiences in gaining leadership positions at Australian universities', *International Journal of Leadership in Education*, doi: 10.1080/13603124.2021.1988717.

Ottsen, C. L. (2019), 'Lucky to reach the top?: Gendered perspectives on leadership acquisition across Qatar and Denmark', *Gender in Management: An International Journal* 34 (7): 541–53.

Patel, D. A., Sanders, G. D., Lundberg-Love, P. K., Gallien, J. A. and Smith, C. D. (2018), 'Issues confronting women leaders in academia: The quest for equality continues', in Florence L. Denmark and Michele A. Paludi (eds), *Women and Leadership*, 79–95, Cham: Springer.

Polkinghorne, D. (1995), 'Narrative configuration in qualitative analysis', *Qualitative Studies in Education* 8: 5–23.

Probert, B. (2013), *Teaching-Focused Academic Appointments in Australian Universities: Recognition, Specialisation, or Stratification?*, Australia: Australian Government: Office for Learning and Teaching. http://www.olt.gov.au/resource-teaching-focused-academic-appointments.

Roxå, T., Mårtensson, K. and Alvertag, M. (2010), 'Understanding and influencing teaching and learning cultures at university: A network approach', *Higher Education* 62 (1): 99–111.

Rao, N., Mace, W., Hosein, A. and Kinchin, I. M. (2019), 'Pedagogic democracy versus pedagogic supremacy: Migrant academics' perspectives', *Teaching in Higher Education* 24 (5): 599–612. doi: 10.1080/13562517.2019.1596078.

Shaked, H. (2021), 'Instructional leadership in higher education: The case of Israel', *Higher Education Quarterly* 75 (2): 212–26.

Svensson, G., and Wood, G. (2005), 'The serendipity of leadership effectiveness in management and business practices', *Management Decision* 43 (7/8): 1001–9.

Part One

Navigating Leadership in Marginalized Spaces

1

Growing into Antiracist Leadership in the American Context

Laurie L. Grupp

Setting the Context

This narrative of my leadership journey has been through several iterations. I wrote, drafted, edited, discarded, talked with colleagues and started over a few times before I realized why the writing was so difficult. I am a white female in the United States who has benefitted from an educational system that was built on principles of white supremacy and designed to privilege white people while oppressing people of colour. I lead, learn, teach and work in this oppressive educational system, and I have benefitted from the privileges that my whiteness has afforded me. At the same time, I am an aspiring antiracist leader who is committed to taking action to challenge and deconstruct racist systems, policies and practices. Focusing on antiracism in my leadership of learning and teaching journey feels risky because I am still learning how to talk about race and racism. The challenge of engaging in antiracist practices while developing self-awareness about whiteness, race, racism and privilege is a primary contested space because this approach runs counter to our dispositions as academics, where we often feel that we need to develop expertise with concepts before we can discuss them with confidence. Several questions came to mind as I tried to settle on an approach to writing about my leadership journey: why is my perspective as a white leader important? What lessons can I share with aspiring leaders of learning and teaching? Is it possible to de-centre whiteness in a narrative about my own efforts to grow into antiracist leadership? I have a lot more to learn about the impact of race and privilege in my work as a leader of learning and teaching, and I grow every day as I gain new understanding. This narrative represents a snapshot of who I am as an antiracist leader-in-development and reflects what I understand currently.

Antiracist leadership involves actively working to challenge and dismantle racist policies, practices and systems while creating pathways and opportunities that promote inclusion and racial equity (Freire, 1990; Kendi, 2019; oneTILT, 2020). For a white person, this antiracism work begins with learning about racism and its impacts while developing self-awareness of whiteness and privilege (Okun, 2006; Singh, 2019). Deepening understanding and undoing internalized beliefs make it possible for white people to develop the self-awareness that is necessary to take action in response to systemic racism. Antiracist leadership requires us to take professional and relational risks by challenging racism and adopting antiracist practices while persisting through mistakes and difficult situations. One of the most important components of growth into antiracist leadership is building relationships by establishing trust, communicating responsively and co-constructing inclusive, equitable solutions (Berila, 2015; Okun, 2006; oneTILT, 2020). My movement towards antiracist leadership began with emerging self-awareness and evolved to include humility, empathy, fear and vulnerability, which helped me to engage authentically and build relationships as I navigated through contested spaces.

The early stages of my interest in antiracism coincided with my development as a leader on my university campus, where I had established myself and my credibility through years of work as a faculty member, educational developer and collaborator. As I grew into leadership roles, I felt the weight of my influence when senior administrators invited my perspective and sometimes followed my advice. They seemed to appreciate the insight that I gained from my close relationships with faculty, which grew through several years as a faculty member and as director of the campus centre for teaching and learning. When students, faculty and staff of colour called for the dismantling of systemic racism at our institution and I agreed with their claims as I spoke against the status quo during meetings with administrative colleagues, I felt that I might be risking my relationships with senior leaders and my own leadership position on campus. As the work to undo racist practices and policies continued over several years with a focus in my home academic department, I felt that I was taking significant professional risks by echoing the voices of students, faculty and staff of colour who advocated for substantial institutional change. I knew that I was also risking long-established relationships with colleagues who did not understand or agree that racism was a problem on our campus. As I learned more about antiracism, power and privilege, I realized that the relational and professional risks that felt big to me were relatively small.

In the work of antiracist leadership, there are several contested spaces. For people of colour, nearly every space in higher education has the potential to be a contested space where racist policies, practices and attitudes marginalize and dehumanize. For a white person in a leadership role, the contested spaces are those where we begin to see the impacts of systemic racism on students, professors and staff of colour; where we understand our complicity within the system; where we challenge racist practices and policies; and where we persist in the face of our own racism, ignorance and need for ongoing development. The contested space for a white person can also be the place where we strive to better understand something that we will never fully know: the experience of race and racism from the perspective of a person of colour. For all who commit to antiracism, we encounter the contested space when persisting efforts to dismantle systemic racism are met with resistance, hostility, rejection and marginalization (Singh, 2019). Contested spaces also occur when we experience uncertainty in the midst of continuing to learn about race and racism. These obstacles to advancing antiracism can make it especially challenging for white antiracist leaders to remain grounded in values of racial equity, inclusivity and humanizing pedagogy. For me, authentic engagement and building meaningful relationships around the work of antiracism provided me with the resources I needed as I navigated through challenges. I learned that once I really heard what colleagues and students of colour were saying about their experiences on our campus, I was invited into relationships that offered me compassion and support as we worked towards the common goal of identifying and eliminating racist practices.

Through this narrative, I share my journey into antiracist leadership of learning and teaching with the hope that the experiences and perspective of a white female working in the US higher education system will provide a pathway for others to consider as they grow into leadership, challenge their own assumptions and strive to address systemic racism. The meaning of my journey into antiracist leadership of learning and teaching is found in the process that I engaged in as I grew into and moved through different professional and leadership roles as a classroom teacher, graduate student, professor at two different institutions, educational developer who directed a centre for learning and teaching, associate provost for faculty affairs, department chair, and academic school dean. More important than the steps on my path are the reflections, insights and relationships that brought me to deeper understanding and helped to solidify my commitment to antiracist leadership of learning and teaching. Throughout my journey, each step that I took never felt as intentional as it might appear. In fact, there were times when I thought that I was floundering because I wanted to grow as a leader, but I was not sure why or how. Simultaneously, I was moving towards antiracism, and I found myself in contested spaces as I was developing skills, dispositions and understandings of an aspiring antiracist leader.

For most of my thirty-year career as an elementary and middle school classroom teacher, higher education faculty member and leader of learning and teaching, my whiteness and privilege within an educational system characterized by systemic racism, inequity and oppression made it possible for me to remain unaware of the impact of my own race and privilege on my everyday work and decision-making. Complex educational and societal systems did not question or diminish my identity because of my race, so I did not have to develop self-awareness of how my whiteness affected my ability to thrive. My limited understanding of my own race and privilege remained unquestioned through decades of leading through learning and teaching until significant events, experiences and interactions during the past several years prompted me to question my lack of self-awareness. As antiracist leaders work to change systems that have been built on principles that promote systemic racism, an important step is to de-centre whiteness while valuing the voices, history and stories of people of colour. Thus, it is important for me to centre the wisdom of my colleagues, students, friends and scholars – people of colour and their allies – who encouraged me to challenge my assumptions, deepen my understanding, and assert myself as an antiracist leader.

Learning and Teaching Identities

My professional identity as an educator and leader has been shaped by my experiences as both a learner and teacher, from my early learning in elementary school to my time teaching children, adolescents and college students. When I faced personal challenges as a high school student, I learned from the teachers who took an interest in me that it was important to recognize each learner as a unique individual with rich prior knowledge and experiences that could serve as entry points and building blocks for new learning (Dewey, 1966; Freire, 1990). Later, as a professional in bilingual special education, I realized that it is essential to adopt learner-centred approaches that value students' rich cultural, linguistic, familial and community experiences (Baca and Almanza, 1991; Gay, 1993). I saw the impact of a personalized approach to teaching that began with meeting students where they were in their learning and experiences in order to challenge them to build on prior knowledge and move their learning to the next level (Vygotsky, 1978). Across various learning environments, I experienced the power of teachers connecting with students through culturally responsive practice, where teachers value students' rich family and community experiences, maintain high expectations for all learners and build on the rich cultural and linguistic foundations that children bring to school (Gay, 1993; Ladson-Billings, 1995). Within classrooms and schools, these approaches enable learners and teachers to create communities that value each individual and engender the belief that learning is interactive, collaborative and social. These early essential lessons about the value of constructivist approaches and building community have followed me into higher education.

My early teaching experiences fuelled my interest in humanizing pedagogy, where learners are valued as unique individuals whose worldview is shaped by their own identities and the systems within which they live, including their families, education and society (Freire, 1990; hooks, 1994). Viewing education through a critical lens generates an understanding of a system that either promotes learning for all, or uses education as a tool to oppress, objectify and marginalize (Giroux, 1988). Critical pedagogy requires learners, teachers and leaders in education to critique oppressive systems and question the status quo in order to promote equity and access for all learners. In recent years, my foundations in culturally responsive practice and critical pedagogy came to bear on my reflections on my whiteness and privilege relative to the systemic racism that surrounded me in higher education.

In the US educational system, meaningful content regarding race, slavery, segregation and racial injustice is often limited or excluded from the curriculum. In fact, in recent years, several states have proposed and/or passed legislation regulating or prohibiting the discussion of critical race theory, race, racism and racial justice in elementary and secondary schools (Kendi, 2021). It is no surprise, then, that white people have not had to reckon with our complicated racist history; we have had few external reasons to confront the privileges and benefits afforded to us through societal and educational systems that are built on principles of white supremacy (Kendi, 2019). In calling for antiracist practice and pedagogy over the past five decades, scholars and activists have been leading a movement for all to take action in response to racist structures and policies, with the goal of working towards racial equity and racial justice (Baldwin, 1963; Brown, 2018; Freire, 1990; Glaude, 2020; hooks, 1994; Kendi, 2019; Singh, 2019; Singh, 2020–1).

During this contemporary era of the Black Lives Matter movement and student protests on college campuses that mirror civil rights and racial justice activism of the 1960s in the United States, students, professors and staff colleagues at my previous institution described racist and oppressive experiences on our campus (The Demands, 2016). Calls for significant change continued through several months of activism, and in my roles on campus I was involved in promoting equity, diversity and inclusion. As I paid more attention to what was happening in the world and at my institution, I sought a deeper understanding of antiracism and white privilege through reading, listening, dialogue, engagement and relationship-building (Brown, 2018; DiAngelo, 2018; Kendi, 2019; Oluo, 2019). Colleagues and students who were committed to significant change on our campus challenged me to engage in the difficult work of developing my own self-awareness to engage in bolder action in response to systemic racism and discrimination. As a result, I felt a significant shift in my perspective and understanding of race, racism and racial justice, and I realized that although I had always valued equity, diversity and inclusion, and my early training and experience instilled values that brought me to culturally responsive practice and humanizing pedagogy, I had not dealt directly with my own race and privilege. Additionally, I was working at a predominantly white institution (PWI) where the campus culture preserved whiteness and privilege rather than creating the conditions for close examination and movement towards antiracism. For example, when students or faculty of colour indicated that they felt marginalized, the response was rarely to question and revise existing policies and practices. Once I began to see and understand systemic racism and racial injustice more clearly, I began to question my role within a system that was built to preserve white superiority while perpetuating oppression.

Moving toward Antiracist Leadership

When I realized that I did not know as much as I needed to know, I did what most white academics would do. I read, listened to podcasts, observed other leaders and talked with colleagues from a diverse range of backgrounds about race, racism, whiteness, privilege, oppression and systemic racism. My understanding deepened as I learned more about the experiences of people of colour in a country where systems are built on the premise that whites are superior, and institutions are organized around whiteness and privilege (Brown, 2018; Glaude, 2020; Kendi, 2019; Oluo, 2019; Singh, 2019). Facts, history and the debilitating effects of systemic racism became more central to my understanding of education, higher education, privilege and power in the United States. Black history, from slavery through Jim Crow laws, school segregation, the civil rights movement, police brutality and Black Lives Matter took on new meaning as I began to better understand the trauma of racism. I learned from people of colour and realized through my readings and reflections that my focus had previously been on individual racism and the question of whether I held racist beliefs or made racist statements. Racist systems, policies and practices that have surrounded me had escaped my attention until I knew how to look for and examine them. My whiteness and privilege made it possible for me to learn, grow and find a career within an educational system that too often fails to educate people of colour. What stood out most to me during this period was that I had not seen systemic racism because I did not have to. I came to understand that gaining knowledge about race and racism is helpful, but it is not enough. Likewise, determining that I am not racist would not be enough, because I would still be complicit as I work in and benefit from systems that perpetuate racism. Most important in my growth into leadership of learning and teaching was my commitment to action through antiracist leadership.

While I was making insights about my growth into antiracism, I was frustrated that many of my white colleagues did not see the systemic racism that I had begun to identify, perhaps because they opted not to see or acknowledge it. They were committed teachers and accomplished scholars who took pride in adopting effective pedagogical approaches that would cultivate students' passion for learning. As we discussed public statements made by professors, students and staff of colour about their experiences with racism on campus, white colleagues often expressed disbelief or offered an explanation that dismissed a claim of racism. In a similar way, colleagues from various parts of the institution frequently resisted changes to long-standing practices, such as those related to recruiting and retaining faculty through the tenure and promotion process, that were proven to have negative impacts on people of colour. In what I understand now as white fragility that centres whiteness (DiAngelo, 2018), white colleagues responded with intense emotions at the possibility that they were being called racist by crying or getting angry in meetings where racism was discussed. There may have been many reasons why my white colleagues in higher education did not see (or choose to see) systemic racism. Like me, they succeeded in systems that valued their whiteness and affirmed their privilege, so they did not need to question how those systems work. Instead, they could remain inattentive to the negative impacts of systemic racism as they fought to preserve policies and practices that they thought worked well. I felt that, in most cases, these white colleagues enjoyed the benefits of white privilege that allowed them to avoid dealing with systemic racism that surrounded them.

As my knowledge and awareness grew, I gained new insights and developed different dispositions around race, racism and relationships. I better understood how systems work, and that when systems fail an entire race of people for generations, it is likely because those systems were never designed to serve people of colour or, even worse, they were designed to oppress. I began to recognize the undue burden that people of colour carry when they are asked to educate white people about racism, reliving racial trauma with each racist incident and subsequent series of conversations explaining the marginalizing and damaging effects of tactics like racial profiling by campus security of professors and students of colour as they entered campus.

In my personal journey towards antiracist leadership, dispositions such as humility, empathy, vulnerability and fear were particularly helpful to explore. It is difficult, especially for a leader in higher education, to admit to not knowing or understanding something. There is so much that I do not understand about the experiences of people of colour, and I will never learn if I do not have enough humility to acknowledge what I do not know about racism and racial trauma. As I entered into campus-wide conversations about race that were labelled as 'difficult dialogues' and as I talked with members of the campus community who were targeted in racist incidents, I experienced the importance of empathy as I endeavoured to listen and engage meaningfully. Additionally, fear and vulnerability took on new meaning for me. Situations and challenges that I experienced during periods of significant growth on my antiracist leadership path taught me to pay attention to fear. Early in my career, fear held me back and kept me silent. In difficult discussions when I felt under pressure in the face of challenge or conflict, I could feel my fear. Committing to antiracism and growing into leadership changed my relationship with fear. Rather than allowing fear to prevent me from speaking up about systemic racism, I learned to feel the fear before I spoke, understand where it was coming from, and assess what was at stake. Certainly, the potential negative impacts of racist policies and practices on people of colour were much bigger than my fear. Recognizing how small my fear was relative to the larger context made it possible for me to acknowledge fear when I felt it, and then move on to question significant decisions and advocate for the dismantling of racist policies. Not far from fear and humility is vulnerability, which for me is difficult to experience in the moment because it leaves me feeling exposed and at risk of getting hurt. But when I have allowed myself to be vulnerable, to express myself openly and honestly, I have felt more authentic, trusting and trusted.

Collaboration and relationship-building are foundational to antiracist leadership of learning and teaching, and my developing understanding of race and racism shifted my ability to connect with colleagues and students. For example, once I understood the need for active resistance to systemic racism, I began to engage differently with a colleague of colour who experienced retaliation after publicly identifying policies and practices that had become obstacles to students' success, such as assessment checkpoints in our teacher preparation program that seemed to disproportionately impede the progress of students of colour. During department meetings, faculty resisted our colleague's perspectives and suggestions and seemed to align themselves with each other as they challenged him. The atmosphere in meetings was tense and uncomfortable as faculty raised their voices and positioned themselves through physical and verbal posturing, and this tension carried over into everyday interpersonal interactions. The retaliation was so significant that my colleague's ability to achieve tenure was in question despite his documented accomplishments that met established criteria in teaching, scholarship and service. While many white faculty members and administrators blamed and marginalized our colleague, I listened more carefully to what he and the students were saying, and I better understood their concerns. After learning about white fragility, I saw everything differently as I watched in meetings while white colleagues took predictable steps in centring themselves as they defended their actions, claimed good intentions and demonstrated emotions such as anger and sadness. My new understanding and approach to antiracism made it possible for me and my colleague to build a friendship and collaboration that enabled us to work together towards a shared vision where we began to dismantle racist policies and practices that were harmful to people of colour. This important work brought me into closer contact with people of colour and their white allies, making new relationships possible and, ultimately, helping me grow.

A specific challenge that I experienced when I was the department chair in an educator preparation programme effectively illustrates my continued growth into antiracist leadership of learning and teaching. A white school administrator at one of our field sites had publicly removed a young Latina intern from a team meeting about one of her students, resulting in her feeling singled out, marginalized and treated differently than others because of her race. My interactions with the administrator began with a phone conversation that was contentious and difficult. He opened the conversation with a defensive stance, claiming that he was determined not to lose his job over the incident. Through many attempts to explain what prompted him to remove the intern from the meeting, he refused to acknowledge that the situation would have played out differently if he had taken an alternative approach, such as asking the intern for a private conversation to let her know that sensitive personnel issues would be discussed in the meeting, and she should not attend. Realizing that I would not make headway in the discussion, I asked the administrator to allow the intern to work and engage as she needed to at the school for the remainder of the term, and he reluctantly agreed. About a month later, as the intern's placement in the school was concluding, I made an appointment to meet with the administrator with the goal of ensuring that we had common expectations of student interns placed at the school. I also hoped that in-person follow-up would provide some closure to this difficult situation. We talked for about thirty minutes and did not reach agreement as the administrator waffled between insisting that he had done nothing wrong and acknowledging that things may not have escalated if he had taken a different approach. The conversation took a turn when he said that he understood what was happening, he knew that potential donors were of value at my institution, and that the intern must have been from an influential family. He assumed that someone at my institution had sent me to the school to make things right. His accusatory tone caught my attention, and I responded with what came to my mind immediately. First, I said that I was there to talk with him on behalf of one of our students, as I would with any student regardless of their financial situation or family background. I then turned to his assumptions, and I said that, since he introduced the topic, we needed to put everything on the table by acknowledging the significant privilege that he had as a white male administrator interacting with a Latina female who was an undergraduate student intern. My statements were met with silence, yet he did not disagree. I wrapped up the meeting by saying that I hoped we shared common commitments to ensuring positive learning experiences for all elementary school students regardless of their racial, economic or family backgrounds.

Several things came to light for me during this interaction with the administrator and in my reflections that followed. It was a powerful experience that has stayed with me because of how loaded it was with challenges and lessons. At first, I was surprised that I had so naturally responded to his assumptions by naming his privilege and position as a white male in an administrative role. In prior situations, if I decided to say anything at all, I would have taken some time to develop a response, and I may have needed to summon the courage to speak. The time between the phone call and the meeting allowed me to process the administrator's disposition and gave me the time I needed to reflect on his stance. My commitment to antiracism and racial equity, and the learning I had been engaged in, gave me the perspective to recognize and address his privilege in the moment. Most important, though I still have a lot to learn, I spoke the language of antiracism without hesitation or rehearsal, a sign to me that I had moved into antiracist leadership and that I was not afraid to challenge racism and privilege.

Choices in Antiracist Leadership

The activism in response to systemic racism on university campuses in 2016 drew me into deeper considerations of my race, privilege, position and agency as a mid-level leader on my campus. At that time, I had been an educational developer and the director of our centre for teaching and learning for nine years, and I had begun to reflect on my interest in leadership and professional growth. I was also involved in campus-wide efforts to promote equity, diversity and inclusion through collaborations with our chief diversity officer, an academic school dean, the director of our centre for engaged learning, the vice president for mission and ministry, and a number of faculty members. We developed and co-facilitated several workshops and dialogues to promote communication and pedagogical decision-making that was more inclusive of all students, especially students of colour at our predominantly white institution. In my role as centre director, I was included in meetings with other campus leaders, which often involved decision-making conversations relative to academics and the student experience. Once the student demands regarding systemic racism were issued (The Demands, 2016), many administrative meetings became more focused on the need to promote an inclusive campus climate and curriculum. My leadership position in the teaching and learning centre gave me perspective on the faculty and student experience, and my work on equity, diversity and inclusion gave me insight into concerns around systemic racism. I also became more aware of my whiteness in those conversations, where many of the other leaders were also white. In retrospect, I believe it was within these meetings that I began to strengthen my voice as a leader as I also began to question my whiteness and privilege.

The choices that I made during that critical time five years ago set me on a path towards antiracist leadership and helped me to grow in ways that I had not imagined. At first, my growth as a leader and my personal commitment to antiracism felt like parallel paths. In the area of leadership, I pursued professional development opportunities that focused on topics such as management skills, competent decision-making, vision, strategy, diversity, problem solving, communication, conflict resolution, team building, networking and interpersonal relationships. I was drawn to the idea of servant leadership, where the emphasis is on the growth and support of members of a community rather than hierarchy and power, and where leaders work collaboratively to cultivate the potential of individuals and the community at large (Greenleaf, 1977). Additionally, the idea that the best team players are humble, hungry and smart resonated with me (Lencioni, 2016) as I realized the value of humility through a desire to learn, build relationships and develop strategies for moving a vision forward. I was encouraged to test my limits by facing fear, taking risks and making big leadership moves even when I felt uncertain (Mohr, 2014; Nichols, 2016; Smith, 2016). I understood through my experience that authenticity generated credibility and trust and that allowing space for vulnerability within authentic moments could be difficult but valuable. Lessons shared during leadership development workshops gave me takeaways that have stayed with me, such as the value of taking risks and the need to stand strong in the face of resistance. These and other ideas shaped my understanding of what it means to be an effective leader. Some of the professional growth opportunities that I accessed included information and reflection on the importance of equity, diversity and inclusion in leadership. For the most part, however, race was not central, and I did not feel prompted to examine my own whiteness and privilege through these leadership-development opportunities.

Exploring my understanding of race, racism, systemic racism, whiteness and privilege began with the campus activism in response to systemic racism and evolved through conversations with students and colleagues of colour and their white allies who challenged me to look more closely at my privilege, position and whiteness. I realized through these interactions and my subsequent learning that there was a great deal that I did not know or understand about race, and I took an immersive approach where I read, listened and watched as people of colour shared their stories, described their trauma, and helped me better understand the impacts of racism (Brown, 2018; Kendi, 2019; Oluo, 2019). I learned about the importance of humility, empathy and de-centring whiteness while questioning systems, policies and practices that are racist and oppressive (hooks, 1994; Kendi, 2019). I developed self-awareness of the influence of my whiteness and privilege in shaping my perspective and informing my actions. While it was difficult at times to acknowledge my biases and mistakes, I learned that sitting with my own discomfort is part of the process of growing into antiracism (Singh, 2020–1). Most importantly, I developed an in-depth understanding of the value of humility, empathy, vulnerability, fear and authenticity. These are all important lessons that not only inform my understanding of antiracism but that have made me a better leader.

Antiracist leadership is daily practice that consists of education, self-awareness, empathy, reflection, relationship building, strategy and action (Kendi, 2019; oneTILT, 2020; Singh, 2020–1). During the early stages of my growth into leadership, I learned that there are many choices to be made in determining what kind of leader I would be and that leaders have different strengths, interests, values and dispositions that affect their interactions, decisions, actions and commitments. My early experience and training provided me with a solid foundation in humanizing and critical pedagogy, and my colleagues challenged and supported me as I moved into antiracist leadership. Within my institutional context in the midst of a widespread call to action in response to systemic racism, I could not imagine being involved in important discussions about student learning, access to resources, humanizing pedagogy, inclusive curriculum, implicit bias and equity without learning about and committing to antiracism.

Closing Thoughts

As I said at the outset, this chapter was challenging to write. I have always embraced reflective practice and I was eager to engage a meta-reflective approach that included review of my journals, correspondence, notes and other materials to get a better sense of how I have grown as a leader of learning and teaching. My learning about antiracism continued as I worked through various iterations of this narrative, and I began to see connections that I had not seen before. The focus of the chapter shifted once I saw the significance of antiracism in my growth as a leader. Some of the resources on antiracist leadership that I cite here are current and were not available to me when questions about whiteness, privilege, race and racism prompted my learning several years ago. Since I was not looking for resources that specifically addressed antiracist leadership at that time, I initially saw my growth as a leader and my commitment to antiracism as related but separate. That feels so naive to say. How could I not see the common threads? How did I not know that in order to lead effectively I needed to adopt principles and practices of antiracism?

While I have found many answers, each learning and insight raises new questions, reminding me that antiracist leadership is a process and daily practice rather than an outcome. In this area, I will always be a work in progress.

As I set the context for this chapter, I asked why my perspective as a white leader is important. I hope that white colleagues who aspire to lead will find some lessons in what I have shared. For those who are beginning the work of antiracism, some of the readings and resources that I reference may be helpful. Additionally, several organizations curate resources on racism and antiracism on their websites and I have found some of those to be the most current, relevant and helpful, such as Racial Equity Tools, Anti-Racist Pedagogy – Methods and Challenges (University of Southern California) and Becoming an Anti-Racist Educator (Wheaton College Massachusetts). For me, the most important lesson is in the process that brought me to where I am now and in my openness to humility, vulnerability, fear, learning and growth. As individuals with unique identities, experiences and dispositions, aspiring leaders need to find and follow their own path. Growth along this path involves humility to admit what we do not know or understand, a mindset to learn in all ways possible, flexibility to adapt and evolve as leaders, and reflective practice that promotes integration of new learning.

My final question in the opening of this chapter asked whether it would be possible to de-centre whiteness in a narrative about my own experience. That feels like a ridiculous question now, as my learning about myself and antiracism has continued while I wrote. I realize that it is not possible to de-centre whiteness, not only because it is the story of my leadership journey and I am white, but because we live, learn, teach and work in a society that was built with whiteness at the centre. Just as addressing individual racism will have limited effect because of the larger context and damaging impact of systemic racism, de-centring my white identity in this narrative is impossible when everything about my story has whiteness at the centre. Writing this narrative has helped me see the centring of whiteness more clearly and has affirmed my commitment to antiracist leadership as a means of addressing the beliefs that allow us to continue to build systems that centre some while excluding and oppressing others.

As leaders in learning and teaching who seek growth, we need to accept that there will always be more to learn. Antiracist leaders understand that the work has very high stakes that will always outweigh the risk, challenge and labour of engaging in antiracist practice.

References

Baca, L. M., and Almanza, E. (1991), *Language Minority Students with Disabilities. Exceptional Children at Risk*, CEC Mini-Library, Reston, VA: Council for Exceptional Children.

Baldwin, J. (1963), 'A Talk to Teachers', *Saturday Review*, 21 December: 42–4.

Berila, B. (2015), *Integrating Mindfulness into Anti-Oppression Pedagogy: Social Justice in Higher Education*, New York: Routledge.

Brown, A. C. (2018), *I'm Still Here: Black Dignity in a World Made for Whiteness*, Colorado Springs, CO: Convergent Books.

Dewey, J. (1966), *Democracy and Education: An Introduction to the Philosophy of Education*, New York: Free Press.

DiAngelo, R. J. (2018), *White Fragility: Why It's so Hard for White People to Talk about Racism*, Boston, MA: Beacon Press.

Freire, P. (1990), *Pedagogy of the Oppressed*, New York: Penguin.

Gay, G. (1993), 'Building cultural bridges: A bold proposal for teacher education', *Education and Urban Society* 25 (3): 285–99.

Giroux, H. A. (1988), *Teachers as Intellectuals: Toward a Critical Pedagogy of Learning*, Granby, MA: Bergin and Garvey.

Glaude, E. S. (2020), *Begin Again: James Baldwin's America and Its Urgent Lessons for Our Own*, New York: Crown.

Greenleaf, R. K. (1977), *Servant Leadership: A Journey into the Nature of Legitimate Power and Greatness*, Mahwah, NJ: Paulist Press.

hooks, b. (1994), *Teaching to Transgress: Education as the Practice of Freedom*, New York: Routledge.

Kendi, I. X. (2019), *How to Be an Antiracist*, New York: One World.

Kendi, I. X. (2021), 'There is no debate over critical race theory', *The Atlantic*, 9 July. https://www.theatlantic.com/ideas/archive/2021/07/opponents-critical-race-theory-are-arguing-themselves/619391/ (accessed 10 July 2021).

Ladson-Billings, G. (1995), 'Toward a theory of culturally relevant pedagogy', *American Education Research Journal* 32 (3): 465–91.

Lencioni, P. M. (2016), *The Ideal Team Player*, Hoboken, NJ: John Wiley & Sons.

Mohr, T. (2014), *Playing Big: Find Your Voice, Your Mission, Your Message*, New York: Avery.

Nichols, 2016. 'How to turn your fear into fuel', 24 November. https://youtu.be/v19rDdIh_kY (accessed 10 July 2021).

Okun (2006), 'From white racist to white anti-racist: The life-long journey', *dRworks*. http://www.dismantlingracism.org/uploads/4/3/5/7/43579015/white_identity_ladder_2013.pdf (accessed 10 July 2021).

Oluo, I. (2019), *So You Want to Talk about Race*, New York: Seal Press.

oneTILT (2020), 'Inclusive Leadership Competencies'. https://drive.google.com/file/d/1l_6ZQhfG4jXIK62-Vr2fL46zu8Yby851/view (accessed 10 July 2021).

Singh, A. A. (2019), *The Racial Healing Handbook: Practical Activities to Help You Challenge Privilege, Confront Systemic Racism, and Engage in Collective Healing*, Oakland, CA: New Harbinger.

Singh, J. S. (Host) (2020–1), 'Antiracism as Spiritual Practice', *Religion News Service*. https://religionnews.com/becoming-less-racist/#readmore-blr (accessed 10 July 2021).

Smith, W. (2016), 'Facing your fears', 9 December. https://www.youtube.com/watch?v=MHnYpcmc2m0.

The Demands (2016), https://www.thedemands.org (accessed 15 February 2021).

Vygotsky, L. S. (1978), *Mind in Society: The Development of Higher Psychological Processes*, Boston, MA: Harvard University Press.

Additional Resources

Racial Equity Tools. https://www.racialequitytools.org/ (accessed 10 July 2021).

University of Southern California, 'Anti-racist pedagogy – methods and challenges'. https://libguides.usc.edu/c.php?g=756583&p=5976568 (accessed 10 July 2021).

Wheaton College Massachusetts, 'Becoming an anti-racist educator'. https://wheatoncollege.edu/academics/special-projects-initiatives/center-for-collaborative-teaching-and-learning/anti-racist-educator/ (accessed 10 July 2021).

2

Establishing Leadership Integrity in Learning and Teaching as a Professor

Susannah Quinsee

Introduction

The inspiration for this chapter came from a comment I received from a long-standing colleague. Over drinks one night, some colleagues were congratulating me on my professorship. As the conversation moved on, one colleague leant over and said to me conspiratorially, 'Well, of course, you are not a real professor, are you?', although he never went on to explain to me what a 'real' professor actually was. I cannot remember my reaction at the time, although I sadly do not think that I countered him on his assertion. I was in my mid-thirties, newly returned from maternity leave, confident enough to apply for a professorship, not confident or perhaps too flabbergasted to counter the assumptions of an older male colleague, who ironically was not a professor. Yet, the comment has stayed with me for years, niggling away at my imposter syndrome and self-doubt at various points.

Why did this comment sting so badly? Perhaps because, I realized on reflection, both my roles as a professor and as the director of Educational Development are not widely understood, and this comment encapsulated the challenges I saw for both myself and others in establishing a credible career in learning and teaching leadership. In this chapter, I explore the role of a leader of educational development and the role of a professor to expose the lack of agreed definitions of these key educational leadership positions. Using my own experience, I consider how this lack of agreed remit can be an opportunity to exercise a different and more collaborative form of leadership which unites and builds bridges. Three leadership strategies are presented that I have found useful in my own practice. The chapter concludes with some advice to aspiring academic educational development leaders.

Before looking at educational leadership in UK higher education more generally, I wish to briefly outline my background to provide the context in which I am working, which takes a qualitative narrative approach and draws on the belief that leadership is very context specific (Inman, 2014). A narrative approach is helpful for aspiring leaders as it enables sense-making to be established beyond the narrative, and I have found that storytelling is a powerful leadership skill (Ancona, 2012; Inman, 2009, 2014).

My role and background are unusual in terms of a 'traditional' academic career path, but not unusual in relation to the field of educational development (Gosling, 2007). My academic 'training' came from completing a PhD in English literature and working as a lecturer in English literature. I worked throughout my PhD as a librarian and IT trainer in another institution, so started to gain a broader skill set and appreciation of the variety of academic and professional service roles. I then took a change of direction and worked in degree administration before taking up a role supporting a newly created online course which was delivered both online and face-to-face. This role particularly coalesced the skills I had developed in academic and professional services. I was heavily involved in content creation and design, as well as student support. I also trained and supported academic staff in creating online content and researched our approach. From this, I moved into an academic educational development role and then became head of e-learning, maintaining my academic position, and later head of learning development (combining e-learning with academic practice), where I received my professorship, and finally director and professor of learning and teaching development. I was recently given the title assistant vice president (educational development) in recognition of the broader role that I take across my university in influencing education strategy.

My professional role, then, is one of educational leadership, both as a head of educational development and a professor; however, neither of these are necessarily well-defined roles in terms of their contribution to strategic leadership, and thus my approach to establishing educational leadership integrity has had to acknowledge and embrace this lack of clarity. Before considering the leadership strategies I have used, firstly, this chapter will consider the evidence defining the leadership roles of both heads of educational development and professors to demonstrate the ambiguity surrounding learning and teaching leadership in UK higher education.[1]

Educational Development Leadership

Educational or academic development teams[2] often occupy an undefined area within a university, acting both as a broker or as an advocate of change for learning and teaching as well as an enforcer of institutional policies (Little and Green, 2012; Sugrue, 2018; Taylor, 2005). The lack of clarity about the role of educational development units (EDUs) can be both positive and negative (Kinesh and Wood, 2013; Little and Green, 2012). This indeterminate space may give EDUs latitude to pursue their values in terms of improving university education and supporting staff, or it may become a realm of conflict as the wider organizational context fails to understand the role that educational developers can bring to the university (Bluteau and Krumins, 2008; Sugrue, 2018). In my own experience, I have found this ambiguity simultaneously positive in terms of enabling freedom to pursue and develop initiatives, but negative in terms of the frustration of being overlooked when we might have a contribution to make, as that contribution is not always understood.

This uncertainty of the function and role of EDUs also brings into question whether they should be involved in leadership and actively promoting strategic goals to improve student learning (Baume and Kahn, 2003). How much EDUs get involved in leadership is, in my experience, often down to the understanding of the role of educational development by senior managers in an institution. Palmer et al. (2011) define strategic leadership as 'the capacity to set directions, identify, choose and implement activities that create compatibility between internal organisational strengths and the changing external environment' (p. 807). I have found that different leaders have variously interpreted the role of an EDU, sometimes seeing us as directly responsible for improving a university's standing in the educational league tables, at other times seeing us playing a more supportive and guiding role. Recent UK government policy focused on measuring the impact of teaching quality through such activities as the National Student Survey and Teaching Excellence Framework, as well as universities' response to the Covid-19 pandemic moving education rapidly online, have all seen EDUs leading on strategic educational decisions. Yet this can lead to tensions, particularly in relation to working with discipline areas where the EDU may act as an intermediary between the discipline and senior management (Palmer et al., 2011). Much of the literature on the role of EDUs refers to turbulent and conflicted priorities in relation to the mission and purpose of their work (Blackmore and Blackwell, 2006; Fraser, 2001; Kanuka, Holmes and Cowley, 2020; Sugrue, 2018). However, in order to be effective, EDUs must play a proactive role in organizational and strategic priorities, and, one could argue, the skills of educational developers are well suited to occupy this role; my leadership has been guided by the desire to create the conditions in which others can act, which fits with this notion of educational developers as bridge builders, facilitators, vision creators and change agents (Kinesh and Wood, 2013; Sugrue, 2018; Taylor, 2005).

Navigating the challenges outlined above is a key leadership skill for heads of educational development (Kanuka, Holmes and Cowley, 2020; Little and Green, 2012; Sugrue et al., 2018; Taylor, 2005). Sugrue et al. (2018) describe how EDUs are engaging more in the language of leadership, which creates exciting and terrifying leadership opportunities as well as increasing the vulnerability of EDUs and their leaders. Blakemore and Blackwell (2006) question whether the role of educational development leaders can ever be conceptualized in a uniform fashion as they have such diversity in approach, discipline background and institutional context. Yet what most research agrees on is that educational development leaders play a key role in bringing people together and the significance of 'value-based' leadership driving this mission to create new working relationships (Blakemore and Blackwell, 2007; Sugrue et al., 2018; Taylor, 2005). In order to do this, educational development leaders are required to take a broad view of a university, understand how different facets of the institution interact with each other and also how to work with these to engender change and progress (Blackmore and Blackwell, 2006). Educational development flourishes when its leaders foresee the growth and potential for the change that their teams can support, particularly where there is a positive correlation between the EDU and the university's mission as this results in more effective relationships (Kanuka, Holmes and Cowley, 2020). During the pandemic, I was able to clearly demonstrate the role of my team in meeting the challenge of delivering the majority of the university's learning and teaching online, which was recognized by us receiving additional resources to support this priority. This activity, and others in my role as a head of educational development, has required me to balance competing demands to carve out space to bring others together to enact strategic change. This can be a challenge when that strategic leadership role is not fully understood. Does adding the title of 'professor' to this role increase the clarity or create further ambiguity?

Is a Professor a Leader?

'Leadership in higher education is a strange field' (Bryman and Lilley, 2009), and the lack of clarity around the role of a professor in UK higher education is a clear example of this. Stereotypically, a professor may be imagined culturally as 'white, male, able, heterosexual, and middle-class' (Fisanick, 2006, p. 326; Fitch, 2020). Whether it is this stereotype or the fact that conferment of the title 'professor' on an individual is an esteem marker, or a combination of both, there is an implication that professors play some kind of leadership role in a university. However, how that role is understood in terms of broader leadership responsibilities and exercising of that within an institutional setting is more challenging (Rayner et al., 2010; Tight, 2002). There is actually very little literature on the definition of a professor's leadership role; even their role as 'intellectual leaders' is not always clearly defined (Esen, Bellibas and Gumus, 2020; Evans, Homer and Rayner, 2013; Macfarlane, 2011b; Macfarlane and Burg, 2018; Rayner et al., 2010). In hindsight, a greater appreciation of this ambiguity earlier in my career would have enabled me to feel more confident in shaping the role of the professor in relation to my own discipline area. Although my professorship is recognized and acknowledged, my seniority in terms of decision-making, I feel, often stems more from my role as a director rather than my academic credentials.

Yet there is a clear case to be made for better recognition of the work professors do for the 'greater good' for institutional leadership (Macfarlane, 2011; Rayner et al., 2010). Drawing on Tight's work from 2002, which makes a case for professorial leadership contributing to 'academic citizenship', Macfarlane and Burg (2019) explore how the role of the professor is a vital one for supporting the broader aims of a university by supporting colleagues. Earlier studies with professors uncover a desire to act as institutional leaders and for there to be more formal recognition of their role in mentoring others (Macfarlane, 2011b; Macfarlane, 2012).

What this analysis and relative paucity of research around the role of the professor demonstrate is that this is a role that is not fully understood in terms of strategic influence and the exercise of leadership capacity. This is a similar situation to that of the head of educational development. Both roles have leadership potential, if not a mandate to exercise leadership in some capacity, yet how this can happen is not always clear. Although professors may not have the positional leadership authority imbued into a head of educational development, they have a motivation and personal power to undertake leadership roles. Whether a head of educational development is also a professor or whether professors are involved in educational development, both roles, if able to establish legitimacy, can be influential in strategic educational change, and not capitalizing these means institutions can miss opportunities. Gaining my professorship was not just a career goal in terms of recognition of my achievements, but I believed it also conferred on me an academic credibility which was vital if I was to play a leading role in working with academics on implementing educational strategy and change. Before considering some strategies I have used to lead with integrity in these circumstances, it is worth briefly considering the impact of gender.

The 'Ivory Ceiling'

There is significant evidence that gender plays a negative role in the opportunities and exercise of leadership for women, particularly in relation to becoming a professor (Macfarlane, 2011b; Macfarlane and Burg, 2019). Given the lack of clarity about what a professor does, it can therefore be even more problematic for women professors to define and exercise their leadership role. Research into women and leadership in higher education has demonstrated that women are more likely to take a collegial and 'rounded view' of professorship, including placing greater emphasis on academic citizenship (Macfarlane and Burg, 2018, 2019). This recognition is notable in that it accords with other research that has found that women exercise different leadership skills and view their responsibilities differently from men in academic settings, often taking on more caring responsibilities such as focusing on well-being, which can be a barrier for promotion (Acker, 1996; Grant and Knowles, 2000; Sanchez-Moreno, 2015). The phrase 'academic housework' (Heijstra, Steinthorsdóttir and Einarsdóttir, 2017) has been used to describe these tasks that are often caring-related, time-consuming and unrecognized, and are predominantly carried out by women. As a female professor of educational development, I certainly identify with that role as an academic citizen, which feels core to my values as an educational leader and a professor. As head of e-learning, new to a leadership role and with a smaller team, that I had 'grown up' with in terms of my career development, I definitely felt a strong caring responsibility to protect and nurture my staff, jokingly at times referring to them as 'my children'. Although I still see it as a vital part of my leadership to advocate for and support my team, experience has taught me that such a familial analogy is not helpful in terms of delegating and sharing responsibilities.

'Women are still heavily under-represented in the professoriate across virtually all subjects' (Bolden, Petrov and Gosling, 2008; MacFarlane, 2011). Yet in educational development, more than 70 per cent of the profession is female (Green and Little, 2016), and although not all of these will be on professorial contracts, this is another factor in establishing the credibility of this kind of work (Niemi and Schwarz, 2019). It could be argued that educational development, and indeed learning and teaching, are further examples of 'academic housekeeping' being caring and emotionally intense development work that is not always recognized institutionally. I found that this can lead to less engagement by academics with the work of an EDU, as it is not seen as vital but rather 'trivial' work that is 'messy' and time-consuming.

What the literature demonstrates is that both the role of a head of an EDU and a professor are unclear in terms of their contribution to learning and teaching leadership. The former may have positional power in terms of an expectation to contribute towards strategic leadership, but a challenge in terms of enacting this; the latter may have expert power and a desire to contribute towards leading strategically, but a challenge in defining this. I have experienced this discomfort about knowing where to 'place' me in the organization – am I a member of professional services as a director or am I an academic? The answer is I am both, but this dual identity often leads to confusion about my role, which can lead to a lack of clarity about my contribution. The fact that educational development is predominantly a female profession adds a further dimension to establishing authoritative leadership for learning and teaching. Whilst the contextual nature of leadership means that there will inevitably be difference in how leadership roles are conceptualized, this lack of clarity around these roles is significant in relation to learning and teaching leadership for three main reasons: firstly, it can be a challenge to be regarded as strategic leaders and therefore gain 'a seat at the table' for decisions relating to education; secondly, the expertise and skills in these roles may not be understood or capitalized upon for the benefit of the institution; and thirdly, incumbents of these roles may struggle with confidence and support in creating an authentic leadership approach. I have experienced all three of these challenges and realized that the key to meeting them, for me, has been to address the third challenge first – my own self-confidence and belief that I should have a seat at the table. Undertaking coaching and leadership development has considerably helped me here. By being more self-confident, I have been able to establish a leadership practice with integrity which has enabled me to demonstrate my value and contribution as a female professor and head of educational development. I have endeavoured to navigate the ambiguous leadership expectations of my role by deploying three strategies which can build confidence to translate undefined boundaries into opportunities: firstly, using a values-based leadership model; secondly, owning the ambiguity of the *Third Space* professional; and thirdly, utilizing playful leadership.

Values-Based Leadership

Understanding what motivates and drives me, what my strengths and development areas are, and taking a reflective approach to my leadership practice are indicative of my values-based leadership approach. Being clear on my values has enabled me to understand how I can work and collaborate with others and what kind of leader I aspire to be. I have written elsewhere how Kouzes and Posner's 1995 (2002) model of exemplary leadership was vital to my leadership practice when responding to the Covid-19 pandemic (Quinsee, 2022). Here, I will discuss more broadly how their model of values-based leadership has resonated with my practice in order to build leadership integrity.

There are five principles that underpin Kouzes and Posner's 1995 model ('model the way', 'inspire a shared vision', 'challenge the process', 'enable others to act' and 'encourage the heart'), which I have found useful touch points for developing and defining my own practice. For example, I have continued to teach throughout my career as this enables me to relate directly to any educational changes I am attempting to lead or influence. I see this as part of modelling the way, exploring hands-on the use of techniques and tools that I wish to see others adopt and to inspire their practice. This also enables me to build trust in others, which is a core part of my authentic leadership practice, and one which also enables others to act. When leading an institutional-wide review of our educational technologies, creating a shared vision was a critical part of the process, and I realized that people needed to own this vision in order to help enact it; thus we allowed considerable interpretation of that vision so that our new technologies could be adopted and adapted across the university (Quinsee and Bullimore, 2011).

I do not slavishly follow a model such as Kouzes and Posner's on a daily basis, but rather see such an approach to be useful as a guiding set of principles which enable me to build confidence around my leadership practice, when my role may not be fully understood. Their model places at its heart leadership skills such as mentoring, bridge building and facilitation, and celebrating and supporting others. As a female academic, professor and educational developer, I find it helpful that owning such 'softer' activities, which are more likely to be undertaken by women, are in fact vital for effective leadership. Values-based leadership has given me the confidence to reconceptualize what leadership might look like for me in my discipline.

Owning the *Third Space*

Drawing on this desire to make sense in ambiguity comes the second approach for academic leaders of educational development to gain credibility and that is to understand and embrace the *Third Space* to seize new leadership opportunities. *Third Space* professionals are 'groups of staff in higher education who do not fit conventional binary descriptors such as those enshrined in "academic" or "non-academic" employment categories' (Whitchurch, 2015). They bring people together to enact change by having an intimate understanding of the organization in which they work and are comfortable with undefined roles, messiness and ambiguity (Whitchurch, 2007, 2008; Veles and Carter, 2016).

Similar to the model of values-based leadership just discussed, *Third Space* professionals also have skills that contribute to effective leadership, such as facilitation, development and 'bringing others on' (Whitchurch, 2009). As we have seen – given the paradoxical ambiguity of the role of a head of educational development and a professor – both of these roles, it could be argued, fit well into the definition of a *Third Space* professional. As a head of educational development, I feel an affinity with the *Third Space*, although professors are not usually seen in this domain; yet, Macfarlane (2012) makes a compelling case for professors being seen as educational developers. Where Whitchurch's analysis is particularly pertinent is the belief that *Third Space* professionals are comfortable about leading without formal power. Professors often find themselves in the position where they have a leadership role in terms of esteem and career culmination, yet without positional power. Although the role of the professor may seem clear in terms of academic discipline, it can be said to have elements of the *Third Space* ambiguity in terms of the exercise of leadership. My dual role combining professorship with my directorship addresses the challenge of positional power to some extent.

I have found an understanding of the operation of the *Third Space* professional and how this can impact on leadership and give me credibility in the area of educational leadership; as I have explored, the Covid-19 pandemic has potential benefits for *Third Space* leadership (Quinsee, 2022). Understanding how *Third Space* professionals have unique skills in bringing people together is a culmination of the role of a leader of educational development coupled with the academic integrity of a professorship. Defining my role as a *Third Space* professional has given me confidence that there are valid new roles in institutions which are needed to help institutions change and grow. Going back to Kouzes and Posner's model, the *Third Space* has given me freedom to challenge and question traditional models and ways of working. From this ambiguity comes opportunity and a way to do things differently.

Playful Leadership

Another way of embracing a different form of leadership is viewing leadership in a playful way. There is very little written about playful leadership as an approach; however, it can be regarded as encouraging and facilitating opportunities for play, approaching problems and challenges with a playful mindset, and encouraging creativity and free thinking (Poulsen, 2015). Ibarra (2015) associates a playful approach with being authentic as a leader, as this is a way for leaders to overcome discomfort about adapting to different roles and expectations. In working with others to understand the perceptions of my team's work, I have been able to use techniques such as Lego Serious Play (Kristiansen and Rasmussen, 2014), where giving adults equitable opportunities to explore the future and different possibilities has had some startling results in terms of engagement and raising challenging questions, as well as changing perspectives. For educational leaders, inspiring curiosity to learn, supporting others and seeking out new opportunities are vital for enacting educational change. Adoption of a playful mindset enables leaders to experiment with different roles and learn whilst doing this. In turn this makes better leaders who are more authentic (Ibarra, 2015).

This notion of playful leadership as supporting leadership development is important in terms of relating back to some of the challenges we have seen concerning the role of both educational development leaders and professors. In my practice, I have started to research into the use of play in leadership to support educational change. Where parameters and expectations of leadership behaviour are opaque, adopting a playful approach can be hugely beneficial in seizing new opportunities and viewing leadership differently. If there are no rules of educational leadership behaviour, who can say that such an approach cannot be done? Playing with identities, creating stories and actively supporting this with others can facilitate bringing people together to solve learning and teaching challenges. These are techniques I have used with my students and staff to support their development as leaders. As we have seen, establishing a vision and engaging others to work towards achieving and realizing that vision is a vital part of leadership. However, what is often less defined is how to actually engage others in creating a vision that is meaningful and one towards which they feel connected. Engaging in play can be a fantastic way of creating meaningful and authentic engagement in vision setting.

Engaging in playful leadership is not without its challenges. There are problems in relation to adults feeling able or allowed to play or seeing the value (James, 2019; Rosen, 2019). I have received feedback that using such techniques is not appropriate and wasting resources, yet a 'traditional' meeting would achieve less and probably cost more. Ironically, in relation to credibility, this could undermine the practice of convincing leadership that the very playful activity is designed to demonstrate. That said, there are so many benefits to play that I would urge educational leaders to be bold and have the confidence to deploy playful techniques. For me, my role as leader and a parent has been instrumental in giving me the confidence to pursue more playful techniques in my practice and enabled me to positively exploit some of the challenges I have found combining leadership with parenthood (Friedman and Westring, 2020). When creating a new team, one of my children's toys inspired me to use it as the metaphor for the culture we wanted to create.

Conclusion: Dancing to a Different Tune

This chapter has explored integrity in learning and teaching leadership from the perspective of a female professor and head of educational development. The ambiguity of these roles can pose challenges establishing credibility as an educational leader whilst navigating tempestuous institutional contexts, yet with that same ambiguity and turbulence comes opportunities to think differently, embrace the ambiguity of the *Third Space* and apply a set of leadership principles to demonstrate an authentic and reflective approach to leadership. Consistency in viewing educational development leaders and professors as bridge builders and mentors gives those occupying these roles latitude to reach out, collaborate imaginatively with others and work free from defined expectations. Whilst initially this may seem daunting to new educational leaders, whether professors or not, the skills inherent in these roles are those that are desperately needed in

UK higher education to move learning and teaching forward. The ambiguity of these roles enables us to establish new identities and create new ways of thinking and engaging with others as leaders. Adapting to the new world of education post the Covid-19 pandemic will require creativity, new thinking and support for change – all skills embodied by educational development leaders. I hope I have demonstrated that there is no agreed way to act as a professor and educational leader; it is up to us to shape and develop these roles so as to meet our skills and the strategic needs of the environment in which we are working.

Am I a real professor? Of course! When I became a professor, I do not think I realized how much freedom and opportunity is contained in this role. If I had, I would have been much more confident to challenge the assumption about what a real professor is. Educational development leaders and professors are naturally aligned as *Third Space* professionals, challenging norms of academic leadership to lead strategic educational change and create new professorial identities. We can find the leadership strategies that enable us to lead with integrity and embrace a different approach, or in other words, to echo Gerald the Giraffe:

> We all can dance … when we find music that we love. (Andreae and Parker-Rees, 1999)

Notes

1 This chapter focuses on UK higher education as that is the context in which I am working, and so the role of the professor is considered in relation to UK universities. However, many of the examples and lessons can be applied to other contexts.
2 'Educational development' is used here to define those activities used for supporting and developing staff. This terminology is more commonly used in the UK and covers the same activities as 'academic development'; see L. Stefani (2003), 'What is staff and educational development?', in P. Kahn and D. Baume (eds), *A Guide to Staff and Educational Development*, 9–23, London: Kogan Page.

References

Acker, S., and Feuerverger, G. (1996), 'Doing good and feeling Bad: The work of women university teachers', *Cambridge Journal of Education* 26 (3): 401–22. doi: 10.1080/0305764960260309.

Andreae, G., and Parker-Rees, G. (1999), *Giraffes Can't Dance*, London: Orchard Books.
Ancona, D. (2012), 'Sensemaking. Framing and acting in the unknown', in S. Snook, N. Nohria and R. Khurana (eds), *The Handbook for Teaching Leadership*, 3–17, Thousand Oaks, CA: Sage.
Baume, D., and Kahn, P. (eds) (2003), *A Guide to Staff & Educational Development*, London: Routledge.
Blackmore, P., and Blackwell, R. (2006), 'Strategic leadership in academic development', *Studies in Higher Education* 31 (3): 373–87. doi: 10.1080/03075070600680893.
Bryman, A., and Lilley, S. (2009), Leadership researchers on leadership in higher education, *Leadership* 5 (3): 331–46. doi.org/10.1177/1742715009337764.
Bluteau, P., and Krumins, M. (2008), 'Engaging academics in developing excellence: Releasing creativity through reward and recognition', *Journal of Further and Higher Education* 32 (4): 415–26. doi: 10.1080/03098770802538137.
Bolden, R., Petrov, G., and Gosling, J. (2008), *Developing Collective Leadership in Higher Education: Final Report*, London: Leadership Foundation for Higher Education.
Esen, M., Bellibas, M. S., and Gumus, S. (2020), 'The evolution of leadership research in higher education for two decades (1995–2014): A bibliometric and content analysis', *International Journal of Leadership in Education* 23 (3): 259–73. doi: 10.1080/13603124.2018.1508753.
Evans, L., Homer, M. and Rayner, S. (2013), 'Professors as academic leaders: The perspectives of "the led"', *Educational Management Administration and Leadership* 41 (5): 674–89. doi: 10.1177/1741143213488589.
Fitch, J. C. (2020), 'Making a college professor film: A case study', *Journal of Creative Communications* 15 (1): 90–105. doi: 10.1177/0973258619866353.
Fisanick, C. (2006), 'Evaluating the absent presence: The professor's body at tenure and promotion', *Review of Education, Pedagogy, and Cultural Studies* 28 (3–4): 325–38.
Fraser, K. (2001), 'Australasian academic developers' conceptions of the Profession', *International Journal of Academic Development* 6 (1): 54–64. doi: 10.1080/13601440110033706.
Friedman, S., and A. Westring (2020), *Parents Who Lead*, Boston, MA: Harvard Business Review Press.
Gosling, D. (2007), 'Context and organisation of educational development', in B. Tomkinson (ed.), *Leading Educational Change*, 11–20, London: SEDA.
Grant, B., and Knowles, S. (2000), 'Flights of imagination: Academic women be(com)ing writers', *International Journal for Academic Development* 5 (1): 6–19.
Green, D. A., and Little, D. (2016), 'Family portrait: A profile of educational developers around the world', *International Journal for Academic Development* 21 (2): 135–50. doi: 10.1080/1360144X.2015.1046875.
Heijstra, T. M., Steinthorsdóttir, F. S. and Einarsdóttir, T. (2017), 'Academic career making and the double-edged role of academic housework', *Gender and Education* 29 (6): 764–80. doi: 10.1080/09540253.2016.1171825.

Ibarra, H. (2015), *Act Like a Leader, Think Like a Leader*, Boston, MA: Harvard Business Review Press.

Inman, M. (2009), 'Learning to lead: Development for middle-level leaders in higher education in England and Wales', *Professional Development in Education* 35 (3): 417–32. doi: 10.1080/13674580802532654.

Inman, M. (2014), 'Bringing life to leadership: The significance of life history in reviewing leadership learning within higher education', *International Journal of Leadership in Education* 17 (2): 237–56. doi: 10.1080/13603124.2013.867076.

James, A (2019), 'Making a case for the playful university', in A. James and C. Nerantzi (eds), *The Power of Play in Higher Education*, 1–19, Cham: Palgrave Macmillan.

Kanuka, H., Holmes, J. and Cowley, S. (2020), 'Teaching development leaders' characteristics and experiences of success in research-focused universities: Narratives of constraint and growth', *Journal of Further and Higher Education* 44 (2): 258–72. doi: 10.1080/0309877X.2018.1529741.

Kinash, S., and Wood, K. (2013), 'Academic developer identity: How we know who we are', *International Journal for Academic Development* 18 (2): 178–89. doi: 10.1080/1360144X.2011.631741.

Kouzes, J., and Posner, B. (2002), *The Leadership Challenge*, 3rd edn, San Francisco: Jossey-Bass.

Kristiansen, P., and Rasmussen, R. (2014), *Building a Better Business Using the Lego Serious Play Method*, New Jersey: Wiley.

Little, D., and Green, D. A. (2012), 'Betwixt and between: Academic developers in the margins', *International Journal for Academic Development* 17 (3): 203–15. doi: 10.1080/1360144X.2012.700895.

Macfarlane, B. (2011), 'The morphing of academic practice: Unbundling and the rise of the para-academic', *Higher Education Quarterly* 65: 59–73. doi: 10.1111/j.1468-2273.2010.00467.x.

Macfarlane, B. (2011b), 'Professors as intellectual leaders: Formation, identity and role', *Studies in Higher Education* 36 (1): 57–73. doi: 10.1080/03075070903443734.

Macfarlane, B. (2012), 'Whisper it softly, professors are really academic developers too', *International Journal for Academic Development* 17 (2): 181–3. doi: 10.1080/1360144X.2012.662465.

Macfarlane, B., and Burg, D. (2018), *Women Professors as Intellectual Leaders*, London: Leadership Foundation for Higher Education.

Macfarlane, B., and Burg, D. (2019), 'Women professors and the academic housework trap', *Journal of Higher Education Policy and Management* 41 (3): 262–74. doi: 10.1080/1360080X.2019.1589682.

Niemi, N. S., and Schwarz, S. L. (2019), 'The gender of innovation: The ascendancy of assessment and technologies in educational development', *New Directions for Teaching and Learning* 2019 (158): 69–81. doi: 10.1002/tl.20340.

Palmer, S., Holt, D. and Challis, D. (2011), 'Strategic leadership of teaching and learning centres: From reality to ideal', *Higher Education Research & Development* 30 (6): 807–21. doi: 10.1080/07294360.2010.539600.

Poulsen, M. (2015), 'What is playful leadership?', *Counterplay*, 9 December. http://www.counterplay.org/what-is-playful-leadership/ (accessed 30 September 2020).

Quinsee, S. (2022), 'Leadership in the *Third Space*', in E. Mcintosh and D. Nutt (eds), *The Impact of the Integrated Practitioner in Higher Education: Studies in Third Space Professionalism*, 33–9, Abington: Routledge.

Quinsee, S., and Bullimore, A. (2011), 'Creating the strategic learning environment at City University London', *Campus-Wide Information Systems* 28 (4): 275–88. doi: 10.1108/10650741111162743.

Rayner, S., Fuller, M., McEwen, L. and Roberts, H. (2010), 'Managing leadership in the UK university: A case for researching the missing professoriate?', *Studies in Higher Education* 35 (6): 617–31. doi: 10.1080/03075070903243100.

Rosen, M. (2019), *Book of Play*, London: Wellcome Collection.

Sánchez-Moreno, M., López-Yáñez, J. and Altopiedi, M. (2015), 'Leadership characteristics and training needs of women and men in charge of Spanish universities', *Gender and Education* 27 (3): 255–72. doi: 10.1080/09540253.2015.1024618.

Stefani, L. (2003), 'What is staff and educational development?', in P. Kahn and D. Baume (eds), *A Guide to Staff and Educational Development*, 9–23, London: Kogan Page.

Sugrue, C., Englund, T., Solbrekke, T. D. and Fossland, T. (2018), 'Trends in the practices of academic developers: Trajectories of higher education?', *Studies in Higher Education* 43 (12): 2336–53. doi: 10.1080/03075079.2017.1326026.

Sutherland, K. A. (2018), 'Holistic academic development: Is it time to think more broadly about the academic development project?', *International Journal for Academic Development* 23 (4): 261–73. doi: 10.1080/1360144X.2018.1524571.

Taylor, K. L. (2005), 'Academic development as institutional leadership: An interplay of person, role, strategy, and institution', *International Journal for Academic Development* 10 (1): 31–46. doi: 10.1080/13601440500099985.

Tight, M. (2002), 'What does it mean to be a professor?', *Higher Education Review* 34: 15–32.

Veles, N., and Carter, M. (2016), 'Imagining a future: Changing the landscape for third space professionals in Australian higher education institutions', *Journal of Higher Education Policy and Management* 38 (5): 519–33. doi: 10.1080/1360080X.2016.1196938.

Whitchurch, C. (2007), 'The changing roles and identities of professional managers in UK higher education', *Perspectives: Policy and Practice in Higher Education* 11 (2): 53–60. doi: 10.1080/13603100701259022.

Whitchurch, C. (2008), 'Shifting identities and blurring boundaries: The emergence of Third Space professionals in UK higher education', *Higher Education Quarterly* 62: 377–96. doi: 10.1111/j.1468-2273.2008.00387.x.

Whitchurch, C. (2009), 'The rise of the blended professional in higher education: A comparison between the United Kingdom, Australia and the United States', *Higher Education* 58 (3): 407–18. doi: 10.1007/sl0734-009-9202-4.

Whitchurch, C. (2015), 'The rise of *Third Space* professionals: Paradoxes and dilemmas', in U. Teichler and W. C. Cummings (eds), *Forming, Recruiting and Managing the Academic Profession*, 79–99, Cham: Springer International.

Developing Higher Education Pedagogy as a Pioneer

Mari Murtonen

Starting My Path to Be a Scholar in University Pedagogy

My personal journey to be a professor of learning and teaching in adult and higher education started after high school, when I worked for a year in an insurance company as an assistant, and learnt that these types of organizations have specific staff training needs. I observed their work and became interested in particular in the staff professional development. My interest in educating adults guided me to study educational sciences and finally to undertake doctoral studies in university students' learning.

Alongside undertaking my master's degree at the University of Turku, I also took courses at the University of Helsinki, the biggest Finnish university. There I participated in a short university pedagogy course in 1996. After the course, I contacted the teacher and joined her research team and worked for a while as an assistant at the Medical Pedagogy Centre that she led. That was the first, and, in those days the only, university pedagogical unit in Finland. There I also met a researcher who later became the leader of the University of Helsinki Centre for University Teaching and Learning. I also met other researchers who later became known as some of the most influential researchers in Finland, and worldwide, within the area of higher education pedagogy research. It is via these colleagues, I have been able to follow the development of this area in another university in addition to my own university, University of Turku. Meeting these people and my experiences in Helsinki were very crucial for my development. They have influenced my conceptions about what university pedagogical education and research should be at the university level.

After finishing my master's degree in 1997, I returned to the University of Turku in my hometown, where I continued to do my doctoral studies under the supervision of a professor who was to become a long-standing teacher and precious mentor in my journey in academia. I continued my university pedagogical studies by participating in a short, basic university pedagogy course in 1998–9, following which I started to teach on the course. At that time there were no long courses on higher education pedagogical training available. However, I realized that in order to teach the university staff, I would myself need the official teacher training of 60 ECTS (The European Credit Transfer and Accumulation System, about 27 hours of work per 1 credit) required by Finnish law. Thus, I completed the official teachers' pedagogical studies programme, offered by the Jyväskylä University of Applied Sciences.

The actual path to becoming a scholar and later a leader in higher education pedagogy started in 2006, when the University of Turku decided to offer more elaborate courses in higher education pedagogy instead of the 10 ECTS basic course that had been available to staff wanting to train in higher education teaching. I was selected to plan, organize and deliver the 60 ECTS programme for higher education pedagogical training to university teachers, and alongside this do research on the topic at the Department of Teacher Training at the Faculty of Education. This was a position and work I was very keen and motivated to undertake.

My visit to the University of Helsinki had made it clear to me that university pedagogy was a new and growing area, and in the 1990s and the beginning of the twenty-first century, the research area of university learning and teaching was growing rapidly. Thus, I believed my own institution, University of Turku, might also be keen to develop it and to invest in its growth. However, things did not go as smoothly as I had anticipated.

Towards High-Quality Teaching in Finnish Universities

Finland is a country with a population of 5.5 million people and with a limited number of universities. Currently there are only thirteen universities, and they all operate under the Ministry of Education and Culture's administrative branch. They are located across the country in main cities, with the biggest universities in the capital, Helsinki. Owing to the limited number of universities and regulation by the law and the ministry, all universities are quite similar in their quality and operation.

Finland has a very high educational status because of its success in the elementary school–level PISA tests (e.g. Sahlberg, 2011; Simola, 2005). This, together with the goals of higher education policy by the European Union (European Commission, 2016), has set high ambitions for Finland to also succeed in higher education. The Finnish Ministry of Education and Culture states in its 'Vision 2030 and Roadmap' the goals of 'Becoming a nation with the most competent labour force' and 'A higher education community with the skills to deliver the best learning outcomes and environments in the world' (Minedu, 2020). Distinctive also is the fact that Finnish university education is free of charge and all students receive a monthly study grant to pursue their studies.

All Finnish universities state in their strategy that they aim to offer high-quality teaching and learning. However, many Finnish university teachers lack any pedagogical training for teaching at university level. This is in strong contradiction with the universities' quality goals as outlined in their strategies. Only a few universities require their teachers to undertake any obligatory pedagogical training to teach in higher education, and if they do, it is usually a short 10 ECTS course. In Finnish universities of applied sciences, the training is more extensive; there, the teachers are usually required to undertake a more elaborate 60 ECTS pedagogical programme.

Pedagogical training for university teachers in its current form, based on constructivist learning theories, started in the 1990s in Finland (see Table 3.1). Earlier, in the 1970s, there was some training based on behaviourist teaching theories, but teachers did not consider this training useful (Järvinen, 2007). The increased focus on research on university learning and teaching in the 1990s probably speeded up the development of higher education pedagogical training. In most universities, some type of pedagogical training for staff became an established practice during the 1990s. The training was usually about 10 ECTS credits and lasted from half a year to one year.

The universities which do not offer the obligatory training in higher education teaching follow the Humboldtian ideal (Simons and Elen, 2007) of a teacher being qualified to teach if they have the subject/disciplinary expertise and knowledge. As per the Humboldtian approach, all skills required for teaching are learnt by 'education through research'. This approach to university teaching is typical in many universities across the world. However, many universities have developed higher education teacher training programmes, and there is already evidence to suggest that such pedagogical training is proving effective (e.g. Chalmers and Gardiner, 2015; Rienties and Hosein, 2015; Rienties and Kinchin, 2014). In addition, staff are becoming increasingly aware of the need to undertake such pedagogical training to support them with their teaching practice (Murtonen and Vilppu, 2020; Sointu, Hirsto and Murtonen, 2019).

Offering voluntary pedagogical courses has been a success, and many universities have found their courses have been so popular that they have not been able to accommodate the growing demand for such courses and not all applicants can be accepted. The typical selection criteria have been the length of experience as a teacher and the amount of teaching responsibility. This has meant that novice teachers often cannot access such training, and this has led to the situation where these novices have to start their teaching career without any pedagogical training. This situation is not ideal, because studies have demonstrated that experienced teachers may change their teaching views very slowly (Postareff, Lindblom-Ylänne and Nevgi, 2007), and that experienced teachers without pedagogical training are not always willing to develop their teaching practices (Murtonen, Virtanen and Vilppu, 2022). This creates a complex situation as when these teachers are novice, they do not have access to the training, and as experienced teachers, they become so established in their ways of approaching teaching that they are reluctant to change their practices when they finally have access to such training. Studies by Vilppu et al. (2020) and Heinonen et al. (2022) show that even short training can have remarkable effect on novice teachers' views of teaching. Thus, pedagogical training should not be optional and left to the later years of teachers' careers.

Establishment of Higher Education Pedagogical Education in Finland and Turku

At the University of Turku, training was organized by the central administration as 'staff training' from the middle of the 1990s until 2006, following which the University gave the task of offering pedagogical education to the Faculty of Education. The move to giving the Faculty of Education responsibility for pedagogical training was driven by two reasons. First, the goal was to offer a more elaborate 60 ECTS pedagogical studies programme which, according to Finnish law, offers formal qualification to work as a teacher. Second, to be accepted and respected by the other faculties, the pedagogical education needed to be research-based. Consequently, two specialist positions for senior researchers became available within the Faculty of Education. Although both positions had a research focus, they were accompanied with a very heavy teaching load.

Establishing university pedagogical education in Finnish universities was not always an easy job, and the development has not been straightforward. In many universities, there were tense negotiations between the faculties of education, who were able to award the 60 ECTS pedagogical studies required by Finnish law, and the educational development units, who in many universities organized these studies leading to the credits. These units were often placed under the university central administration, and often they had not collaborated before with the faculty of education at their university. Nowadays, the faculties of education in most universities are responsible for developing and researching university pedagogy, and in many cases also responsible for delivering the courses.

At the University of Turku, there were many negotiations in the beginning as to how pedagogical education would be organized. The Faculty of Education's Head of Studies wanted to offer only the whole 60 ECTS education, not smaller packages, because all other pedagogical studies offered by the faculty were organized in that way. Usually these pedagogical studies require participants to study pedagogy full time for one year. That kind of a model had been tested at the University of Eastern Finland (former University of Joensuu). The experience was that many teachers wanted to participate in smaller bite-size courses rather than undertake the whole 60 ECTS education, because many were doubtful of their ability to complete (or did not want to undertake) the whole 60 ECTS package (Meriläinen, 2006).

Other Finnish universities were offering smaller packages (10 or 25 ECTS), so in my role as the senior researcher who was assigned to oversee the development of this programme, and who knew the situation in other universities, I suggested the University of Turku should adopt a more flexible approach. I believed university staff would not leave their job for one year to study pedagogy. Instead, as I suggested, the studies should be offered in smaller packages of 10, 15 and 35 ECTS, which would be possible to complete in around three to four years. As a compromise, the faculty started to offer 25 and 35 ECTS packages which together formed the 60 ECTS pedagogical studies. However, most of the teachers were keen to only undertake 10 ECTS packages, so the university central administration continued offering this smaller package alongside the larger packages being offered by the Faculty of Education. This resulted in a situation where the participants had many types of study rights, that is some had a right to study only 10 ECTS, while other had applied directly to the 25 ECTS package. This caused problems for us as organizers, because we needed to keep several different records on different type of students' credits. After a few years, the faculty started to offer all three packages, 10, 15 and 35 ECTS. Later, there has been even smaller packages of 5 ETCS, and the participants can collect their first 25 ECTS in many ways, and these comprise both obligatory and optional courses. We still have developmental issues with issuing the credit points, and hope that micro credential or badge systems will help us in the future.

My Rocky Road to Becoming a Leader

When looking back to 2006, when I was selected as a university researcher, I see a naive belief in me, in trusting that there would soon be a pedagogical centre at the University of Turku like the one I had seen at the University of Helsinki. There, we would have sufficient resources to offer high-quality pedagogical courses for staff, and there I could do research on the pedagogical topics alongside a motivated research group. Looking at the situation now, that is about what has actually happened, and where I am now in 2022. However, the journey has not been as straightforward as I believed it would be, and it has taken fifteen long years.

The two things which have kept me driven in these turbulent times are my passion to work with university staff and conducting research on higher education pedagogical issues. In my journey, I have faced the typical problems of any working community, such as differences in goals and conceptions from my colleagues and sometimes even the institution about the work (Laack, 2021; Maier and Brunstein, 2001), and lack of sufficient resources and help (Clarke and Reid, 2013; Stupnisky, Weaver-Hightower and Kartoshkina, 2015).

The cultures in different Finnish universities have been different in relation to, for example, how much and in which phase of the career responsibility was given to staff. I had seen at the University of Helsinki many kinds of leadership positions being given to early career academics, but this was not the case at my university, faculty and indeed my department. I was myself not interested in leadership positions in the beginning, which probably was a mistake. Later I realized that such a position was the key to the functions I wanted to do, namely, organize high-quality teaching and do research on it, so with time this desire sparked my interest in leadership positions. In practice, I was the leader of the entire university's staff pedagogical training from the beginning of 2006. I was responsible for negotiating resources that would ensure the best learning experience for students, for the curriculum and most of the teaching, for writing applications to request funding to support pedagogical interventions and research, and finally for reporting on the success of such initiatives. At times I have been, and currently am, supported by great colleagues with whom I share this responsibility, but there have been changes in personnel and this has sometimes even led to increased workload.

When I compare my tasks at the time when I began as a researcher with focus on university pedagogy, and now when I have become a leader of the University of Turku Centre for University Pedagogy and Research (UTUPEDA), my tasks were actually more demanding in the early years. Then the whole area of university learning and teaching was new and required several negotiations with university central administration, the Faculty of Education and its two Departments, all other faculties and the doctoral school. I had, of course, some support in this task; for example, the vice rector of the University was interested in pedagogical studies, the dean of the Faculty was supportive, and my former supervisor was a great help, but there were actually not many who had a complete understanding of the area.

It has been the most burdening thing both emotionally and in terms of time in the whole path, that not many understand and appreciate the tasks running the university's pedagogy education entails. This has led to the situation where I have often needed to fight the corner for pedagogical education, having to explain the whole thing over and over again to different and changing actors and working hard to convince them of the need to act in a certain way. Sometimes I have felt like it was my own idea and wish to offer university pedagogical courses instead of the university hiring and asking me to do this job.

Placing the university pedagogy education under the Department of Teacher Education was, on the one hand, suitable for the education and research tasks but, on the other hand, organizationally a compromise. The departments of teacher education in Finland have a long tradition of focusing only on elementary school teacher and subject teacher training. As the university pedagogy education task is quite different to the massive task of training teachers for schools, university pedagogy has not always been at the top of the priority list of departmental decisions.

Another source for stress has been the limited possibility for conducting research. Although my title was a senior researcher, which in Finland is a good position and should allow the worker to conduct research, in practice I had almost no time to do research. In my work, I was either alone or accompanied by one colleague, and the task was to offer the 60 ECTS education for the whole university, comprised of six faculties. This left me with no time for research.

In personal life, becoming a mother to three children (in 2003, 2008 and 2010) made conducting research even more difficult, since there was less time in the evenings, weekends and holidays to do research. Luckily, my husband has always shared the household chores with me and shared responsibilities for childcare. He also stayed at home with the children for some years, allowing me to return to work after my maternity leave. Without his support, being a mother, a researcher and developing as a leader in teaching and learning would have been impossible. According to a study by Prinz et al. (2020), supporting partners are a necessity for many women to succeed in academic life.

The most important positive development in my research career was funding that we secured from the Finnish Ministry of Education and Culture in 2017 to develop and study a digital pedagogical solution for university teachers and doctoral students. Within this University Pedagogical Support (UNIPS) project, I was finally able to have some help to conduct research. The outcomes of this project gave me sufficient credibility to apply for professorship and thus to progress in my career. Another instance that has been very important for both my personal development and for the whole Finnish higher education pedagogy development has been the network of educators and developers called Kouke.

Finnish Kouke Support Network for Educators and Developers of Higher Education Pedagogy

As one of the pioneers in university pedagogy teaching, there were not many models or much help available to me when designing and creating pedagogical studies courses. It was typical that those who designed and organized university pedagogical training in Finland were themselves not educated in higher education pedagogy. The developers of such courses usually do not have a background in teacher education. The developers of university pedagogy thus themselves suffered from the same lack of pedagogical training and help as other university teachers (e.g. Brownell and Tanner, 2012; Kane, Sandretto and Heath, 2002; Murtonen and Vilppu, 2020; Remmik et al., 2011). Absence of pedagogical guidance combined with limited teaching preparation time has been found to drive many new teachers to copy their former teachers' style (Knight, 2002). However, lack of models could sometimes be considered as a good thing, as

Table 3.1 Development of Finnish University Pedagogical Education and my Personal Career Path since the 1970s

Year	Pedagogical Staff Training in Finnish Universities	My Career Path
1970s	Some training —Emphasis on behaviouristic theories —Faced criticism among staff	
1980s	Almost no training	
1990s	Short training courses (about 10 ECTS) offered by many universities —Expansion of research based on constructivist theories on university learning and teaching —Staff very interested in participating	—Studying in Turku during 1993–6 —Visit to Helsinki in 1996–7 —Master's degree in 1997 and starting doctoral studies, University of Turku
2000s	Expansion of trainings —Many universities start to offer longer trainings (20–60 ECTS) —Strengthening pedagogical research on the basis of trainings	—PhD 2005. Selected in 2006 to university researcher position to plan, organize and research the new 60 ECTS pedagogical studies at the University of Turku
2010s	Consolidation of trainings —Departments of teacher education approving university pedagogy trainings as official pedagogical training regulated by the Finnish law. —Some universities requiring obligatory pedagogical training (usually 10–25 ECTS) —Finnish Ministry of Education and Culture funding the development of research-based higher education pedagogy	—Selected as a professor of higher education pedagogy at Tampere University in 2018, starting in 2019
2020s	Continuing consolidation —Even stronger emphasis on pedagogical training in many functions, such as strategies of universities, work plans of staff, new workers' selection processes, etc. —Plans about continuing pedagogical education paths for staff	—Selected as a professor of higher education pedagogy at the University of Turku in 2020 —Selected as director of the University of Turku Centre for University Pedagogy (UTUPEDA), starting in 2021

in this case it forced us develop something new together and really consider justifications for all choices.

In the beginning of creating the University of Turku pedagogical programme, we benchmarked all Finnish, the available Scandinavian, and some other pedagogical education programmes. However, we also needed other colleagues to discuss the more complex problems and get support for our ideas. While feeling a bit lonely in leading the developmental task, a support network was more than welcome. In Finland, a network called Pedaforum has been in operation since the early 1990s. The network is well known in universities and has been engaged in organizing pedagogical conferences each year in some Finnish universities. Many higher education teachers present their developmental pedagogical innovations and research at this conference.

Under the Pedaforum network, there has been a sub-network for teachers and developers of university pedagogy education called Kouke (In Finnish *Kouluttajien ja kehittäjien verkosto*). At the same time as when we developed the higher education pedagogical programme at Turku, other Finnish universities were also developing their university pedagogical training programmes. The network has offered the participants both collegial support and ideas on how the training should be organized. With the Kouke network, we, for example, created together the central learning outcomes for a 10 ECTS basic university pedagogy course.

In recent years, the Finnish Ministry of Education and Culture has emphasized collaboration between the Universities and Universities of Applied Sciences. In line with this emphasis, the higher education pedagogy developers have started to collaborate, and the Pedaforum network has been replaced by KoPe (Higher Education, in Finnish *Korkeakoulupedagogiikka*) network.

In most Finnish universities, like at Turku, the number of staff dedicated to running the university pedagogy education programmes has been limited, with typically one to three persons, so those engaged in developing and running such programmes have all felt the need for and benefited from the help from this network. The network has been important for me personally and for the development of pedagogical education at the University of Turku. However, the times have changed now, and we could say that the Finnish university pedagogy education is not in its early years anymore but has become an established educational programme. This also means that new members of the group of educators and developers need new kinds of support. This type of network will probably offer that support also in the future.

UNIPS – the Finnish Innovation for Organizing Pedagogical Training Together

One of the innovations that originated in the Kouke meeting during early 2000 was the idea of organizing pedagogical education together through digital devices. Most universities suffered from limited resources in organizing the training and high number of applicants to courses. Foreign workers and doctoral students, in particular, were asking for courses in English. With a limited number of personnel, it was hard to offer courses for all who were willing to participate, and simultaneously in many languages, whilst also ensuring high quality content.

I presented the idea of small digital pedagogical courses to the University of Turku, and we got strategic funding for a project called the University of Turku Pedagogical Support (UTUPS) in 2015. I was the main designer and hired a project researcher to develop the digital environment alongside me. We were able to offer short pedagogical modules in English for international staff and doctoral students via UTUPS. In 2016, the vice rector encouraged us to submit an application to the Ministry of Education and Culture for getting funding to collaborate with other Finnish universities in creating these digital modules. The application was informed by the work of the UTUPS, and in collaboration with the members in the Kouke group who expressed a desire to participate. The ministry allowed a key funding project for the University Pedagogical Support (UNIPS) for the years 2017–19 (Murtonen et al., 2019). With this funding, the UNIPS solution was developed in collaboration with eight (out of thirteen) Finnish universities (see unips.fi). I was selected as the leader of the project, and this position allowed me to develop a further understanding of Finnish university pedagogy education.

The funder, the Finnish Ministry of Education and Culture, has declared often that all development and decisions in educational solutions should be evidence-based. The UNIPS project was thus research-based, meaning that we not only had feedback from the participants in the end saying that they enjoyed their studies in the UNIPS environment, but also that developments and changes were informed both by student evaluations and research evidence (Murtonen et al., 2019). We secured rich and rigorous research data with quantitative evidence from questionnaires, qualitative data from open-ended questions and eye-tracking data on watching videos on teaching and learning situations. These data showed that in addition to the benefits of prior pedagogical training (Murtonen, Anto, Laakkonen and Vilppu, in press), these short pedagogical modules were able to change participants' conceptions and ideas of teaching

(Vilppu et al., 2019). For me, personally this was a very important step in my career: finally, I had an opportunity to do research; hire someone to help me with data collection, analyses and writing; and publish in high-quality journals. This also offered me recognition in the promotion process by being appointed as the professor of higher education pedagogy based on the outcomes of this research.

The UNIPS modules are currently offered in many Finnish universities, and new modules are constantly developed. The main idea of UNIPS is to develop module content in collaboration with other universities, ensuring collaboration also in the future. The modules can be used by the teachers for self-study, or the universities can offer them as guided studies with a possibility to earn 1 ECTS per module. The future goal is to develop discipline-specific modules and to work together with universities from other countries in order to give teachers the opportunity to develop their pedagogical expertise in collaboration with their international colleagues. I believe international collaboration between teachers in pedagogical issues would raise the quality of teaching in higher education.

Lessons Learnt and Future Perspectives in University Pedagogy

Now, after fifteen years since I was selected to plan and offer a university pedagogy 60-credit programme at the University of Turku, I am still partly struggling with the same issues that I had at the beginning, such as insufficient resources compared to the scale of the task. I know the situation is quite similar in most Finnish universities, but this does not offer an excuse for under-resourcing. Everybody seems to agree that these courses are important, and the participants are very satisfied with their training. In discussions with faculties and university leaders, it is typical that many new, important pedagogical and research ideas and development goals arise, but when it comes to the question of who pays for it, there are not anymore so many comments. I have found it quite hard to draw the line between important development tasks and research, since I would like to do both, but there is not enough time to do justice to either.

On becoming a professor, I have now managed to secure some more time to conduct research than what I had as a researcher, but rejecting an interesting teaching or development project due to limited time has not come easily to me. I often struggle with the syndrome of trying to do everything – I have tried to learn to say 'no', a skill that many of us try to learn, and to remember that

I have my tasks listed in my work plan, and none can expect me to do all the extra work that comes up. I would say that this is the lesson to be learnt for new academic developers and researchers in this area, that the university defines which functions it wants to fund, and if there is no funding for something, it does not mean that you need to do it in your free time.

Being a pioneer in university pedagogy has been both demanding and rewarding. Having to work with a variety of stakeholders – the university central administration, the university vice rector of education, doctoral school representatives, the faculty of education and its two departments, and naturally all other faculties at the university who are our 'customers' – the expressed wishes and requirements from all these actors have sometimes been overwhelming and even contradictory. The over twenty years history has been a constant process of explaining and justifying our activity for all instances, and when the representatives of these instances change, the whole process usually has to be started all over again. It feels almost like I have my own agenda to promote at the university, although the situation is that I have been hired to do work that the university wants me to do. This has all taught me a lot about a university and its functions, although sometimes this does become frustrating.

Maybe the biggest individual disappointment in my journey to a professor has been when I was not selected as a tenure professor in 2017 at the University of Turku. The challenging thing to accept was that although the domain was higher education pedagogy, the selection was made by emphasizing the h-index value (a research impact metric) of the applicants. Being burdened with a heavy teaching load during the years, I could not compete in that aspect very well. However, the person who was selected as a tenure professor was familiar to me and working with her in Turku was great. She brought to Turku just the kind of research-directed attitude that I had missed.

One year later, a higher education pedagogy professor position opened at Tampere University, a new university coalition of three former universities. I was selected for this position. It appeared to be a wonderful experience, because working in another university and seeing the practices of a new, innovative university coalition taught me a lot. I began to know many interesting people and began research projects and collaboration that are still ongoing. Working in Tampere, however, ended quite soon. The person who was selected as a tenure professor to Turku got another job and the professorship in Turku was opened again, and I applied for this, because my family still lived in Turku. This time I was selected. Working at Tampere physically ended suddenly due to Covid-19. When I left my office for the last time in March 2020, I did not know that

I would be selected for the position of a professor at the University of Turku and that I would not be able to access my Tampere office before June 2020, when I emptied my office.

As a conclusion, I would say that the actual work of interacting with university teachers and other staff from different faculties involved in teaching and supervising students has been very interesting and rewarding. The participants in pedagogical courses are usually very motivated and eager to develop their pedagogical expertise. Doing research with them and about them and their students has been very exciting and satisfying. In addition, collaborating with other pedagogical developers and researchers in the domain has been very motivating.

The future of university pedagogy in Finland seems to be in search for new directions. Processes such as lifelong or continuous learning, personalized learning environments and digitalization have already been shaping the education offered. Sudden changes in society, such as those due to Covid-19, may have dramatic consequences for teaching and university pedagogy, which need to be addressed quickly. We need to offer our teaching and supervising staff the right support at the right time to be able to help them, and in turn the learning of students. It is important that there is recognition that training in higher education pedagogy is a lifelong endeavour and should be ongoing and not delivered via one package of courses. We need much more research on both teachers' and students' learning to be able to develop the right kind of training and materials for them. Research is the way to ensure that university teachers' training will be proactive, not just reactive, meaning that we can offer them tools for their expertise development before they face the challenges and problems with their teaching. I am happy to be currently in a position where I hope to be able to lead this new direction of teacher development.

References

Boice, R. (1991), 'New faculty as teachers', *Journal of Higher Education* 62 (2): 150–73.

Brownell, S., and Tanner, K. (2012), 'Barriers to faculty pedagogical change: Lack of training, time, incentives, and tensions with professional identity', *CBE – Life Sciences Education* 11: 339–46.

Chalmers, D., and Gardiner, D. (2015), 'An evaluation framework for identifying the effectiveness and impact of academic teacher development programmes', *Studies in Educational Evaluation* 46: 81–91.

Clarke, C., and Reid, J. (2013), 'Foundational academic development: Building collegiality across divides?', *International Journal for Academic Development* 18: 318–30. https://doi.org/10.1080/1360144X.2012.728529.

European Commission (2016), 'Communication from the Commission to the European Parliament, the Council, the European Economic and Social Committee and the Committee of the Regions. Improving and modernising education', European Commission, Brussels, 7 December, COM(2016)941 final. https://ec.europa.eu/transparency/regdoc/rep/1/2016/EN/COM-2016-941-F1-EN-MAIN.PDF (accessed 12 October 2020).

Heinonen, N., Katajavuori, N., Murtonen, M. and Södervik, I. (2022). Short pedagogical training in supporting university teachers' professional vision: A comparison of prospective and current faculty teachers. Instructional Science. https://doi.org/10.1007/s11251-022-09603-7.

Järvinen, A. (2007), Anna Raija Nummenmaa interviewing Annikki Järvinen on the history of university pedagogy in Finland, 23 March, Pedaforum meeting at Tampere.

Kane, R., Sandretto, S. and Heath, C. (2002), 'Telling half the story: A critical review of the research on the teaching beliefs and practices of university academics', *Review of Educational Research* 72 (2): 177–228.

Knight, P. (2002), *Being a Teacher in Higher Education*, Maidenhead, UK: Society for Research into Higher Education & Open University Press.

Laack, N. N. (2021), 'Aligning your goals with your colleagues, department, and institution', in R. A. Chandra, N. Vapiwala and C. R. Thomas Jr. (eds), *Career Development in Academic Radiation Oncology*, 121–9, Cham: Springer International Publishing. https://doi.org/10.1007/978-3-030-71855-8_10.

Maier, G., and Brunstein, J. C. (2001), 'The role of personal work goals in newcomers' job satisfaction and organizational commitment: A longitudinal analysis', *Journal of Applied Psychology* 86: 1034–42.

Meriläinen (2006), interview by phone on university pedagogy education at the University of Joensuu, 1 November.

Minedu (2020), 'Universities in Finland', Ministry of Education and Culture. https://minedu.fi/en/universities (accessed 15 September 2020).

Minedu (2020), 'Vision 2030 & Roadmap', Ministry of Education and Culture. https://minedu.fi/en/vision-2030 (accessed 15 September 2020).

Murtonen, M., Anto, E., Laakkonen, E. and Vilppu, H. (2022), 'University teachers' focus on students: Examining the relationships between visual attention, conceptions of teaching and pedagogical training', *Frontline Learning Research* 10 (2): 66–87.

Murtonen, M., Laato, S., Lipponen, E., Salmento, H., Vilppu, H., Maikkola, M., Vaskuri, P., Mäkinen, M., Naukkarinen, J., Virkki-Hatakka, T., Pajarre, E., Selänne, S. and Skaniakos, T. (2019), 'Creating a national digital learning environment for enhancing university teachers' pedagogical expertise – The case UNIPS', *International Journal of Learning, Teaching and Educational Research* 18 (13): 7–29.

Murtonen, M., and Vilppu, H. (2020), 'Change in university pedagogical culture – The impact of increased pedagogical training on first teaching experiences', *International Journal of Learning, Teaching and Educational Research* 19 (3): 367–83.

Murtonen, M., Virtanen, H. and Vilppu, H. (2022). Connections between higher education pedagogy developers' regulation skills and the concrete ways they develop their own pedagogical expertise. A paper presentation at the Earli SIG Higher Education, Gadiz, Spain, 27–30 June 2022.

Postareff, L., Lindblom-Ylänne, S. and Nevgi, A. (2007), 'The effect of pedagogical training on teaching in higher education', *Teaching and Teacher Education* 23 (5): 557–71.

Prinz, A., Zeeb, H., Flanigan, A. E., Renkl, A. and Kiewra, K. A. (2020), 'Conversations with five highly successful female educational psychologists: Patricia Alexander, Carol Dweck, Jacquelynne Eccles, Mareike Kunter, and Tamara van Gog', *Educational Psychology Review* 33: 763–95. https://link.springer.com/article/10.1007/s10648-020-09552-y.

Remmik, M., Karm, M., Haamer, A., and Lepp, L. (2011), 'Early-career academics' learning in academic communities', *International Journal for Academic Development* 16: 187–99.

Rienties, B., and Kinchin, I. (2014), 'Understanding (in) formal learning in an academic development programme: A social network perspective', *Teaching and Teacher Education* 39: 123–35.

Rienties, B., and Hosein, A. (2015), 'Unpacking (in) formal learning in an academic development programme: A mixed-method social network perspective', *International Journal for Academic Development* 20 (2): 163–77.

Sahlberg, P. (2011), 'PISA in Finland: An education miracle or an obstacle to change?', *CEPS Journal* 1 (3): 119–40.

Simola, H. (2005), 'The Finnish miracle of PISA: Historical and sociological remarks on teaching and teacher education', *Comparative Education* 41 (4): 455–70.

Simons, M., and Elen, J. (2007), 'The "research–teaching nexus" and "education through research": An exploration of ambivalences', *Studies in Higher Education* 32: 617–31.

Sointu, E., Hirsto, L. and Murtonen, M. (2019), 'Editorial: Transforming higher education teaching and learning environments – Introduction to the special issue', *International Journal of Learning, Teaching and Educational Research* 18 (13): 1–6.

Stupnisky, R. H., Weaver-Hightower, M. B. and Kartoshkina, Y. (2015), 'Exploring and testing the predictors of new faculty success: A mixed methods study', *Studies in Higher Education* 40: 368–90. https://doi.org/10.1080/03075079.2013.842220.

Vilppu, H., Södervik, I., Postareff, L. and Murtonen, M. (2019), 'The effect of short online pedagogical training on university teachers' interpretations of teaching–learning situations', *Instructional Science* 47 (6): 679–709.

4

A Leadership Journey in Change and Uncertainty

Jeni Fountain

Introduction

My learning and teaching leadership journey has certainly required a lot of deep breaths! In fact, my career footsteps have been eclectic, walking down many different paths entirely. I initially trained and worked as a primary school teacher, mostly teaching young adolescents. I progressed into school management and leadership positions, then moved into secondary school education, again with leadership roles. Then after thirteen years, I took a new path and completed my law degree, and was admitted to the bar. Due to family commitments, I next ventured part-time into tertiary education and was an owner/operator of two hospitality businesses. But the part-time venture quickly became full-time once I completed my master's, and I felt the pull of education once more. After experiencing different professional fields and roles, I knew I had found my best 'fit' as a lecturer and programme lead for a suite of legal qualifications. I knew the subjects, I knew the industry and I knew how to manage staff and lead a business unit. What I *didn't* know was the veritable tsunami of change, barely glimpsed on the horizon, but moving rapidly and inexorably to our shores.

It began in 2017, six months prior to the institutional merger of two well-known legacy institutes. I had already moved from the classroom – an online one at that – to full-time management, through a series of incremental career progressions as roles became vacant, or team re-structures created new positions. I found that I enjoyed managing day-to-day service delivery as well as tackling longer-term planning and strategic development, looking for efficiencies and hunting down new opportunities. With a business background, I wasn't fazed by managing budgets and on-the-fly decision-making; my time in the hospitality sector had also honed my interpersonal and communication skills, so that I found forging a team culture and positive morale somewhat less challenging than other new managers in my own organization. However, I had barely moved offices, let alone gotten my feet under my new desk, when I needed to assume some of the leadership responsibilities as the post-merger new entity strove to consolidate curricula, staff and resources.

Organizational structures in New Zealand's larger higher education providers are generally 'taller' than many commercial enterprises, with a cascading executive-management hierarchy reflecting several levels of authority and responsibility from 'Tier 1' Chief Executive governance and oversight, to classroom delivery and learner support (Toi Ohomai Institute of Technology, 2019). In terms of my position description, I started and ended 2017 in different Tier 4 leadership positions, in different institutes, and by June 2018 was in a different acting Tier 3 position. By August 2018, I had applied for and secured the role as faculty leader Business Management and Legal Studies and was now leading a team of fifty-two staff and approximately two thousand students across twelve different delivery sites.

In January 2019, the majority of my faculty staff were relocated to a different campus within the same city, and with our merger barely two years old, February 2019 saw the Education Minister announce a major proposal to reform vocational education and training in New Zealand. Whilst waiting for this reform to be finalized over a projected five-year timeframe, our merged institute undertook an all-faculty structure and management review. In 2020 I find myself barely a year in my current seat as dean of a 'mega-faculty' group incorporating health, education and environment qualifications, yet all but submerged by the challenges of keeping the institute afloat in the floodwaters of a global pandemic.

Change has been the constant in my own higher education learning and teaching leadership journey, just as it has been across the sector; indeed, change is a constant in almost all our lives. Unlike Lewin's (1947, 1951) classic change management model of 'unfreeze, change and refreeze' for effective organization change, my higher education organizational change experience has mostly been stalled in the unfreeze stage. With an inability to resolve organizational or societal uncertainty in order to change and move to refreeze, my leadership has focused on the connection with students and creating a faculty that nurtures sound learning and teaching practices. This chapter will reflect on the journey so far and share three key learnings that have helped me to catch my breath, against the backdrop of our country's cultural, economic and social milieu. I also share examples of learning from my own vulnerability when things have not gone so well.

Part 1. Organizational Change – in Theory and in My World

Kurt Lewin, a social psychologist who arguably pioneered the study of organizational culture in the 1940s and 1950s, developed a simple three-step change model to explain the assumptions underpinning changes in human systems (Lewin, 1947, 1951). More than fifty years on, and despite extensive critique, for example, that it is misleadingly over-simplistic, linear and/or episodic, Lewin's model is still widely taught and widely applied (Cummings et al., 2016). In the broadest sense, the model offers a base from which to consider the group dynamics of social change, the forces that impact leaders and the different actions required of them in response. Lewin's model, summarized by Esa et al. (2017), proposes three basic levels in the process of efficient change implementation: unfreeze, moving/change and refreeze. 'Unfreeze' refers to the process of 'melting' the behaviours, beliefs or established status quo in an organization; 'moving' or 'change' occurs with some form of restructuring or pivoting of strategic intent; and 'refreezing' describes the embedding or settling of new culture and practices within the organization (Esa et al., 2017).

In this model, change is envisaged as a flow from stasis to a period of dynamic change, and then returning to some manner of (quasi) equilibrium (Verhulst and Lambrechts, 2014). This is more or less aligned with some parts of my experience, less so with others. Until I encountered this time of rapid change, my assumptions about change management and leadership which underpinned my role had been largely unexamined. I had a philosophical understanding about what it meant to be a 'change agent' (Cummings et al., 2016), but, in examining the particular cultural, social and economic/political goals of my new organization, I came to better appreciate the need to rethink the rhetoric. Day-to-day, I needed to focus on what was achievable, rather than purely aspirational. As I questioned the expectations of my new environment, I came to examine my own practice as a manager and leader, and began to adapt the way I was working.

The first 'unfreeze' that I encountered in 2017 provides a good illustration. As the position progressions described above meant that I was now one of the senior leadership team, I was party to many of the challenges which came with the merger of two institutes of technology and polytechnics (ITPs), which although geographically close, had very different organizational cultures, policies, management structures and educational programmes. Even where there was overlap, there was dissonance – staff and stakeholders may have talked the same language, but interpretations and inferences often differed. The rationale for the merger was only partly to reduce costs, and more presented as a mechanism for sustainability and growth. However, some staff, and some stakeholders in each city where the two main campuses were based, did not see it that way. There were visits from the sector's academic and administrative staff unions, stories in the media, and a high level of disengagement and lack of trust reported in our annual staff engagement survey.

Verhulst and Lambrechts's (2014) study of higher education from the perspective of organizational change management emphasizes the human factors at play: 'resistance, communication, empowerment and involvement, and organisational culture' (p. 4), and these were all evident in my setting. In the early days of joining staff from both legacy institutes into a new, combined faculty, I had expected that I would simply be stepping forward and 'leading from the front' (Hill, 2010), doing the job that I already knew but in a different environment. But there will always be a difference between those who have been a long time in a work environment and those who arrive later, and it takes time to learn 'how we do things around here'. I had to address the human factors, definitely, but first I had to address my own 'otherness' – the unconscious assumption of 'Us' and 'Them' which Ideland and Malmberg (2014) say can lead to 'exclusion through intentions of inclusion' (p. 369). I was 'other' not only to half my new staff from the previous partner organization I had not been a part of, but also to my own new role as a leader and modeller of a new, nascent, post-merger culture. I could not show hesitation or deviate from the merger's chosen path, so I chose to embrace it.

My nature has always been to be an active rather than passive participant. For me, then, embracing this new journey meant that I got involved and looked for ways to synthesize my old and new experiences, all the while accepting that there were areas in which I needed to be a learner, not the leader. I focused on building relationships and noting those around me who were ready to grow and take on projects, responsibilities and distributed leadership roles to build capacity for change and improvement. To do this, I travelled to our various campuses. I asked to be included in team meetings, conducted my own management meetings, alternating the physical location and enabling join online options. I met with individual staff to understand who they are, their personal journey in the organization and what they do in the faculty. I met both committed team members and some who were less engaged, all the while piecing together the big people picture of what the team needed from me as a leader, in order for our faculty people and programmes to best survive the nationwide change to vocational education delivery.

Hill (2010) calls this 'leading from behind', citing the metaphor of a shepherd, employed by Nelson Mandela: 'He stays behind the flock, letting the most nimble go out ahead, whereupon the others follow, not realizing that all along they are being directed from behind' (Mandela, cited in Hill, 2010, para. 2). The concept here is about not being the source of all decision-making, but rather standing back and fostering people's 'collective genius' (Hill, 2010). This is a strategy I have been consciously fostering in my personal leadership repertoire, and is the first key learning which I believe has played a key part in my development as a leader.

Another approach I adopted early during this period of 'unfreeze' was developing strong and transparent communication lines, avoiding any sense of there being 'insiders' who were privileged with foreknowledge of initiatives or opportunities. A sense of equity and 'fair play' has always been important to me personally, and is shared, I believe, by the majority of staff in any business: an impression gained from years of anecdotal feedback and coffee-break conversations. I began what has become a tradition of sending an emailed newsletter to all staff in my faculty, at irregular intervals, but at least monthly. The newsletter is deliberately written informally, to distinguish the tone from chief executive, council, or marketing all-staff emails. I am writing to my team in both their personal and professional identities, and I carefully balance my topics. I might include some statistics from our institution's reporting 'dashboard' about how our faculty is tracking against others, and against budgeted targets, for enrolments, course completions, survey responses, graduations – and more. If I have noticed some general slippage, I will take the chance to remind all staff of professional responsibilities, with items like marking turnaround, or working from home protocols. I include notices about functions and events, reminders about applying for leave, or external programme monitor visits. I also try to make it personal, even more so since the arrival of Covid-19 and associated restrictions, with reminders about wellness and links to support. And there's always humour – I love a good GIF or witty cartoon or pithy saying – if I can make it fit our teaching and learning setting, I'll use it! I have found these faculty emails a highly effective way to stay in touch when it might be weeks between face-to face encounters. Regular communications also counter the management style 'out of sight, out of mind', which I have myself been subjected to earlier in my career and rate as one of my more frustrating professional experiences.

Along with leading from behind and clear and collective communication channels, a third key learning is my personal mantra that sometimes 'the answer is not the right answer, it's the right answer now'. When living with uncertainty becomes the new norm, we need to have confidence and courage to back ourselves, to do the best job we can, and then to let it go. If leaders can't sleep at night, how can we sincerely tell our teams that wellness matters, and that they need to make the same leaps of faith with their students' best interests in mind, as we are doing for them?

As I write this three years on, our merger is behind us and there are only occasional reminders of the 'Us' and 'Them' culture (Ideland and Malmberg, 2014) we have worked so hard to diffuse. Physically we have combined administrative functions, information technology systems, executive management and programme curricula. Managers, teachers and support staff work across campuses, video-conference meetings are the norm, and collaborative projects and secondments have grown collegiality amongst staff from both legacy organizations. If I was reporting solely on the outcomes of this internal upheaval, I might be tempted to say that Lewin's model has signposted my journey – that we have arrived at a new state of 'freeze' and that I can breathe freely once more. However, there is more to my story beyond the metaphorical walls of my organization, and this is where the limitations of what I can do to unfreeze entrenched ways of thinking really hit home – in the unique cultural, political and social changes being called for in contemporary New Zealand's higher education sector.

Part 2. Aotearoa New Zealand and Higher Education

Bi-culturalism

Aotearoa New Zealand, like many countries across the globe, has been shaped by the spread of Western culture, as immigrants from primarily the UK and Europe arrived in large numbers from the late 1700s to establish settlement colonies and farming, trading and commercial enterprises. In addition, numerous other ethnicities came to New Zealand, beginning gradually with Asian, South Asian and Pasifika groups, with numbers and diversity of arrivals increasing dramatically in recent decades. The impact of this influx of peoples on Māori, the indigenous *tangata whenua* (people of the land), has been far-reaching and long-term; there have been benefits, certainly, but also losses and struggles, many related to cultural differences and misunderstandings (Podsiadlowski and Fox, 2011).

The need for Māori and non-Māori to find a way to coexist civilly led to the signing of one of the country's founding documents, *Te Tiriti o Waitangi* (the Treaty of Waitangi), in 1840 by representatives of the British government and forty-six Māori *rangatira* (chiefs). There have been disputes over versions and wording, breaches, apologies and settlements, but through it all, *Te Tiriti o Waitangi* remains pivotal in New Zealanders' conception of ourselves as a bi-cultural nation which honours the traditions and dual heritage of both groups. *Te Tiriti o Waitangi* is taught in schools, threaded throughout curricula in higher education and is central to all legislation and public policies (Ministry of Justice, 2016).

True equity for Māori and non-Māori remains aspirational, rather than realizable, in the face of continued disparities and contested issues. In higher education, Māori participation rates are still below average: 16 per cent of Māori under twenty-five participate in study at level 4 and above, compared to 23 per cent of the total population. Completion rates, while increasing, remain below the total population: 62 per cent of Māori completed a qualification at level 4 or above within five years after beginning full-time study, compared to 74 per cent of the total population (Ministry of Education, 2014). Boosting achievement of Māori learners is a high-priority area for New Zealand's government (Ministry of Education, 2013), a reporting requirement for all higher education providers, and hence a focus area for faculty leaders like myself.

The Cultural Driver for Change

I therefore found myself as a leader charged with meeting key performance indicators in intercultural relations and Māori success strategies where I had no first-hand experience. Our geographic location makes this leadership vulnerability especially pertinent: our regional base on the northeast coast of New Zealand's North Island, the Bay of Plenty, has a significantly higher proportion of the population (27.5 per cent) who identify Māori, compared with 15 per cent of the national population (Statistics New Zealand, 2018). Many of the learners are characterized by a poor past schooling experience, and are 'second-chance' and 'first-in-family' students, with little familiarity with the world of higher education (Bidois, 2011; Fraser et al., 2020).

Clearly what we have been doing isn't working, and/or isn't working fast enough. In New Zealand, there is an extensive literature documenting the 'deficit theorizing and pathologizing practices, especially through the education system ... [as] schools attempt to "fix" the problem of Māori under-achievement' (Berryman et al., 2017, p. 476). When our merger occurred, one of the ways in which our Council described our unique offering was our commitment to be regionally relevant and serve the needs of our communities, and to do this through our vision to 'be an exemplar bi-cultural organisation' (Toi Ohomai, 2019, p. 3).

Yet I am *Pākehā* (the Māori word for non-Māori New Zealanders); my ancestors came to Aotearoa from European shores. However, my own upbringing was relatively culturally inclusive due to public servant parents and rural living, when compared to many others in my organization. I was shocked at the level of indifference and ignorance that many staff had to our *Te Tiriti* obligations and the significant efforts we should be making to improve outcomes for our Māori learners. Unfreezing this space was, and remains, difficult, slow paced and frustrating – due to the necessity to shift the mindsets of staff, and to my own vulnerability in advocating for initiatives to improve Māori achievement from outside their culture and protocols.

In order to counter this, my management team and I have emphasized that 'fixing' is not the starting point. We have had to 'unfreeze' a 'closing the gap' mentality, and, through programme analysis, identify where Māori success is occurring and understand the key factors influencing this. For example, we found that programmes with significant emphasis on *whanaungatanga* (building and nurturing relationship and connections) had higher success rates – mostly due to student retention. Further conversations with staff and students suggested that students in these programmes were more confident and felt safe communicating with teaching and support staff about pressures, challenges or issues they may be facing. Our team also found that programmes with higher use and acknowledgement of Māori *tikanga* (practices), *reo* (language) and case studies, regardless of whether programme design specified directed bi-cultural emphasis, also had higher success and retention. None of these programme delivery practices were aimed at Māori or intended to combat the 'gap' between Māori and *Pākehā*. They had simply been adopted as good practice, and therefore avoided some of the resistance which might have met more overtly targeted interventions.

With commitment to meeting our bi-cultural organization intentions, I have also focussed on 'unfreezing' the current approach to staff professional development. Rather than starting with individuals identifying their own professional development plans, potentially avoiding activities to improve bi-cultural practice, we are starting with the needs and gaps of the faculty, our programmes and teams. This collective approach to PDP (Professional Development Planning) involves approving a wider faculty goal, a team goal and then an individual goal. Whilst the individual staff member remains the beneficiary of development, they have been 'unfrozen', so professional goals have wider impact. For example, one team goal was for staff to improve *te reo* (Māori language) usage within programme delivery. The staff members enrolled in one of our organization's language programmes, engaged through online learning and attended *noho marae* (face-to-face one- or two-day learning days on the *Marae* – Māori meeting grounds). However, most learning occurred in the shared office space and walking around campus as staff practiced their *te reo* with each other due to the shared goals.

Economic Drivers for Change in Our Higher Education Institutes

In New Zealand, we have an array of provision and provider models: universities, ITPs, private training establishments (PTEs), industry training organizations (ITOs) and *wānanga* (publicly owned tertiary institutions that provide education in a Māori cultural context). There are also multiple provider agreements where introductory courses and entry-level qualifications from one institute receive credits and ensure enrolment in higher-level qualifications awarded by another. There are currently sixteen ITPs across New Zealand, all autonomous Crown entities, mandated by the Education (Polytechnics) Amendment Act (2009). Various ITPs offer qualifications from foundation studies to masters, with considerable overlap and competition for enrolments – with one another and with other higher education providers.

In a country of 4.8 million, this number of providers was probably always going to be unsustainable (Vosse and Aliyu, 2018), and over the past decade there has been an overall decline in ITP sector profitability. By 2018, over half the ITPs were posting deficits requiring taxpayer-funded bailouts and four were under government intervention; worse, 'most were not expecting a major material turnaround in fortunes for 2019' (Redmond, 2019, para. 15). The education minister announced findings from a wide-ranging review of vocational education with the February 2019 decision to amalgamate the sixteen ITPs and eight ITOs (responsible for 140,000 apprentices and workplace trainees) in a single entity, the 'New Zealand Institute of Skills and Technology', more recently renamed officially as *Te Pūkenga*. The intention was not only to avert financial disaster but also to create a new, more streamlined funding system, better coordination of vocational training and a sector that can better respond to technology-driven workplaces (Redmond, 2019; Tertiary Education Commission, 2020).

Such a radical change to our national higher education product is unprecedented in this country, and it has certainly influenced my own leadership journey. Understandably, there has been considerable resistance to this imposed change, from organizations which value their autonomy, from those which are bucking the trend and operating profitably, from staff who see considerable job losses, and from local bodies and communities which suspect that a centralized approach will not serve or safeguard their regional character. Instead, I have deliberately chosen to be an early advocate for the amalgamation, as (despite pre-election pledges of opposition political parties) this decision is highly unlikely to be reversed, with planning and Tier 1 and Tier 2 executive appointments already in place. Put differently, we cannot control the narrative, but we can be part of it. For me, this means seeking to be an active participant in the unfreezing process, even if there is still considerable uncertainty about how the structure will look, and how roles, tasks and responsibilities will be distributed. Our senior leadership team is endeavouring to make sure we have a strong representation in various committee and consultation groups, and encouraging colleagues to contribute to efforts in benchmarking performance, or compiling national registers. This is an example of 'leading from the side' (Hill, 2010), supporting those doing the work, clearing their path for them, and cheering from the side lines. As Cummuta (2017) notes, organizations need to avoid a culture where every time something new or unusual needs to be done, the leader is expected to do it first. This, he says, is not only unrealistic; it can cause a bottleneck in development and reduce productivity. Recognizing that I do not have to do it all, or do it first, has been a key lesson in my leadership development.

Social Drivers for Institutional Change in the Time of a Pandemic

The sudden arrival of a highly contagious virus has had a significant, and likely enduring, impact on universities, ITPs and other providers in this country as almost everywhere else. When I began my leadership-in-higher-education journey, I managed a number of 'legal' programmes which were offered online, to students in-country and off shore. My small team was well versed in blended and flexible remote learning; we had the appropriate technology and digital capability. Yet when Covid-19 arrived in New Zealand in February 2020, I was responsible for a much wider range of programmes, including those with labs and extensive practical requirements, and internships and practicums. Responding to the need to staff and students to work from home was not as simple as posting videoed lectures and hosting class 'chat' meetings.

However, due to the immediacy of change that a Covid-19 New Zealand lockdown thrust upon us, I found myself in a position to 'unfreeze' an area of usual constraint – IT. Recognizing that staff were going to need to work from home during the government-imposed lockdown, our executive leadership team gave permission for staff to take workspace equipment – for example, computers, desks, chairs – for use at home. The usually frozen rigour of IT procurement documentation shifted to one of trust management as staff literally loaded their vehicles with workplace assets. We quickly identified our programme delivery into three categories: (1) those programmes already online or with enough resource to continue remotely with little change, (2) those programmes that with a little time could deliver remotely either online or through the supply of workbook-type learning material and (3) those programmes unable to deliver in a lockdown situation. From this categorization our institutional support services targeted support to the staff and students in the category 1 and 2 areas. Laptops, data top-ups and internet connections were distributed across our *rohe* (geographical area), whilst staff were provided additional technician and technical guidance. The whole atmosphere and environment of our institution unfroze within the three days prior to lockdown, and much of this was for the better.

As we emerge from the changes forced upon us during this period, we will continue to take stock of work which needs to be undertaken to redress the imbalances made apparent during this worldwide time of change. There are issues of rising student debt, a shrinking employment market for graduates in many fields, students who have suffered mental health challenges related to isolation, and international students whose separation from family impacted their learning outcomes. Equity gaps in higher education and its connection to work have always been a challenge for educational leaders (Fain, 2020); in this country, work to reduce the disparity between Māori and non-Māori academic achievement continues. It is likely that it will be a long time before any of us in higher education leadership will suggest that we are ready for a 'refreeze'.

Owning up to Vulnerabilities

Just as I have learned from my own career to date, from my colleagues and from the cultural, economic and social milieu in which we operate, I have also learned important lessons in leadership from my own shortcomings. In one example,

I was 'managed up' by one of my team leaders, who had shared an issue with one of her staff, but not expected me to enter the fray and oversee a resolution process. She made a meeting, and told me that rather than helping, she felt undermined and that I had overridden the reporting line of authority. I listened, put myself in her place, and instantly understood. Leadership means delegation, that is, empowering and trusting subordinates, and this incident was a timely reminder. I am a 'fixer': I see solutions and want to take action, but leadership also means ensuring others build capability. Listening, mentoring and guiding from the side lines will ensure that my faculty are high achievers whether I am there or not, a hallmark of good succession planning, and, I believe, another attribute of leadership.

In a second, possibly related, example, I have also been 'managed down' by my chief executive, who asked me to consider some feedback following a senior leadership meeting early in my inclusion in the group. He told me that when I participated in strategic planning dialogue, especially with people I was meeting for the first time, and others I didn't know all that well, my impatience with discussions and haste to arrive at a decision, assign actions, and move on to the next item, were affecting the mood in the room. I was coming over as a little too forthright, and preventing others airing alternative ideas, even if the final solution was going to be the one I had wanted to jump to straight away. Again, by listening and reflecting, I was able to recognize that what I had seen as being decisive, effective and efficient could be perceived differently. I also came to see that ideas were more readily embraced when everyone had contributed to their genesis.

In both examples, I have had to be humble, to be vulnerable and to hear truths that were otherwise not apparent. In both cases, I like to think that my leadership has improved as a result. Moreover, I recognize that these will not be the only times a critique of my managerial approach is justified, but I hope I am at least more alert to the need to continuously check in, and step back, instead of always forward

Concluding Thoughts

My background is in teaching and learning, not research or change-management, but this focus on the core business of education – our students and the staff who teach them – makes my desire to lead from within the higher education environment even stronger. Whether the occasion calls for me to lead from in front, from the side or from behind, or to be part of the system that educates people in order to provide them the skills and knowledge to adapt, survive and thrive through lives of constant change is a path worth navigating.

There are distinct challenges related to the Aotearoa New Zealand context: our higher education sector and the bi-cultural, economic and social milieu in which it operates. There are also organizational and sector restructures, which are likely to be generalizable beyond my own institute and this country. I have shared some of the strategies I have found useful, some learnings that I came to as a result of the odd misstep and hopefully imparted some sense of a generally positive outlook. However, I concede that try as I might, it is hard at this time of writing in the midst of considerable shifts in our bedrock to frame an unfreeze – change – refreeze narrative in which I return comfortably to controlled space. Rather, I see that a climate of change is likely to continue to prevail, and will likely shape my leadership practice for the foreseeable future, perhaps to the end of my career.

What have I learned by living through these planned and unplanned drivers of change? First, that rules and often 'best practice' go out the window! When our country moved to lockdown with forty-eight hours' notice, there was little time to plan, to consult or to pilot our response. As a leadership team, we have had to learn to make quick decisions – and then to sell, defend or retract these as required. Words like 'nimble' and 'agile' sound fine in management texts, but can be difficult to adopt when they go against our preferred leadership styles. Nonetheless, reflecting on the learnings outlined in this chapter helps me to stay 'centred'. The implications for my development as a learning and teaching leader are above all about self-awareness. I need to share leadership, I need to communicate clearly and consistently, and I need to model a wellness approach.

Change, we are told, is as inevitable as death and taxes. We won't live, let alone lead through it unless we keep breathing!

References

Berryman, M., Eley, E. and Copeland, D. (2017), 'Listening and learning from Rangatahi Māori: The voices of Māori youth', *Critical Questions in Education* (Special Issue) 8 (4): 476–94.

Bidois, V. (2011), *Māori Student Engagement: Voices from the Margins*, Unpublished report, Bay of Plenty Polytechnic.

Blair, E. (2018), 'Contextualizing the new teaching environment', in A. Hosein, N. Rao, C. S-H Yeh and I. Kinchin (eds), *Academics' International Teaching*

Journeys: Personal Narratives of Transitions in Higher Education, 13–24, London: Bloomsbury Academic.

Cummings, S., Bridgman, T. and Brown, K. G. (2016), 'Unfreezing change as three steps: Rethinking Kurt Lewin's legacy for change management', *Human Relations* 69 (1): 33–60. doi: 10.1177/0018726715577707.

Cummuta, T. (2017), 'Leading the way or Leadership from behind?' *About Leaders* [Blog], 7 December. https://aboutleaders.com/leading-the-way-or-leadership-from-behind/#gs.inh9cz.

Esa, N. A., Shaladdin, M., Ibrahim, M. Y. and Mansor, N. R. (2017), 'The application of Kurt Lewin's model of change in the implementation of higher order thinking skills in school', *International Journal of Academic Research in Business and Social Sciences* 7 (8): 109–15. doi: 10.6007/IJARBSS/v7-i8/3212.

Fain, P. (2020), 'Higher education and work amid crisis', *Inside Higher Ed*, 17 June. https://www.insidehighered.com/news/2020/06/17/pandemic-has-worsened-equity-gaps-higher-education-and-work.

Fraser, C., Bright, P., Keogh, J. and Aliyu, O. A. (2020), 'Moving culture to the center of the curriculum: A strategy for regional relevance and organization sustainability', in E. Sengupta, P. Blessinger and T. S. Yamin (eds), *Introduction to Sustainable Development Leadership and Strategies in Higher Education* (Innovations in Higher Education Teaching and Learning, Vol. 22), 67–82, Bingley: Emerald Publishing. https://doi.org/10.1108/S2055-364120200000022005.

Hill, L. A. (2010), 'Leading from behind', *Harvard Business Review* [Blog], 5 May. https://hbr.org/2010/05/leading-from-behind.

Ideland, M., and Malmberg, C. (2014), ' "Our common world" belongs to "Us": Constructions of otherness in education for sustainable development', *Critical Studies in Education* 55 (3): 369–86.

Lewin, K. (1947), 'Frontiers in group dynamics: Concept, method and reality in social science; social equilibria and social change', *Human Relations* 1: 5–40. https://doi.org/10.1177/001872674700100103.

Lewin, K. (1951), *Field Theory in Social Science: Selected Theoretical Papers*, ed. Dorwin Cartwright, Oxford: Harpers.

Ministry of Education (2013), *Kahikitia: Accelerating Success 2013–2017. The Māori Education Strategy*, Wellington, NZ: Ministry of Education.

Ministry of Education (2014), *Tertiary Education Strategy 2014–2019*. https://education.govt.nz/further-education/policies-and-strategies/tertiary-education-strategy/.

Ministry of Justice (2016), *The Principles of the Treaty of Waitangi as Expressed by the Courts and the Waitangi Tribunal*. https://www.waitangitribunal.govt.nz/treaty-of-waitangi/principles-of-the-treaty/.

Podsiadlowski, A., and Fox, S. (2011), 'Collectivist value orientations among four ethnic groups: Collectivism in the New Zealand context', *New Zealand Journal of Psychology* 40 (1): 5–18.

Redmond, A. (2019), 'Shock, apprehension and hope: Can the radical plan to fix New Zealand's polytechnics work?', *Stuff News*, 16 February. https://www.stuff.co.nz/national/education/110582413/shock-apprehension-and-hope-can-the-radical-plan-to-fix-new-zealands-polytechnics-work.

Statistics New Zealand (2018), *Quickstats about Māori*. https://www.stats.govt.nz/topics/ethnicity.

Tertiary Education Commission (2020), *Reform of Vocational Education (RoVE)*. https://tec.govt.nz/rove/reform-of-vocational-education/.

Toi Ohomai Institute of Technology (2019), 'Strategic framework', Internal policy document, Unpublished.

Verhulst, E., and Lambrechts, W. (2014), 'Fostering the incorporation of sustainable development in higher education. Lessons learned from a change management perspective', *Journal of Cleaner Production* 106 (1): 189–204. doi: 10.1016/j.jclepro.2014.09.049.

Vosse, B., and Aliyu, O. A. (2018), 'Determinants of employee trust during organisational change in higher institutions', *Journal of Organizational Change Management* 31 (5): 1105–18.

5

Participative Leadership as an Early Career Academic

Andrew Kelly

Introduction

Most teaching and learning leaders in higher education occupy such leadership roles in the middle to latter stages of their respective careers. This trend is logical, as it usually takes time to be able to demonstrate leadership expertise in learning and teaching (as opposed to research-focused roles, whereby excellence is normally evidenced by more tangible outputs such as number of publications and citations). Indeed, multiple studies globally have found that the average age of those in senior academic leadership roles is between fifty and sixty, normally with at least two decades of disciplinary expertise before occupying deanships or similar positions (Behr and Schneider, 2015; Breakwell and Tytherleigh, 2008; Coll et al., 2018). The current literature, however, largely overlooks the experiences of younger managers and leaders in a university context because it is uncommon for one to act in such roles without establishing a significant scholarly reputation before appointment.

To this end, this chapter focuses on my personal experience as an early career academic (ECA) and transition into leading a large learning support team at an Australian university. Using the concept of participative leadership, it explores how I navigated this role in a range of challenging circumstances. It also explores the tensions between participative and directive approaches, and the types of situations in which one worked more effectively than the other during my early experiences as an academic leader. Sharing both genuine successes and shortcomings, this chapter serves as an authentic guide for other prospective leaders in the early stages of an academic career interested in a path towards university leadership and management in teaching. In this context, management is defined as a position focused mainly on operational day-to-day tasks whereas leadership is focused on strategy and inspiring others, though these roles are often intertwined (Riggio, 2017).

This chapter is structured in three parts. Through considering DeRue and Ashford's (2010) concept of leadership identity and the ways in which leadership can be socially constructed, the first part focuses on participative leadership and its applications for ECAs starting a teaching and learning leadership position. More specifically, by building on Bosanquet et al.'s (2017) definition of ECAs, it draws upon my personal experiences leading a new learning support team in late 2018 and the challenges I faced in this new leadership context. Secondly, this chapter discusses a new distributed model of leadership that was implemented shortly after I began in this new role, including reflections on the successes and limitations of participative leadership in such a model. Finally, the third part skips ahead twelve months and explores the impact of Covid-19 on leading a teaching and learning team during a period of great change and uncertainty. This section also considers the role of shared expertise in team decision-making and the extent to which this is effective during time-sensitive crises. The chapter then concludes with some overarching reflections of the key lessons I learned during these experiences and how these learnings can inform future practice for both myself as well as others.

Participative Leadership in a New Role

In December 2018, I resigned from my teaching-focused lectureship and accepted a management position at a different Australian university. In almost every way this experience fundamentally shifted my personal and professional circumstances, to the point where nothing felt familiar or comfortable. Though both roles were similar insofar as each focused on academic skills development and student support, this new position was in another institution with entirely different responsibilities. Instead of teaching first-year university students about academic communication skills, I would be leading others to provide academic skills support. The new role also sat within a centralized learning and teaching unit rather than a teaching faculty, and I was managing a team of over twenty professional staff that provided student learning support across the entire university. In addition to leading staff rather than teaching students, the position required significant strategic thinking and negotiation with a wide variety of academic staff and university leaders for the delivery of student support services – neither of which were really required when I was simply responsible for teaching classes at my previous institution. In accepting the role, I also relocated interstate. I left my family behind in tropical Darwin (they would join me several months later) and began a new life in Perth. Even though I was still based in Australia and had visited the campus once before formally accepting the position, I felt completely out of my comfort zone as I had no local personal support networks available.

At the start of my first day, I first reported to my line manager. As pro vice chancellor (education), she held a senior position at the university and had very clear expectations in the early stages of my appointment. Within the first month, I had to ensure that my team of learning advisers, who had just relocated into a new centre, had a workable service delivery model that met the needs of the new space. I was also tasked with preparing that same team to deliver new orientation programmes for the coming semester, chairing a working group on embedding communication skills in the curriculum across the university, recruiting a new team member, and revising the intervention processes for the institution's post-entry language assessment programme. Outside of work, I also had to find a place to live and organize other simple yet rather important things, such as the location of nearby supermarkets and bus stations. The expectations and stakes felt high. I did not want to fail, nor want to feel like this career move was a mistake. There were a few times where I missed the simplicity of my former teaching life in Darwin.

I was also very conscious that I came into this role with less experience than many staff within my team. At the time I was still in my late twenties, and had staff that were older than my parents who had decades of experience in academic skills support. I quickly learned that this can be a double-edged sword; staff with such experience have a wealth of knowledge to share, but they can at times be attached to particular ways of working and resistant to change. As DeRue and Ashford's (2010) leadership model highlights the socially constructed nature of leadership within organizations, I realized that I needed to facilitate situations in which staff felt they had opportunities to contribute to important decisions while still respecting the need to defer to any final decision made by myself. This type of model rejects the notion of leadership as purely top-down and hierarchical, but rather posits one in which leader and follower identities can be granted regardless of a position within an organization (DeRue and Ashford 2010). It means that leadership does not simply exist by virtue of position; a leader's role is constructed by the person and the followers that recognize that role relationally. Leadership in this context, then, is best conceptualized as a complex behavioural process rather than a simple organizational structure of leader–follower (Li, Liu and Luo, 2018). Reflecting on this model and the highly experienced profile of my new team, I considered that the best way to build cohesiveness and trust was to collaborate on all important decisions and give each staff member a chance to draw upon their expertise and experience when making such decisions whenever it appeared possible to do so.

This approach is a core component of participative leadership, by which I intentionally attempted to make decisions collectively rather than unilaterally. While often taking longer than simply making decisions individually, participative leadership has shown to improve job satisfaction, motivation and trust within teams (Benoliel and Barth, 2017; Huang et al., 2010; Chan, 2019). Each of these were important considerations while I was still in the very early stages of navigating a new role and building my own identity within it. Actioning these collaborative decisions in practice, however, can be a challenging process. Even if decisions are shared, it still requires team members to acknowledge that managers are ultimately responsible for final decisions. This can present challenges when staff disagree with the majority of team or managerial decisions, which can often happen with leaders at a younger age who lack a natural 'status cue' (Buengeler, Homan and Voelpel, 2016). I observed that these challenges applied to both daily operational management decisions as well as attempting to lead new directions, the latter of which focused on long-term strategies for improving learning support at the institution. I noticed that I tended to act and feel more like a manager than a leader in this early period. I felt I did not yet have the experience or time in the role to conceptualize a clear and purposeful vision for how I wanted my team to deliver high-quality and impactful student support practices. My initial priority was simply surviving day-to-day management challenges rather than leading new ways of working.

In these very early stages, every type of disagreement or form of resistance I encountered with my team also felt somehow connected to my lack of experience, even though there was never any implicit or explicit suggestion from anyone that my age was a factor. I reflected that this was own personal lack of confidence about my own abilities, and that I needed to continually remind myself it was only my self-consciousness that was negatively focusing on my age. Autoethnographic accounts of other ECA experiences suggest that it is indeed quite common to feel self-doubt, nervousness and a heightened awareness of looking too young in academia (Wilkinson, 2020). These feelings are also often referred to 'imposter syndrome', a term first coined by psychologists in 1978 as an internal experience of intellectual phoniness (Clance and Imes, 1978). The first time I started teaching in academia, I felt like an imposter to my students, but as I grew in experience and confidence those feelings subsided over time. In this new role, however, these feelings were manifesting again in different ways. I felt like a new type of imposter – one in which I was more self-conscious about the perceptions my team and colleagues might hold about me.

In any case, I attempted to put these feelings aside and focus on the outcomes with which I was tasked. To build my confidence, I read books and articles about leadership, which led to adopting a participative approach to leading my team. In practice, participative leadership manifested into regular team meetings, distributed responsibilities and actively inviting recommendations about solving collective challenges. Organizing new operations for an academic skills centre was perhaps the most complex challenge, as there were many stakeholders involved and it required a coordinated rostering system to ensure that students were able to access timely support. All learning advisers contributed their ideas, and we developed a shared roster with agreed appointment hours to manage workloads. Staff members also had designated responsibilities for designing an optimal operational model, such as overseeing a central email address, coordinating the delivery of orientation workshops and booking our general academic skills workshops for the upcoming semester. Through this method, I observed that staff had a stake in how the team operated and shared responsibility for the decisions that were made. We shared positive feelings when something was working well, and had to own our decisions when something did not go according to plan.

Not all staff members were happy with these types of decisions, such as working in a new open-plan environment. Some ultimately decided to leave the institution, whereas others continued to resist changes because it did not align with the ways in which they had worked in the past. Responding to insubordinate and recalcitrant staff members was the largest test I faced as a young manager. I had no practical experience in resolving these challenges in a higher education context. I fit within the normal definition of an ECA as someone working in academic context within five years of receiving my doctorate, and also resonated with common themes within the ECA literature such as feeling uncertain, overwhelmed and pressured (Bosanquet et al., 2017; Osbaldiston, Cannizzo and Mauri, 2019; Price, Coffey and Nethery, 2014). However, my pressures felt somewhat unique. Most ECA pressures stem from individual teaching and research responsibilities, whereas my pressures stemmed from managing new people in an uncertain environment.

When scanning for guidance within the current scholarship, I learned that acting in a management role as an ECA seemed to be quite rare as there was hardly any literature on the topic to read. There were internal university training sessions available, but they did not meet my immediate support needs. I needed a mentor. Formal mentorship programmes are not commonplace across the academic sector, even though the evidence suggests such programmes can play a crucial support role and prevent talented staff from leaving higher education (Thomas, Lunsford and Rodrigues, 2015). Indeed, due to the formative nature of these types of roles, ECAs tend to learn through experience in forming a leadership identity (McAlpine, Amundsen and Turner, 2013). To that end, I needed to find my own solutions and mentors. The informal support from my line manager and the human resources department was especially invaluable. The former was the closest person I had to acting as a mentor, though as she was the pro vice chancellor (education) – the busy nature of her role made it difficult to find times to receive feedback and guidance about my progress as a new manager. Nonetheless, the advice I did receive assisted greatly in navigating difficult conversations and moving forward despite ongoing interpersonal professional challenges. I received additional informal mentorship support from the other managers within the unit in which I worked, which made me feel less isolated in managerial challenges.

As volatile situations continued to evolve, I continued to grow and build my own identity as an academic leader. While relevant guiding literature appeared scarce, I found Monk and McKay's (2017) use of Alice's experiences in Wonderland as a metaphor for developing academic identity and agency as an ECA quite reassuring. As these authors point out, Lewis Carroll's famous character of Alice experiences events and feelings similar to ECAs when navigating academia for the first time: the pursuit of an elusive 'white rabbit' into a strange land, learning the new rules of a game, feelings of being small and seeking advice from strange sources. Each of these characterizations were relevant for my initial experiences in a new role. I felt that while my individual circumstances were quite unique – as unlike most ECAs, I was not focused on research or teaching – I was not alone in feeling challenged. Those feelings were normal, and similar to many other young academics navigating their own identity in higher education.

Navigating a New Team Leadership Model

After several months, I started to feel more settled and confident in my new role. Delegating tasks and having individual conversations with staff about workload priorities felt constructive and natural. Leading team meetings became easier to facilitate after I learned about each team member's strengths, experiences and perspectives. In this regard, I found that a participative leadership model worked quite well. In each meeting, I would present a key set of challenges that required further discussion and an accompanying decision. By opening the floor and inviting input as well as suggestions for decisions, I aimed to let the team develop ideas and debate strategies. Occasionally I would intervene to steer the conversation back to its intended focus, yet this did not seem to detract from developing constructive solutions with which my team felt satisfied. In most cases we were able to reach unanimous decisions, and in the event we could not reach an agreed solution, I either made the final decision or adjourned the meeting for future discussion. I was purposefully not telling them what we were doing; instead, we collectively decided what to do. At times there were some situations in which decisions needed to be more directive, although these were fairly infrequent. It was a slow process, but it was producing results.

One challenge that required a more directive approach was the structural organization of the learning adviser team. When I arrived, eight senior learning advisers each supported a university teaching faculty directly and seven other team members provided general academic skills support across all campuses. In addition to supporting a university teaching area, one of the senior learning advisers also line managed all of the general learning advisers. This caused significant workload issues and required managerial intervention. It was not a simple problem to solve. All other senior learning advisers would have similar workload challenges if they were tasked with line management duties, and it was beyond the scope of the role of a general learning adviser to undertake supervisory responsibilities. Finding a balance between clarifying new roles without compromising service quality would be crucial, as directive leadership tends to decrease staff commitment to service quality but increase role clarity whereas the inverse tends to be true for participative leadership (Dolatabadi and Safa, 2010).

After consulting with key staff, I decided to realign the line manager roles into three disciplinary areas. Instead of one manager for all learning advisers, the role would be split into thematic areas. There would be a supervisor for the learning advisers that specialized in English-language skills, another for mathematics and numeracy and one for general academic skills support. On the one hand, this approach supported a distributed model whereby greater leadership roles were internally recognized. It also empowered each learning adviser to think strategically about how their respective disciplinary area would be supported across the university. On the other hand, as DeRue and

Ashford (2010) articulated, hierarchical position alone does not necessarily equate to adopting a leadership role. In other words, relational and social factors also contribute to building leadership identity, such as whether learning advisers recognize their role and how they build their own capacity to lead even if they do not occupy a formal leadership position. There were also additional logistical challenges when implementing this structure, as managers required regular meetings to coordinate rosters and schedules across each team.

I reflected that this decision solved a short-term problem but was not an ideal long-term solution. At some point in the future the model would need further reconsideration after it was implemented in practice, and in that regard, there may have been other options that were not properly considered before the first decision was made. While there was some team participation in deciding upon this leadership model, it was far more directive than it had been in the past. Some staff accepted this new model whereas others resisted, both implicitly and explicitly. Implicit resistance included noticeably disengaged body language in team meetings, whereas explicit resistance included passive aggressive or unconstructive comments about the merits of this structure that were openly shared with others. These were challenges in themselves, but I also felt challenged in taking such an approach because directive management did not align with my values of making team decisions *with* the team, rather than *for* the team (Rok, 2009). I reflected that directive leadership was useful in some situations, but perhaps greater staff involvement in this decision-making process would have produced higher engagement and commitment to the direction I was attempting to lead.

Creating these new leadership roles also led to another challenge I had not fully realized: I now had to lead others to lead. There are numerous benefits of leaders coaching new managers, yet leaders are often not fully equipped to take on such a role at times when it is most needed (Ahrens, McCarthy and Milner, 2018). In early 2019, I certainly felt unequipped to provide this type of guidance to my new managerial team as I had less than three months of personal leadership experience in a higher education context. While DeRue and Ashford (2010) stress that hierarchical position is only one aspect of being a leader, practical expectations are quite different when it is a formal requirement of one's role to be supervising and managing staff. I had little personal experience and had to draw from other sources for guidance. Advice from my own manager, other managers in the learning and teaching unit and support from the human resources department were all critical.

It was not the original intent of this team structure to accommodate such an approach, but I quickly observed that participative leadership at a managerial level was equally valuable. By having three managers supervise learning advisers instead of one, it necessitated that decisions were made collectively rather than individually. Through participation in regular meetings with this team of managers, we navigated several operational and personnel challenges together as well as provided a support structure to each other. The main challenges usually related to balancing this workload alongside supporting the needs of individual teaching areas rather than any challenges specific only to management duties. I found myself learning about leadership and the key characteristics required from those that were also quite new to acting formally in such a role.

Leading during Covid-19: Participative Leadership during Time-Sensitive Crises

It took approximately twelve months before I felt comfortable working in university management. I had gathered enough experience to feel reasonably confident when I needed to make decisions myself or request team input and discussion. This was important, as despite the fact that team decision-making was working well to date, it was not an efficient use of time to use a participative approach in every situation. Discussing issues was time-consuming and would ultimately disadvantage students if too much time was spent on staff meetings. Major challenges that would likely have operational impacts were discussed as a team as a matter of course, although it was not always obvious when a participative approach would need to be used. Sometimes decisions were made entirely collectively, sometimes entirely individually, and other times with some form of combination of both. Each approach's usefulness depended on the context, as conceptualizing the directive-participative paradigm as mutually exclusive and at opposing ends of a continuum does not fully capture the dynamic nature of leadership (Somech, 2006). There was no clear delineation when one approach would work better than the other, but as a general principle, I attempted to maintain the belief in team decision-making as my core approach when deciding between the two.

This line of leadership thinking was strongly tested during the first half of 2020. In March and April of that year, the university, and indeed the rest of the world, had to respond rapidly to the Covid-19 pandemic. Government health responses to the global spread of this virus caused significant and unprecedented disruptions to multiple sectors, leading to significant revenue loss and subsequent unemployment in industries such as retail, hospitality and tourism (Coibion, Gorodnichenko and Weber, 2020). The Australian higher education sector was similarly exposed, due to an overreliance on international students as a revenue source. This led to hundreds of redundancies being announced across the sector. Similar to other institutions, my university experienced a pause in international student mobility, transitioned all teaching and learning to move to an online delivery model within the space of one month and organized all staff to work remotely from home during the same time period. Needless to say, tensions and anxieties were high in my team and across the broader university.

During the weeks leading up to moving entirely off-campus, work intensified greatly. The unit in which I worked was responsible for providing teaching and learning support to the university, and there were a large number of staff and students that were entirely unprepared for online delivery. Training sessions and self-access materials needed to be delivered incredibly rapidly. New operational systems also needed to be put in place at short notice, including online learning adviser appointment options using Microsoft Teams. As a result, decisions needed to be made quickly, often within hours. The seriousness and time pressures of the situation simply did not allow for many team-based decisions to occur in the early stages of the university's response to Covid-19. Feelings of uncertainty and pressure, reminiscent of my first period as a new manager, began to resurface. There was much at stake, after all. However, as the situation was unprecedented, collective support from my managerial colleagues built my confidence. As none of us could claim we had experienced this type of situation before, there was a clear sense of unity and togetherness.

Once my team started working at home, the pace of work began to slow dramatically into a new type of 'normal'. After several weeks of remote work, the initial panic associated with Covid-19 had largely subsided. Staff had adjusted and could appreciate some of the benefits of working from home, such as shorter commute times and more flexible work schedules. Interestingly, despite the physical distance between each of us, I found that we communicated and collaborated more frequently than when we were based on-campus. I implemented brief daily meetings every afternoon to provide updates on key university developments, but this was then scaled back to every three days (and finally weekly) once the pipeline of new information and challenges to discuss slowed down. It also facilitated a way in which to connect socially with my team, as we were all sharing similar new professional experiences. I observed that maintaining these connections and inviting stories of home-based work was also a form of leadership, as shared experiences play a key role in building team identity. As DeRue and Ashford (2010, p. 627) described, the team's experiences becomes 'shared property' of the group members rather than those in formal leadership roles.

Using collaborative technologies such as Microsoft Teams opened up new ways of discussing shared challenges. It enabled seamless online conversations, greater ease in scheduling meeting times and brainstorming solutions to problems. This also facilitated an ability to reinstate a more participative approach to decision-making. For example, decisions about improving operational processes for student support during off-campus teaching arrangements as well as the frequency and structure of team meetings were made collectively. I felt that this approach shared the responsibility of improving online support services and built team cohesion at an important moment. Staff had an ability to provide input and shape the nature of their work, which offered some degree of agency at a time where heightened government health restrictions temporarily limited other aspects of life.

One aspect of this approach that needed further adjustment upon reflection, however, was balancing the quantity of meeting times alongside achieving outcomes. My team and I were participating in a record number of online meetings each day, which, like many other workers during this time, started to cause screen fatigue (Deloitte, 2020). I wanted to feel like I was present and available to support them, yet I was also mindful of the blurred boundary of an 'always-on' culture while working from home (Waizenegger et al., 2020). Team feedback about limiting the number of meetings and using an agenda proved helpful, as it allowed time and space for staff to achieve outcomes. It also ensured there was a clear purpose for meetings and any subsequent discussions.

Key Lessons Learned

I learned many lessons during these experiences as an academic leader, some of which are beyond the scope of this chapter to explore in further detail. One critical learning that flowed throughout each experience was the value of support networks. Their importance in teaching and research ECA roles is already well established, but my experiences highlight that this also extends to those working in academic, managerial, supervisory or coordinator roles. I had excellent informal support from other managers and human resources professionals and would have felt even more challenged if these were not available. Previous formal training provided some degree of professional development and leadership preparedness, but in my experience it was most often informal advice from colleagues at the point of need that was the most valuable. Tasks such as responding to sensitive emails, having difficult conversations, and setting strategic priorities all hinged upon sound advice from more experienced colleagues.

As a general principle, I also learned that taking a participative approach to leadership was a useful strategy in tertiary education contexts. Teams of highly educated and experienced professionals have much to offer and involving them in the decision-making process will generally produce better results if given an opportunity to contribute. This, of course, can never be a blanket rule – as Covid-19 highlighted, the time-sensitive nature of some decisions requires a more directive approach – yet in my experience it provided a helpful framework for building my own identity as an academic leader and advancing the objectives of my team. At the very least, even if staff disagreed with a final decision, this approach ensured team members were given the opportunity to express their views before it was made for consideration. Through this approach, I learned that my age did not act as any significant barrier in practice even though I had early self-doubts about my lack of experience. As long as I invited team discussion and collective decisions wherever possible, I was able to develop a greater sense of unity and subsequent stronger learning outcomes for the students that my team supported.

Conclusion

As the landscape of higher education and the academic workforce continues to shift, so too will the attributes and experiences of those employed to manage and lead academic teams in universities. While still relatively uncommon, there will be future opportunities for ECAs to step into supervisory roles and develop capabilities to lead. To that end, this chapter provided personal experiences of the challenges I faced in an effort to guide others that are interested in working in learning and teaching leadership roles in a university context. As I navigated finding the right balance between participative and directive approaches, I learned the value of support networks and involving an academic team in decisions that affected them. Looking introspectively, these experiences have all contributed to my own academic identity. This identity is now not just a product of my research and teaching background, but also one based on the contributions and experiences of the team in which I lead.

References

Ahrens, J., McCarthy, G. and Milner, T. J. (2018), 'Training for the coaching leader: How organizations can support managers', *Journal of Management Development* 37 (2): 188–200.

Behr, M., and Schneider, J. (2015), 'Gender and the ladder to the deanship', *Diversity and Democracy* 18 (2). https://www.aacu.org/diversitydemocracy/2015/spring/behr (accessed 8 September 2020).

Benoliel, P., and Barth, A. (2017), 'The implications of the school's cultural attributes in the relationships between participative leadership and teacher job satisfaction and burnout', *Journal of Educational Administration* 55 (6): 640–66.

Bosanquet, A., Mailey, A., Matthews, K. E. and Lodge, J. M. (2017), 'Redefining "early career" in academia: A collective narrative approach', *Higher Education Research & Development* 36 (5): 890–902.

Breakwell, G. M., and Tytherleigh, M. Y. (2008), 'UK university leaders at the turn of the 21st century: Changing patterns in their socio-demographic characteristics', *Higher Education* 56: 109–27.

Buengeler, C., Homan, A. C. and Voelpel, S. C. (2016), 'The challenge of being a young manager: The effects of contingent reward and participative leadership on team-level turnover depend on leader age', *Journal of Organizational Behavior* 37 (8): 1224–45.

Chan, S. C. (2019), 'Participative leadership and job satisfaction', *Leadership & Organization Development Journal* 40 (3): 319–33.

Clance, P. R., and Imes, S. A. (1978), 'The imposter syndrome phenomenon in high achieving women: Dynamics and therapeutic intervention', *Psychotherapy: Theory, Research & Practice* 15 (3): 241–7.

Coibion, O., Gorodnichenko, Y. and Weber, M. (2020), 'Labor markets during the Covid-19 crisis: A preliminary view', CESifo Working Paper, No. 82387, Munich: Center for Economic Studies and ifo Institute. https://www.econstor.eu/handle/10419/216634 (accessed 19 August 2020).

Coll, K., Niles, S. G., Coll, K. F., Ruch, C. P. and Stewart, R. A. (2018), 'Education deans: Challenges and stress', *Journal of Organizational & Educational Leadership* 4 (1): 1–16.

Deloitte (2020), 'Remote Collaboration: Facing the challenges of COVID-19' [Presentation]. https://www2.deloitte.com/content/dam/Deloitte/de/Documents/human-capital/Remote-Collaboration-COVID-19.pdf (accessed 22 September 2020)

DeRue, D. S., and Ashford, S. J. (2010), 'Who will lead and who will follow? A social process of leadership identity construction in organizations', *Academy of Management Review* 35 (4): 627–47.

Dolatabadi, H. R., and Safa, M. (2010), 'The effect of directive and participative leadership style on employees' commitment to service quality', *International Bulletin of Business Administration* 9 (1): 31–42.

Huang, X., Iun, J., Liu, A. and Gong, Y. (2010), 'Does participative leadership enhance work performance by inducing empowerment or trust? The differential effects on managerial and non-managerial subordinates', *Journal of Organizational Behavior* 31 (1): 122–43.

Li, G., Liu., H. and Luo, Y. (2018), 'Directive versus participative leadership: Dispositional antecedents and team consequences', *Journal of Occupational and Organizational Psychology* 91 (3): 645–64.

McAlpine, L., Amundsen, C. and Turner, G. (2013), 'Identity-trajectory: Reframing early career academic experience', *British Educational Research Journal* 40 (6): 952–69.

Monk, S., and McKay, L. (2017), 'Developing identity and agency as an early career academic: Lessons from Alice', *International Journal for Academic Development* 22 (3): 223–30.

Osbaldiston, N., Cannizzo, F. and Mauri, C. (2019), 'I love my work but I hate my job' – Early career academic perspective on academic times in Australia', *Time & Society* 28 (2): 743–62.

Price, E., Coffey, B. and Nethery, A. (2014), 'An early career academic network: What worked and what didn't', *Journal of Further and Higher Education* 39 (5): 680–98.

Riggio, R. E. (2017), 'Management and leadership', in A. Wilkinson, S. J. Armstrong and M. Lounsbury (eds), *The Oxford Handbook of* Management, 276–92, New York: Oxford University Press.

Rok, B. (2009), 'Ethical context of the participative leadership model: Taking people into account', *Corporate Governance* 9 (4): 461–72.

Somech, A., and Wenderow, M. (2006), 'The impact of participative and directive leadership on teachers' performance: The intervening effects of job structuring, decision domain, and leader-member exchange', *Educational Administration Quarterly* 42 (5): 746–72.

Thomas, D. J., Lunsford, G. L. and Rodrigues, H. A. (2015), 'Early career academic staff support: Evaluating mentoring networks', *Journal of Higher Education Policy and Management* 37 (3): 320–9.

Waizenegger, L., McKenna, B., Cai, W. and Bendz, T. (2020), 'An affordance perspective of team collaboration and enforced working from home during COVID-19', *European Journal of Information Systems* 29 (4): 429–42. https://doi.org/10.1080/0960085X.2020.1800417.

Wilkinson, C. (2020), 'Imposter syndrome and the accidental academic: An autoethnographic account', *International Journal for Academic Development* 25 (4): 363–74. https://doi.org/10.1080/1360144X.2020.1762087.

6

Clarifying the Fuzzy Lines of Programme Leadership

Patrick Baughan

Introduction

In twenty-five years of employment in the higher education (HE) sector, I have worked in a variety of leadership positions in universities, in my recent work at a cross-sector organization and in several ancillary and external roles. My experience includes managing institutional initiatives, leading teams to develop specific pedagogical innovations, line management of staff, coordinating large-scale events such as conferences and international visits and, most recently, leading collaborative projects involving multiple universities.

However, in spite of this breadth of experience, no other leadership position I have occupied has been so complex and ambiguous as the role of the Programme Leader (PL). Normally, a PL is a member of staff responsible for the day-to-day management of a given programme of study (Cahill et al., 2015). In my case, it might be that the longevity of my time as a PL (in three different roles) partly explains the number of challenges I faced, but as I shall argue, there are many other reasons for which programme leadership may represent a 'difficult' example of academic leadership and much that could be done to clarify some of the 'fuzzy lines' by which it is characterized. It is undoubtedly the case that many PLs, myself included, enjoy leading and nurturing a university programme, before, in some instances, being promoted to more senior roles. However, it is also the case that others report mixed experiences, having been unclear about their roles. My own experiences straddle these two positions: success and fulfilment on the one hand, ambiguity and frustration on the other.

In this chapter, drawing primarily on my leadership experience, but also on conversations with colleagues and on relevant literature, I will argue that the PL role is often problematic and that more could be done to improve the experiences of those undertaking it. Having completed my time as a PL, this chapter provides an opportunity to reflect on some of my experiences and offer words of advice to existing PLs and colleagues responsible for organizing these roles. Many PLs need clearer aims and boundaries for their work, or else they risk not developing their own leadership skills, but merely enacting the decisions of others.

In this chapter, I define and contextualize the role of the PL and present a model of programme leadership which I used to inform my leadership approach. I outline my own leadership journey based on my work at three (UK) universities. Finally, drawing on the successes and challenges I have encountered, I conclude with several recommendations.

A note on terminology: Different terms are used to denote the PL role, such as Programme Leader, Programme Director and Course Leader. I use the term 'Programme Leader' for the sake of consistency and because it is widely adopted. When I began drafting the chapter, I decided to use the word 'fuzzy' to describe the ambiguous and messy nature of the PL role, one which is not always defined sufficiently in job descriptions. At the time, I was not aware that the same term has been used to describe programme leadership before. In fact, it was used in Mitchell's (2015) work, suggesting that some of the experiences I write about are shared by others.

Contextualizing the Role of the Programme Leader

Whilst the study of academic leadership attracts on-going interest (see, e.g. Bracken and Novak, 2019; McCaffery, 2019), less attention has been given to programme leadership. Johnston and Westwood (2009) explain: 'There is a paucity of published literature that specifically addresses either the programme leader role or their professional development needs' (pp. 1–2). This paucity is surprising in view of the fact that all higher education institutions employ staff in these positions, and that it represents a vital one in the delivery of learning and teaching. It also leaves open the question as to what the role means and what the duties of a PL are: is it about leadership of programmes, people, processes or a combination of these? In reality, it may be all or any of these, at different times, in different organizational contexts. Of course, it needs to be recognized that programmes vary in terms of focus, level, size and composition and that this forms part of the explanation for variations. Further, staff become PLs at different stages of their careers: for some, it forms an early part of their leadership journey; for others, programme leadership may come at a later juncture. Yet in spite of these factors, the PL role is fluid and ill-defined (Lawrence and Ellis, 2018; Murphy and Curtis, 2013). Further, whilst programme leadership refers to a commonly used role title, it leaves open what styles and approaches of leadership the person in that role will adopt or will be able to adopt within their work. Thus, in reality, PLs vary significantly in how, what and the extent to which they really do 'lead'.

Cahill et al. (2015) provide a useful attempt to encapsulate the PL role, as 'an experienced academic and/or senior practitioner responsible for the day-to-day management of a particular programme of study leading to an academic award' (p. 273). The same authors add that 'the role has wide ranging responsibilities, as programme leaders have to deal with complex, academic, pastoral, moral, administrative and pragmatic decisions on a daily basis' (p. 283). Indeed, it might be some of the softer or 'people' skills, so important in being an effective PL, that are often overlooked in formal definitions and job descriptions. Vilkinas and Ladyshewsky (2012, p. 123) emphasize the 'people' aspect, stating 'PLs are widely identified as occupying a unique and pivotal role within HEIs [Higher Education Institutions]'. PLs have a direct impact on the student experience and normally represent translators of policy into practice (Ellis, 2019; Milburn, 2010). Fotheringham (2019) has commented on how, more recently, many PLs are required to work with significant data in relation to issues such as retention rates, pass rates, national benchmarks and student evaluations. In the UK, this includes the annual National Student Survey (NSS), a scheme run by the Office for Students which provides students with an opportunity to answer questions about the courses they are taking. Robinson-Self (2020) interprets the role as 'essential, but also amorphous, unbounded and singularly difficult to perform' (p. 118).

Thus, even at this explanatory level, we see the complexities that characterize the role. Consequently, authors including Lawrence and Ellis (2018), Cahill et al. (2015) and McLeod (2010) have all pointed to the need for a clearer articulation of what programme leadership constitutes. My own experiences support these points and will be expanded on below.

Approach and Framework

In total, I was a PL for nine years (not continuously) at three institutions, for which I have used pseudonyms in this chapter, referring to them as University A,

University B and University C. All three universities are UK-based. University A is a well-established, medium-sized, campus-based institution. University B is a city-centre institution with close links to business. University C is a large, research-focused and prestigious organization.

At University A, I worked as a course leader in a large distance learning department, with students studying for postgraduate degrees. Here, the PL role was organized not by programme but by the country in which the students were based. Many students were based in, for example, Hong Kong (where there were often a few hundred students), Malaysia and Singapore, and at different times I was PL for courses and students in one or more of these geographical locations, until I became the overall head of distance learning. After leaving University A, I moved to University B, where I was PL for a postgraduate staff development programme – provided for colleagues with a teaching role. Learners generally combine study with their work and undertake modules leading towards their qualification. More recently, I worked as a PL at University C, where the programme I ran was structured into a suite of routes and development opportunities. All three programmes which I ran were internally validated within their respective institutions, whilst those at universities B and C were both staff development programmes focused on learning and teaching issues, and were also externally accredited by Advance HE (UK).

Each of the above programmes was quite distinct in its overall structure and organization. Much of my working experience in these settings was positive and enriching, but I also encountered challenges. Perhaps as a result of this, as my work developed, I became interested in the varied nature of the PL role itself. I made it my priority to seek out, meet and work with other colleagues in similar positions through both formal channels, such as at meetings or in specific work-projects, and informal ones, such as in 'café conversations' or by email. One initial observation to be made is that each of my PL roles was distinct, and so what I learned from undertaking each of them was different. At University A, where my role involved managing distance learning courses in various countries, a key focus was student support for a diverse, 'at distance' student body. It was fascinating, but strategic decisions about pedagogy and programme development were led elsewhere. At University 'B', my role was more pedagogically grounded – from the outset, I strove to improve the learning, teaching and assessment components of the programme. And at University C, more strategic approaches were needed for reviewing the programme in light of the pace of change in teaching and learning in higher education more generally. Looking back, I therefore tend to view my PL experience as comprising three independent journeys as opposed to a single one, which itself suggests the disparate nature of these roles. Whilst this might appear to have been personally enriching for me, it does lend evidence to support points I make about the extent of role variation within and amongst institutions – which may be a source of confusion or cause mismatches of expectations and suggests a need for greater clarity.

In the sections that follow, I have drawn on a guiding framework to inform aspects of the discussion. As Senior (2018) informs us, there is little bespoke theory to guide discussions about programme leadership: 'The small pool of literature that does exist acts as a critical launch pad, and has the potential to further raise the profile of programme leadership. The findings of these exploratory studies are very much in alignment, and demonstrate that a firm theoretical basis for programme leadership is yet to be established' (p. 11). The same author has therefore proposed a model comprising nine categories as core components for the role. These are programme delivery and quality assurance; student liaison, support and guidance; staff liaison; committees; external stakeholder engagement; external examiner and examination boards; managing internal and external student feedback processes; programme design, approval and modification; and curriculum and programme reviews. Collectively, these items represent a substantial workload for PLs who usually have other responsibilities to fulfil too. Senior's framework can be applied most readily to a British context (especially with its reference to external examiner systems), although many aspects of it should resonate with those leading programmes in other countries too. The model is illustrated in Figure 6.1.

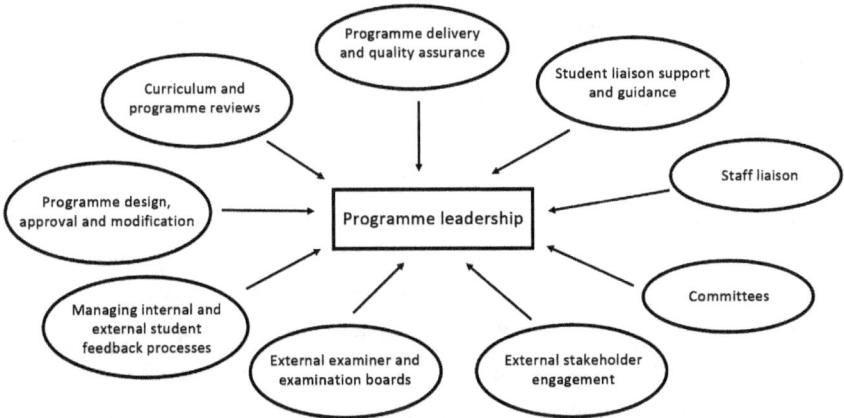

Figure 6.1 Core components of programme leadership (adapted from Senior, 2018).

Reflections on a Personal Leadership Journey

An example of a significant leadership challenge I faced, which resonates now (in light of the Covid-19 pandemic present at the time of writing), occurred when I had to determine whether I should continue with or cancel an overseas teaching visit to Hong Kong at the start of the SARS outbreak, a decision which would impact several hundred postgraduate students and a team of visiting staff. This provided early-career evidence to me of the responsibilities associated with the PL role. The following represents a sample of other experiences from my PL roles organized under a set of 'vignettes'. These are all intended to show significant moments of my work, providing opportunities for reflection and learning.

Determining What the Roles and Responsibilities Are

At the start of the chapter, I explained how I have been involved in a range of academic leadership activities. However, programme leadership was the hardest because it is often not clear what the parameters of the role are. In the first week of my PL duties at one institution, a sheet of paper was left on my desk indicating a vague list of 'to do' items for the next few months. There was a lack of any formal role description. In another episode, in spite of some responsibilities being defined in the original job profile, an 'updated' list of 'expectations' was sent to me a few weeks later. This email comprised a list made by an earlier PL more than a year before. Thus, a clear problem that I have experienced is a basic failure to determine what the PL role is. This type of situation – in which I was assigned a position without a formal job description – elicited in me feelings of discomfort but, at the same time, determination. As specific responsibilities for the role were left unclear, this could lead, and indeed did lead, to inconsistent understandings about it amongst other staff. My first response was to note down key 'known' aspects of the job or aspects that were, in my interpretation, central to it. Then, I spoke to colleagues in the department about their experiences and where they felt the needs and priorities lay. However, a difficulty with consulting with other staff was that they themselves would produce different accounts. These perspectives contributed to my view that the role needed clarification: there were not enough reference points from which to develop priorities. Whilst not a desirable situation, I learned quickly that I also had an opportunity to exercise leadership in determining to others how I saw the role, let colleagues know what my priorities were and enable people to come back to me if they were unhappy with this. If the PL role was fuzzy or ill-defined, a positive action that could be taken was to make the decisions. In spite of all these positive intentions, gaps and ambiguities did occur, as other offers or tasks presented themselves, and it was not clear whether these fell under a PL remit or were to be taken forward by someone else, such as someone with a specialist interest in the area. For example, should a possible project involving the earmarking of departmental funds to work with a publisher on a bespoke pedagogic initiative be led by the PL, the departmental head, someone else, or a combination of staff? In sum, a 'scrap of paper' (or equivalent) approach in which a few notes or actions are given to the new PL 'to get on with' is inadequate – a lack of information leads to multiple interpretations of what a role entails. To avoid these circumstances from arising, the PL can act, yet that action may only delay ambiguities if undertaken in isolation from senior colleagues. More positively, these ambiguities contributed to the development of my own leadership approach – a need to be vocal, to make decisions about the role, and to let people come back to me if they needed to. I can now advise others, with some authority, about becoming a PL. Further, my experiences align with arguments expressed by McLeod (2010), who spoke about uncertainties which occur over the remit of the PL role. Similarly, emphasizing the importance of role descriptions, Mitchell (2015) found that, even when an institutional role description has been written, PLs are not always made aware of it. To conclude, the basic need of defining what an individual PL's role means is where much of the fuzziness of programme leadership lies.

Induction, Training and Development

In the previous section, I have explained how difficulties can emerge for PLs in cases where their roles and responsibilities are not sufficiently defined. Here, I elaborate on one possible explanation for this: according to Cahill et al. (2015), one of the reasons that PLs may be unclear on their roles and priorities is that they are insufficiently inducted. Indeed, in conversations I have had, PLs often reflected on the 'double disappointment' of both the lack of a clear job description *and* the absence of adequate induction and initial training. This resonates with one of my experiences, where I was parachuted into the PL position very suddenly: I arrived in the office for my third week of employment at that university, and suddenly – I was PL. It was August, where, here in the UK, most students and many staff are away for their vacations, so there were few people around to seek guidance from. I recall taking some long walks to think through a plan for my new programme, safe in the knowledge that no one would notice my absence. I looked for a job description. I made my own job description. Reflecting on some of my early days in this position, I began to perceive myself as something of a 'loner-leader', dropped into an undefined role at a time when everyone else seemed to have left for holiday. To be fair, I am sure that my imagination has exaggerated the circumstances – and the situation felt as though it lasted for much longer than it did. Yet the experience is a reminder of the need to support someone appointed into a new role. It all changed a few weeks later when I met and spoke to a senior academic in the school, also newly appointed, also confused, and, as the vacation receded and the new academic year approached, we worked together to establish some proper processes and embed ourselves fully. These changes came about because I acted, and I was supported by the other new appointee, but I also felt fortunate to come through the episode: I had been teetering. For a PL, the willingness to be proactive and meet new colleagues is important, but it cannot act as replacement for early induction and training. Cahill et al. (2015) suggest that approaches that might be useful here are preceptorship, mentorship, a package of staff development, a handbook and/or a 'toolkit' for PLs. Moore (2018) adds that formal development activity should be complemented by opportunities to learn on the job, mentoring schemes and tailored support for programme teams, also suggesting that transdisciplinary networks maybe useful. The situation is improving: Ellis and Nimmo (2018) examine professional development needs and opportunities for PLs and discuss the introduction of a bespoke provision at one university (Glasgow Caledonian) based on an earlier academic development framework by Sharpe (2017). Robinson-Self (2020) also observes that training and development opportunities are increasing for PLs: in the UK-based organizations such as Advance HE and the Staff and Educational Development Association (SEDA) offer specialist courses. Pulling together both my experience and the evidence, most new PLs offer ability, commitment and enthusiasm – but institutions must ensure that their PLs are suitably inducted. Without this, there is a danger that early commitment may be lost, and we risk providing our newest academic leaders with a poor first leadership experience.

One possible source of development for new PLs might be the academic development community. These staff focus upon 'enhancing teaching and learning, promoting high quality teaching through academic programmes and seminars, and supporting staff in areas of pedagogy' (Baughan, 2015, p. 3). Academic developers cannot advise on all aspects of leadership development but might be a source of support on pedagogic issues, such as curriculum design, teaching methods and assessment. However, my case here is not based on previous experience of seeking support from academic developers but that, for some years, I was a PL *and* an academic developer and indeed mentored a number of new PLs. For me, the dual role of PL and academic developer presented additional benefits and challenges: on the one hand, I was immersed in academic development, with particular interests in areas such as assessment and feedback, academic integrity and student support – all useful areas for a PL. Conversely and understandably, expectations on me were higher – to model good practice in the pedagogic aspects of programme leadership, such that if something was perceived as 'not right', it was quickly pointed out. An additional lesson I took from my role as both PL and academic developer is that it leaves limited time to take on further duties and interests: I found it difficult to fit in much research or engage as much as I wanted to with other academic developers (though I did both, to an extent). But for those leading programmes in other disciplines, an academic developer may provide a further, informed source of support.

Committees, Meetings and Working Groups

I chaired or was a member of numerous committees and working groups. This represents an inevitable part of the role of most PLs, yet a common assumption, echoed to me repeatedly by fatigued colleagues, is that a PL 'needs' to be included on numerous committees and boards. For me, these included all programme-related meetings such as programme management teams, staff student meetings, external examiner meetings, as well as many short-term but intensive task groups. These committees typically ran alongside many others: departmental meetings, school or faculty events, away days – the list went on. Meetings offered some positive opportunities – for networking, for developing a cohesive, motivated programme team, and for understanding and following up student feedback. Attending and contributing is a good strategy for a PL seeking to get to know colleagues across their institution – yet such a strategy can only be pursued to an extent and diminishing returns may set in; there could be little time to *do* the work in between the meetings. When I found myself attending meetings, morning and afternoon, not all of which were relevant, I knew something had to be done. Thus, an aspect of 'unwritten' leadership would involve making judgements about how to manage all these meeting requests, and what I, in my role as PL, could most effectively contribute to. Was my time in preparation for and at these committees either beneficial to my PL work or was I merely filling a space? Sometimes, it was the latter. I became more strategic in my approach, an important skill to harness in programme leadership: I would either accept the invitation, suggest that an alternative member of the programme team could attend, or decline. As my leadership evolved, and I became more confident, I would be ready to explain and defend my decision. For a newer PL, declining a committee membership may be difficult, but if there is a strong case, it should be made. In sum, priorities need to be accorded, but at the same time visibility and good networking skills represent important attributes. All these issues are to be weighed up, and good programme leadership necessitated assessing competing demands. These less-documented skills of persuasion and persistence are important. Still, it took me longer to learn some of them than it should have done: soft skills are crucial for navigating the competing expectations inherent in leading programmes.

Quality and Curriculum Development

Quality assurance refers to the safeguarding and improvement of standards in higher education. For the PL, it includes activities such as programme reviews, quality audits and external accreditations. Cahill et al. (2015) explain that, amongst their tapestry of skills, PLs need to have a sound knowledge of institutional quality procedures – and so it proved for me. As my roles evolved, more of my time was dedicated to quality and development of the programmes I was leading. At one level, I enjoyed many aspects of curriculum review: it encouraged me to remain up-to-date with the relevant academic issues and in touch with my students and alumni. If I had ideas, I could put them forward and canvass opinion (usually to staff and students involved in the programme, but sometimes more widely), and many of these ideas were adopted. At University B, I introduced education for sustainable development as a topic, since there was clear evidence of growing interest amongst students. It would be gratifying if curriculum changes which I had led received positive student feedback. It wasn't always noticed, but collecting feedback from students and staff provides a key part of programme leadership. Still, there were more mundane aspects to managing programme reviews and accreditations: the sheer bureaucracy involved could be a test of resilience. Universities and accrediting bodies can set a lot of hoops to jump through, making it difficult to enact changes in a timely way. Accreditation could be a demanding process: it was often reflective and therefore of value, encouraging programme teams to assess strengths and development areas for a programme, bringing in a diverse range of views. But again, there would always be a lot of data to collect and administration to fulfil. At these times, it would be important to call on and consider ideas of the programme team, external colleagues and students. And in this, ideas offered differed amongst members of the programme team – and I had to navigate these tensions. At first, I wasn't particularly good: I can recall one meeting I chaired as a new PL when tempers flared and views about new modules differed. I lost my nerve, in a cacophony of noise made by colleagues, most of whom had more experience than I did. It was an awakening – it wouldn't happen again. Since this time, I have been a very structured chair, who enacts effective chairing in *all* my activities. It's another of those unspoken skills of programme leadership that may serve well in later, more senior roles. However, there were fewer straightforward strategies for managing the impact on time: I had to invest plenty of my own time in work that was not always visible to the outside world. Still, for the new PL, I would make the point that although many find quality assurance unappealing, it does provide the chance to understand the 'inner workings' of an institution. It may help the PL prepare for other types of academic leadership. Again, support from and working with a wider programme team is necessary, illustrating the people-oriented focus of much of the role.

Students and Other Stakeholders

Of all the PL roles I undertook, the opportunity to work with such a diversity of students was the most enriching. Early in my PL career, I was fortunate to work in places including Singapore, Hong Kong, Shanghai, Trinidad and Tobago, and the United States of America. It was a privilege to work with so many overseas students and staff, experiencing their countries and cultures. These international adventures at the start of a higher education career left a strong mark on me and certainly influenced my conception of what leading a programme should involve. In particular, it led me to understand that programme leadership should be about the students – understanding and prioritizing student needs, taking actions to ensure that each had a fulfilling learning experience, and acting upon their ideas and feedback. Also, most of the students on the distance programmes that I led were more experienced and further into their careers than I was at the time, such that I learned from them – this strengthened my view that students may have vital contributions to make in developing a programme. Mitchell (2015) examined student perspectives about PLs and found that 'Students recognized the broad remit of PLship ... they emphasized PLs' role in supporting students, whether academically or otherwise ... Students placed a high value on the work of PLs' (p. 730). The PL–student relationship should be valued by both parties: for many of us, the students make the role worthwhile, or even special. However, there may be difficulties too. Cahill et al. (2015) commented on the complexities of PLs working with different groups of people, one of their participants referring to being 'sandwiched' in a 'complex matrix dealing with multiple levels of staff and students' (p. 278). This takes us back to an issue discussed earlier: while many PLs may have little managerial authority, they are expected to offer wide-ranging interpersonal skills with students and staff. PLs represent their institutions in their interactions with numerous staff and student groups, again demonstrating the importance of training and support.

Discussion and Recommendations

In the sections above, I have reflected upon my experiences of programme leadership at three universities. I have shared my enjoyment of developing programmes but also documented the challenges, often concerning the manageability of a role which was not sufficiently defined. To address these issues, I formulated some of my own strategies and made attempts to give clarity to the roles myself. Also, my PL experiences were varied, and I question whether they can simply be joined up and understood as a linear 'leadership journey'. It may be better to view them as different journeys, all rich in learning (and work), but also presenting distinct activities, successes and challenges. I suggest that it is the ambiguities and blurred boundaries of these roles, rather than any formal job descriptions, that represents the best example of their interlinking and continuity in my leadership journey. I now build on these points with a series of recommendations.

First, I would encourage any new PL to ask for a written role description. This might include a generic institutional job description, but should also be tailored to the specific needs of the programme. It should be remembered that a full PL role is demanding, so other aspects of work will need to be considered around this role and should be realistic. Second, in the changing HE environment, PL duties need to be reviewed periodically. This too is an area that should be discussed between the PL and the head of the department or line manager. For example, the migration to remote learning has affected the work of PLs as much as it has changed all other roles in universities. Next, the new PL should check what support or guidelines are available. Is there a network, by which ideas can be shared and concerns addressed? When new to the role, try to talk to the outgoing PL or others who have worked on the programme. Find ways to talk to students – PLs have a genuine influence on student work and welfare, and students may offer some excellent ideas.

Looking back at my time as a PL, there are areas in which I might have done better. In my early years, I could have made better use of feedback from students. I learned that it is useful to take a long view of feedback and evaluation received about the programme concerned. I would advise other PLs to carefully use feedback received to generate ideas and priorities for programme development and note down ideas as they come in and how often they are raised. If help is needed with pedagogic aspects of the role, for example, curriculum design, most institutions employ teams of academic developers – it may be helpful to seek their support. Also, there remains a lack of research into programme leadership. As I have established above, this is now changing, but it would be useful for us to learn more about PL experiences and innovations from those at the 'coal face'. Finally, the PL must have some ownership of the programme that they run. What vision of the programme do you have? An effective PL needs to work through the melee of bureaucracy and regulation, and should have something to show for their efforts. Keep a record of achievements and consider too what you may like to do next.

I also have some recommendations for colleagues organizing PL roles within institutions. As discussed, PLs are often not clear on the boundaries of their work. Roles are 'fuzzy' because they are not clearly defined. Inductions and mentoring systems are useful, and PL support networks or working groups are easy to set up. Training needs should be considered. This will benefit the PLs, potentially benefit students as well, and provide larger numbers of staff equipped for leadership roles. Further, in accordance with recommendations by Moore (2018), structures can usefully be put in place to empower PLs to meet and share ideas, views and experiences with a range of other colleagues, including senior learning and teaching leaders and managers. In other words, many senior leaders could do more to support and understand the important work of the PL community. By doing so, they may also provide a valuable learning opportunity for themselves.

Senior's framework (Figure 6.1) illustrates the breadth and detail of the PL's role, but the author acknowledges that we need more help from theory for casting additional perspectives. Still, in showing this breadth and complexity, Senior's framework is useful. It correlates both with the work I undertook in my PL positions in terms of its diversity and the sheer amount there was to simply 'get done'. It may be useful to PLs as a reference point, and to institutions as a guide to help construct PL role descriptions and training.

Closing Points

This chapter has focused on the role of the PL in higher education. Drawing on excerpts from my own professional experience and other sources, I have argued that although the role can be rewarding and varied, it might also be characterized by 'fuzziness' – ambiguity and uncertainty – in areas including where the parameters of the PL role lie. Improvements have been made in programme leadership but work still needs to be done in many institutions to support the role, because these staff represent a vital interface between university management and students. For many, myself included, managing a programme represents a first leadership opportunity such that this training and development may bear long-term positive impacts. Looking back, I have reflected above on some unique experiences – many positive, others less so. Collectively, I think these experiences demonstrate that investment in programme leadership is an investment into the sector and its students, and that there is still work to be done to enable PLs to be the best they can be. I hope that this piece provides a fresh and more personal perspective for supporting the growing body of research which argues for the need for our sector to develop and support its PL community.

References

Baughan, P. (2015), 'Sustainability policy and sustainability in higher education curricula: The educational developer perspective', *International Journal for Academic Development* 20 (4): 319–32.

Bracken, S., and Novak, K. (eds) (2019), *Transforming Higher Education through Universal Design for Learning: An International Perspective*, Abingdon: Routledge.

Cahill, J., Bowyer, J., Rendell, C., Hammond, A. and Korek, S. (2015), 'An exploration of how programme leaders in higher education can be prepared and supported to discharge their responsibilities effectively', *Educational Research* 57 (3): 272–86.

Ellis, S. (2019), 'Programme leadership: A review of evidence and an agenda for action', Quality Assurance Agency for Higher Education. https://www.enhancementthemes.ac.uk/docs/ethemes/evidence-for-enhancement/programme-leadership---a-review-of-evidence.pdf?sfvrsn=97f4c381_6 (accessed 25 October 2020).

Ellis, S., and Nimmo, A. (2018), 'Opening eyes and changing mind-sets: Professional development for programme leaders', in J. Lawrence and S. Ellis (eds), *Supporting Programme Leaders and Programme Leadership* (SEDA Special No. 39), 35–9, London: Staff and Educational Development Association.

Fotheringham, H. (2019), 'Engaging staff and students with data', Quality Assurance Agency for Higher Education. https://www.enhancementthemes.ac.uk/docs/ethemes/evidence-for-enhancement/engaging-staff-and-students-with-data.pdf?sfvrsn=e392c781_8 (accessed 25 October 2020).

Johnston, V., and Westwood, J. (2009), 'Academic leadership: Developing a framework for the professional development of programme leaders', York: Advance HE. https://www.advance-he.ac.uk/knowledge-hub/academic-leadership-developing-framework-professional-development-programme-leaders (accessed 26 September 2020).

Lawrence, J., and Ellis, S. (2018), *Supporting Programme Leaders and Programme Leadership* (SEDA Special No. 39), London: Staff and Educational Development Association.

McCaffery, P. (2019), *The Higher Education Manager's Handbook: Effective Leadership and Management in Universities and Colleges*, 3rd edn, Abingdon: Routledge.

McLeod, C. (2010), *Developing and Supporting Programme Leadership at Edinburgh Napier University*, Edinburgh: Edinburgh Napier University.

Milburn, P. (2010), 'The role of programme directors as academic leaders', *Active Learning in Higher Education* 11 (2): 87–95.

Mitchell, R. (2015), '"If there is a job description I don't think I've read one": A case study of programme leadership in a UK pre-1992 university', *Journal of Further and Higher Education* 39 (5): 713–32.

Moore, S. (2018), 'Beyond isolation: Exploring the relationality and collegiality of the programme', in J. Lawrence and S. Ellis (eds), *Supporting Programme Leaders and Programme Leadership* (SEDA Special No. 39), 29–33, London: Staff and Educational Development Association.

Murphy, M., and Curtis, W. (2013), 'The micro-politics of microleadership: Exploring the role of programme leader in English universities', *Journal of Higher Education Policy and Management* 35 (1): 34–44.

Robinson-Self, P. (2020), 'The practice and politics of programme leadership: Between strategy and teaching', in J. Potter and C. Devecchi (eds), *Delivering Educational Change in Higher Education: A Transformative Approach for Leaders and Practitioners*, 116–25, Abingdon: Routledge.

Senior, R. (2018), 'The shape of programme leadership in the contemporary university', in J. Lawrence and S. Ellis (eds), *Supporting Programme Leaders and Programme Leadership* (SEDA Special No. 39), 11–14, London: Staff and Educational Development Association.

Sharpe, R. (2017), 'SWEET strategies for developers working in the third space', *Educational Developments* 18 (1): 1–5.

Vilkinas, T., and Ladyshewsky, R. (2012), 'Leadership behaviour and effectiveness of academic program directors in Australian universities', *Educational Management Administration and Leadership* 40 (1): 109–26.

Part Two

Engaging Values, Resilience and Serendipity in Leadership

Towards a Community for Teaching Excellence at a Research-Intensive University

Stephanie Laggini Fiore

In thinking about my career trajectory and what led to my leadership position as assistant vice provost at the Centre for the Advancement of Teaching (CAT), I realize that I followed in my father's footsteps, but in an unanticipated way. My father was an Italian professor at a research-intensive (R1) institution[1] and I thought I was following in his footsteps when I too entered the field as a newly minted PhD in Italian. In a time of depressed opportunities for tenure-track positions in the liberal arts, I was grateful to land a full-time non-tenure-track position at my current R1 university. The dean tasked me with increasing retention in my department's major,[2] a challenge I took on fully because I was passionate about the importance of world languages and literatures, and because I relished the opportunity to modernize our programme offerings. I began building a co-curricular student community by offering weekly coffee discussion hours in Italian, reviving a defunct Italian Club that sponsored cultural events, and creating a peer-tutoring service. Later, as programme head, I updated the course inventory, revised the core curriculum to address proficiency gaps and improve retention of students into upper-level courses, and provided opportunities for students who did not speak the language to engage with the literary and cultural content of our discipline. I also acted as advisor for our majors and minors,[3] hired and mentored non-tenure track academics and represented the department on college curriculum committees.

In this first leadership experience, I learned to accomplish things despite the naysayers. When the senior academics in our department told me that they had tried creating a student club and 'it just doesn't work here', I tried anyway. When they told me that non-tenured academics didn't normally serve on committees and had never been considered for roles as programme heads, I asked 'why not'?

Then I asked them to consider it. When department colleagues questioned the wisdom of designing courses for students not proficient in the language, I argued that our rich literary and cultural tradition should be more universally accessible. And it worked! Our programme's enrolment grew by 33 per cent overall and 50 per cent in upper-level courses. I followed in my father's footsteps, I realize now, by emulating his dedication to educating students and to the benefits of learning, and his passion for the discipline. This is how I imagined the life of an academic, and all of my work mirrored that vision.

So of course, in an R1 institution, my career suffered for it. I threw myself into building the programme, as the dean had instructed me to do, and never changed course even as we went through five deans and three chairs in ten years, each with his or her own view of what success meant. I published but did not meet the level of output that someone intent on a tenure-track role should produce. The ironic result of my success in increasing programme enrolment and retention was that it allowed the department to recruit a tenure-track academic for the first time in decades, but that position would not go to me. My journey to learning and teaching leadership began in the work I had done to improve student success in my programme. But the catalyst that led to re-examining my career trajectory and finally embracing fully the role of a teaching leader was when I lost the bruising bid to gain this tenure-track position because I had prioritized teaching over research. When the director of our teaching centre approached me about an open associate director position (a full-time administrative role), I jumped in feet first.

I was hopeful that my transition to educational development would be the right path for me, as this new role would afford me the opportunity to focus on great teaching and work with others who cared about student success. But the transition off the academic track into administrative work still felt risky. I worried that, in this role dedicated to developing academics, I would no longer be impacting students directly through teaching and, frankly, would miss them. I fretted that I might be isolated in my new role, part of a small team instead of a larger college setting. There was no small amount of imposter syndrome, as I was unfamiliar with the literature on learning, and the scholarship of the field had cultures and traditions that were alien to me ('What's a poster session?' I asked when planning our annual conference). In addition, I had to work out of my comfort zone, facilitating programming for those who taught in large lecture classes, clinics, studios and labs. In my years leading a centre, I perceive the same doubts in new developers, but they come to understand, as I did, that the skills we gain as teacher, mentor and researcher are transferable. I saw that facilitating workshops for academics is another form of teaching, mentoring experience gained in my department was useful for consultations with colleagues, committee work prepared me to evaluate the curriculum of other disciplines with a practised eye, and research skills – while needing to be adapted – were applicable across disciplines. I also found, to my immense pleasure, that the learning and teaching world was supportive of newcomers. I distinctly remember my astonishment at how willing to share and assist others the Professional and Organizational Development (POD) Network[4] members were the first time I attended the annual conference. No intellectual property boundaries slowed down this spirit of common mission, and I remain even today grateful for POD. Most of all, I found great purpose in the ripple effect that educational development creates – I impact academics, which impacts every student they will ever teach. My fear of leaving students behind disappeared with the awareness that this impact on academics and on their students is profound. A short while after joining the centre, I ran into a former colleague from my college, and she commented that it was clear I had made the right career choice as she could see that I was glowing (her words) with newfound purpose. We are trained to believe that only one path equals success, but my 'failure' to earn the tenure-track position led me to truly fulfilling and inspiring work.

An Ode to (Teaching) Joy

In this new role, most striking for me was the revelation that many academics do not live the joyful and purposeful life of teaching that I had been fortunate enough to experience, but instead live that part of their professional lives with trepidation or ambivalence. The core of my personal journey to learning and teaching leadership became the desire to facilitate a change in teaching that enables joy. One of the first anchors for me as an educational developer was Dean McManus's *Leaving the Lectern: Cooperative Learning and the Critical First Days of Students Working in Groups*, which I used for my very first book group discussion. In it, McManus describes his journey from sage on the stage lecturer to a facilitator of active learning. He identifies themes for switching one's teaching from a nineteenth- to a twenty-first-century model: accept risk, use feedback, reflect, adapt and be flexible, establish a partnership, accept that you are teaching in a different world, and welcome the joy! (McManus, 2005, pp. 166–73). The description McManus gives of his transformation from a professor who dreaded teaching to one who 'welcomes the joy' is compelling. He describes his early teaching trials this way:

> For several years, I wore a white lab coat to class, not because I had just come from the lab, but because it concealed the damp tension blotches that waxed darkly on my shirt as I lectured. Teaching was not a joy. It was a duty. (Years later I read and enjoyed Parker Palmer's inspiring book, *The Courage to Teach* [1998]. But when he adverted to 'the passions that took us into teaching' [p.21], I'm afraid a big snort of derision escaped me.) (McManus, 2005, p. 8).

As his dive into educational development deepens, and the evolution of his teaching unfolds, McManus chronicles the meaningful change that occurred for his students and for him as a teacher.

> A student walked into the computer room, greeted another student, and said, 'Man, that pattern looks nothing like what I got yesterday.' He apparently pulled out his map and the two students proceeded to discuss what the differences in the two patterns at different times meant. And they knew what they were talking about. To me they were expressing self-assessment of their learning. I leaned back in my desk chair with a limitless smile, punched my fists at the ceiling, and hissed to myself, 'Yes-s-s-s-s!' They had learned it. I was doing something right. Oh, the joy of it! The pure joy! (McManus, 2005, p. 97)

McManus's story has stuck with me throughout my years as an educational developer. It illustrates my ultimate goal and constant hope as a learning and teaching leader, that academics find that kind of positive, life- and career-changing, attitude-improving shift that brings benefits both to them and to their students. The educational philosopher Louis Schmier describes clearly the transformative potential of feeling true joy in our teaching:

> When I had begun to believe that there was joy for me in working with and for each student ... rather in just working for myself, and experienced that joy, the classroom truly became a significant and even momentous place of joyous celebration. (Schmier, 2007)

The generative effect of educational development is the central core of our work, in my opinion. If we haven't helped academics to find more joy in teaching, we have utterly failed.

A recent encounter reminded me that helping colleagues find that joy informs my vision of teaching leadership. Professor Smith,[5] an academic with a reputation as a professor who cares about students, joined a cohort working with our centre to redesign courses with high failure rates. She was willing to participate but expressed scepticism that it could make a real difference, especially in courses such as her introductory, required quantitative course. In her view, the (much-criticized) online maths placement test placed students into courses when they were unprepared to handle its rigours and probably lacked the talent to persist in STEM courses.

In my centre's redesign work,[6] I espouse evidence-based practices such as active learning, collaborative work and targeted practice and feedback, but I also emphasize heavily the research on motivation.[7] I encourage academics to consider questions such as: How can I assist students to develop a growth mindset? How can I build community in large classes? What strategies might foster more equitable outcomes? What messaging will signal support for students and a reminder that learning takes struggle and hard work? For the academics involved in this type of course redesign, there is struggle and hard work too, as learning new ways to think about teaching takes mental energy and a willingness to push old teaching habits aside. I remember distinctly a particular moment when participants role-played a conversation in which the academic needed to convince a student to take the course relying solely on the value the course would bring to the student. The maths academics were stumped. 'They take pre-calculus because it's a prerequisite for calculus.' 'Can't use that,' we responded. 'Why should they take pre-calculus? What is its beauty and usefulness as a course? How does it help them grow?' I could see the wheels turning as it dawned on them that they had never considered the value of this course, other than as a hoop that students needed to jump through to complete the maths sequence. Professor Smith worked diligently through our exercises, redesigned the course and piloted the new version. She remained unconvinced that the changes could make a difference, but then a curious thing happened. As the semester wore on, she noticed that students' test results were appreciably better and that they could use the language of maths more effectively. She saw them persisting at problem-solving where they would have given up before. She also felt her own sense of confidence growing in being able to move students forward in their maths literacy skills. Soon, she was our most enthusiastic convert. She submitted a poster for our annual teaching conference and a disciplinary conference detailing her experiences of teaching the redesigned course. In departmental meetings, she proselytized about the benefits of redesigning courses according to evidence-based practices. In fact, she was such a prophet for change that she swayed her formerly resistant department to send more academics to the next iterations of the programme. Recently, she worked with her department to scale up the improvements to generalize the impact across the curriculum.

What happened here is why I do what I do. It is no accident that I use words like *convert* and *proselytize* to describe what happened to Professor Smith. As

I see it, I am in the business of guiding people to an alternative path, one they are yearning for but are not sure is within reach. And when they see what a difference it can make in their lives and in their students' lives, they experience a joy that they may not have felt for years in teaching, if at all. Conversion and joy! What better use of my career than to convert others to something that brings them greater joy in their work! I often use that word – JOY – when talking about the feeling we get as academics when the light bulb goes off over a student's head, when a class discussion becomes rich and nuanced, leading students in new directions, when a particularly difficult problem is solved or when a student feels a great sense of accomplishment. These moments turn into the stories Linda Shadlow (2013) references in *What Our Stories Teach Us: A Guide to Critical Reflection for College Academics*. Shadlow reminds us that the stories academics tell are integral to the lived process of creating a professional life. Yes, there are certainly stories of frustration and failure. But the stories that we want to tell are those moments of triumph and joy that inform our work, give us energy to keep moving, and remind us that our efforts matter. The essential nature of my learning and teaching leadership is anchored in supporting my institution's 4,600 academics and teaching assistants to create a teaching life replete with the professional satisfaction and joy derived from effectively fostering student learning, success and development, both as learners and as people. But how to do this at an R1 university, of course, is the rub.

Cultural Barriers to Change at R1 Universities

Brownell and Tanner (2012) provide an overview of the literature on the recognized elements needed to overcome academics' resistance to change and enable meaningful reform in undergraduate teaching – training, time, and incentives – and describe in which ways these factors are lacking at R1 universities. But they also point to a more difficult barrier to overcome – the disciplinary culture and values implicitly taught in graduate school 'that defines … professional identities primarily as research identities to the exclusion of teaching identities', and in which embracing a teaching identity 'can be perceived as a liability and something to be hidden', as it implies to others in the disciplinary culture that you are not serious about research (Brownell and Tanner 2012, p. 342). In my experience, this cultural barrier to change is central to the stubbornness of the problem. Beginning in graduate school in R1 universities, resistance to teacher training can arise out of a concern that graduate students focus their energies on research and not 'waste time' on teaching. Graduate students are groomed to follow in their mentors' footsteps as high-level researchers and professors at similar institutions, what the Modern Language Association (MLA)[8] Task Force on Doctoral Study in Language and Literature calls the 'narrow narrative of success' (2014, p. 7). At my own institution, despite the availability of a Teaching in Higher Education Certificate[9] intended to prepare graduate students to be educators, it has been an uphill climb to convince departments to allow it as an elective in the graduate curriculum. Yet, according to a report from the Association of American Colleges and Universities and the Council of Graduate Schools,

> Approximately 75 percent of faculty[10] positions are in … institutions where teaching and professional and community service roles are of equal or greater importance. Doctoral programs seldom adequately prepare students for the realities of faculty life, particularly in these different sorts of institutions. (Gaff et al. 2003, p. 15)

This culture is exacerbated in the formative years of junior academics' careers by a system that rewards research production by reducing teaching load, signalling that teaching is an undesirable part of our professional lives. As noted extensively in recent years, the structures at research-intensive universities de-incentivize time spent on teaching, thereby perpetuating long-standing ineffective teaching practices:

> A critical factor impeding systemic improvements of undergraduate education … is how teaching is considered in the rewards structure … 'Neglect of undergraduate education had been built into the postwar university, in which faculty members were rewarded for their research output, graduate student Ph.D. production, and the procurement of external research support, but not for time devoted to undergraduate education' (Lowen, 1997, p. 224). This reality is frequently reinforced by a lack of support and feedback about teaching (Gormally et al., 2014). (Dennin et al., 2017, es5.2)

This cycle perpetuates inattention to teaching, to the detriment of academics' own professional teaching competence, their students' learning and, ultimately, their job satisfaction. From my perspective as a leader of learning and teaching at an R1 university, this neglect presents a continual need to overcome the perception of educational development as remedial instead of a necessary part of a talent-development philosophy that encourages professional growth as a teacher in higher education.

In this environment, then, how can teaching leaders effect change? Attend any conference for educational developers, and you will have a choice of sessions that offer strategies on how to engage academics in the work of teaching centres. There are helpful tips on how to improve attendance at events, effectively communicate the value of educational development and advertise available services. (Is social media beneficial? Do incentives work? What about recognition like micro-credentialling?) Like all teaching centres, my staff and I pay attention to these concrete ways of connecting academics to our services. But what I have found is that the key to the ability to connect with academics and reach into seemingly remote and resistant parts of the university is relationship-building and providing a community of champions for change in which sometimes isolated academics can openly pursue teaching excellence, find collegial support and then influence others to join this community.

Developing Champions for Change

Robert Diamond states that a teaching centre is an 'institutional change agency' that supports transformational change (2005, p. 33). In order to accomplish this mission, the teaching centre must both create a space for an interdisciplinary, university-wide community to form and, also, facilitate the formation of intra-disciplinary teaching communities located within departments and colleges. In leading the CAT, therefore, I lean into Lee Shulman's idea of the importance of making teaching 'community property'. In Shulman's (1993) *Teaching as Community Property: Putting an End to Pedagogical Solitude,* he describes the realization that his image of academic life – of solitary research work and communal teaching work – was backwards.

> What I didn't understand as a new PhD was that I had it backwards! We experience isolation not in the stacks but in the classroom. We close the classroom door and experience pedagogical solitude, whereas in our life as scholars, we are members of active communities: communities of conversation, communities of evaluation, communities in which we gather with others in our invisible colleges to exchange our findings, our methods, and our excuses. (Shulman, 1993, p. 6)

McManus's (2005) reference to 'establishing a partnership' as one of the themes that will lead to twenty-first-century teaching is about this exact need for a community in which academics can benefit from colleagues' shared wisdom. It is through professional discourse within this community that academics in an R1 university find like-minded colleagues who want to deliver powerful learning experiences, solve teaching challenges, receive feedback that helps them improve, and test new ideas. This community in turn forms new networks of influence inside their colleges and departments. It is not enough to just host workshops that bring evidence-based teaching practices to academics who seek them out; one must begin a network of relationships that will bloom into communities of practice[11] throughout the university and bring broader and deeper change. When people tell you that it can't be done at an R1 institution, try anyway, because it can be. In fact, my fear of isolation in the educational developer role was unfounded. My team and I have worked closely with this dedicated community of academics as change-agents, tackling retention, inclusion and other learning issues head-on.

As the leader of the centre, I have been intentional about prioritizing communities of practice that develop 'champions for change', dedicating funds and staff time to these efforts. In my mind's eye, I see a network of change-agents developing new networks wherever they are situated and amplifying the message of teaching excellence. One of the primary avenues for these campus-wide communities of informed advocates – both for evidence-based teaching and for our centre's mission – is the Provost's Teaching Academy (PTA),[12] a yearly six-week deep dive into evidence-based curricular and pedagogical practices. *Informed* is the essential word here as these academics immerse themselves in an intensive survey of the research on teaching and learning, evidence-based practises in integrated course design, teaching methodologies that promote deep learning, reflective teaching and inclusive teaching practices including Universal Design for Learning (UDL).[13] They read a significant amount of literature on teaching and learning, complete collaborative activities that make them reflect on their own teaching methods, consider evidence-based alternatives and participate in a micro-teaching exercise with feedback from peers. In the process, participants find that their beliefs and action-possibilities around student learning and development are honed and grown.

While CAT programming is typically open to all academics at any level, for this particular development opportunity, I intentionally choose applicants with significant curriculum development and/or course coordination responsibilities (often full-time non-tenure-track academics), or known influencers in their departments or colleges with the ability to promote change (those in key positions like department chair, or tenure-track academics who will lead future generations of academics in that department). Every year, I strategically invite a handful of academics and academic administrators to the programme because they represent an area that I feel is not yet well-represented in the CAT's network.[14] As an important part of the learning experience involves getting out of our silos and hearing new perspectives on teaching, there is special attention paid to forming cohorts that represent racial and gender diversity as well as a mix of ranks and disciplines. In this interactive, interdisciplinary and highly collaborative environment, people get to know each other well, and they often maintain those contacts beyond the six weeks. This is one of the few CAT programmes that targets a particular population because its purpose is to be the vehicle for creating an interdisciplinary community of practice made up of champions for change, who will in turn build their own intra-disciplinary communities to support great teaching.

PTA participants, all of whom have significant teaching experience but who have probably never had the opportunity to delve deeply into thinking and talking about teaching, express great satisfaction with what the experience does for them as teaching professionals. This note from one of the participants, an academic for fifteen years, is emblematic of the kind of joyful and empowered growth academics experience:

> I am now in the process of writing my teaching philosophy and I realize how much I have grown since last year. The Provost Teaching Academy was one of the most life changing experiences in my career and I cannot thank you enough. This semester I have changed completely the way I teach ... Now I use the flipped classroom, and I am amazed with the level of participation so far. It is too soon to talk about results, but the vibe in the classroom is incredibly positive; the students spend most of the time solving problems in groups. The most amazing part is that they work an average of 15 problems per hour, which is three times as many as I used to do when I was lecturing this same class. Having said all this, I know that there are many things that I could do better. I would ask you if you could come to one of my classes so that I can get your input on how to make this class the best experience my students have in their college life, both as a learning experience and as a life experience. (22 September 2016, email)

During a recent panel discussion with recipients of our university's teaching awards, almost all these recognized great teachers talked about their transformative experience in PTA and how it was responsible for their success as instructors. The joy PTA graduates feel is our best advertisement.

Building community through a programme such as PTA is one thing; maintaining a sense of community 'aliveness' (Wenger et al., 2002) that encourages continual engagement with educational development and an enduring willingness to act as change-agents within their own spheres of influence is another.

> How do you design for aliveness? ... Many intentional communities fall apart soon after their initial launch because they don't have enough energy to sustain themselves. Communities, unlike teams and other structures, need to invite the interaction that makes them alive. (Wenger et al., p. 49)

Thoughtful attention must be paid to nurturing the persistence of the larger community of PTA graduates by taking steps to acknowledge the participants as important members of our centre's community, inviting their continued contributions, and helping them to develop and maintain the connections they have begun to forge with each other and the centre.

The first step is to recognize the extraordinary commitment to teaching excellence that PTA participants have undertaken by participating in this intensive programme. At PTA's concluding luncheon, we award a certificate and an engraved glass apple to acknowledge participants' hard work and dedication and ask them to display that apple in their offices as a visible symbol of their membership in PTA. Some have proudly posted the picture of the apple on social media. Each year's graduates are publicly listed in our annual teaching conference brochure and permanently on our website, and are featured in our *Provost's Teaching Academy Spotlight* social media series. The CAT hosts periodic luncheons, coffee hours or open houses to help them maintain a sense of belonging and to connect and reconnect them with us and with their colleagues.

In order to build persistent community engagement over time, I follow the guidance of Wenger et al. (2002) by allowing for flexible and cyclical participation in a variety of ways. I intentionally invite concrete contributions – be they small or large – to advance teaching, transform university culture and supplement the bandwidth of my modest-sized team. For example, when launching new major initiatives, such as our Inclusive Teaching Institute, I invite PTA graduates to experience them first and solicit their feedback on possible improvements before launching them for their colleagues. I recruit CAT fellows from this community, who take on faculty developer roles, leading workshops and conducting consultations with colleagues. Others take on smaller tasks: they are invited to share their insights on teaching by writing for our *EDvice Exchange* teaching blog, to act as reviewers for the poster and breakout sessions at our conference, as well as to facilitate sessions and collaborate with my team on initiatives, publications and presentations. I especially encourage them to form what Block calls the 'network of networks' (Block, 2008, p. 79), that is, smaller, disciplinary communities of practice around teaching that are drivers for evidence-based teaching practices. When they lead educational development opportunities in their own departments and colleges, we provide our expertise or resources to support them, and also act as a sounding board for their ideas. This is, of course, the ultimate goal: to create a network of informed advocates who will go out into their own communities to form new networks in which to incubate ideas.

PTA graduates feel clearly that they are part of a special community who are essential collaborators in the struggle for joyful and meaningful change. The result has been remarkable. At this point, we have almost two hundred PTA graduates embedded in departments across the university. PTA graduates regularly host teaching brown bags or other events in their colleges or departments, invite the CAT into departmental decision-making, identify areas that need improvement in their departments and either develop programming to address it or connect me with the department to support change. One associate dean PTA graduate immediately began thinking up new ways of engaging her academics in teaching development opportunities, identified great teachers who could lead the way (all of whom were also PTA graduates) and encouraged departments to implement formative peer review of teaching protocols. Some members have urged me to invite department colleagues to participate in PTA as they need to build informed allies around them for the reforms they envision facilitating. A recent restructuring of one of our colleges put PTA graduates in every chair and academic associate dean position, a clear sign that those academics are recognized voices for a new way of thinking about the future of teaching. My attachment to this network of full-throated advocates has solidified my leadership position on campus as the primary voice for teaching and learning, so much so that in the recent move to remote learning due to Covid-19, the deputy provost and I were charged with ensuring academic continuity for the university. The provost then announced to university academics that the deans and I would be reaching out to support the transition online.

Final Thoughts

As educational developers, we focus on the research on how students learn, as we should. We are interested in how to improve educational experiences so that all students can succeed academically and so that we can help them value what we are teaching. We provide academics with strategies to make that happen (how to engage students in the learning opportunities, how to promote self-regulated learning in students, how to design well-aligned courses that promote deep learning, how to create more inclusive classes, etc.). For the course redesign institute at my university, the research study was initially set up to measure the success of these strategies. Were students failing less? What kinds of shifts did they exhibit in growth mindset or task value? These are all important questions that must be pursued and refined.

But I missed something in developing the research questions – I missed asking how the academics themselves had shifted. There were anecdotal stories from academics that they felt more confident, empowered, successful at their teaching and that they felt as if they had served their students better. But there was no way to measure it. In essence, I needed to figure out the answer to this question, 'How do I measure the joy?' My decision to add research questions designed to examine this shift for the following year's iteration of course redesign produced data that revealed a meaningful, transformational impact on academics' identity, actions and beliefs. Were the academics more successful at accomplishing the goals they had set out for their courses? Had they developed more of a growth mindset around teaching? Did they feel empowered to adapt their teaching to support student learning? In order to develop a comprehensive strategy for meeting the centre's mission, as a learning and teaching leader, I need to encourage deeper enquiry into these questions and the larger questions that McManus posed and that have been my guidepost throughout my educational development career. 'Does your class bring you joy? ... If not, why do you settle for receiving less than joy or gladness in what you do?' (McManus, 2005, p. 162).

I believe the key to progress is to think of yourself, in the parlance of today's social media world, as an influencer who asks the question, 'How can I, as a learning and teaching leader, help you discover your teaching joy?' In that positionality, plant the seeds of meaningful change by building positive relationships with willing academics, engaging them in deep learning about evidence-based teaching and connecting them to each other in a rich network of encouragement and support. Then send them out to catalyze and nurture teaching excellence in their disciplinary communities. The tangible joy that blooms when academics experience newfound teaching prowess will in turn sustain your own purposeful and joyful work as educational developers.

Notes

1. According to the Carnegie Classifications of Institutions of Higher Education, an R1 institution has 'very high research activity', at least $5 million in total research expenditures, and confers at least twenty research/scholarship doctorates.
2. In the United States, a 'major' is the equivalent of a 'course of study' in the UK, that is, the specialization a student pursues for the undergraduate degree.
3. A minor in the United States is an optional course of study in a secondary academic discipline. The requirements for completing a minor are about half as many credit hours as a major.
4. The POD (Professional and Organizational Development) Network is North America's largest educational development community.
5. An alias to protect her privacy.
6. I remain grateful to Dr Johanna Inman, formerly of the CAT, for partnering with me to develop the programme's curriculum.
7. To introduce these theories to academics, I rely on the excellent summary of the research on motivation in Ambrose et al.'s *How Learning Works: 7 Research-Based Principles for Smart Teaching* (2010).
8. The Modern Language Association (MLA) is a professional organization dedicated to the study and teaching of languages and literatures.
9. This Certificate consists of a three-credit graduate course on learning and teaching theory and practice, and a nil-credit practicum that pairs students with mentors.
10. The term 'faculty' is used in the United States to refer to academics.
11. Wenger et al. (2002) identifies three characteristics of communities of practice: (1) Shared domain of interest; (2) Sharing of information, activities, relationships, and learning; (3) Members are practitioners.
12. This model originated with Dr. Pamela Barnett, dean at LaSalle University and former director of our centre, who created PTA to develop a cadre of academics prepared to teach graduate students in the Teaching in Higher Education Certificate.
13. UDL is.an approach to learning that focuses on proactively implementing teaching methods that remove barriers to student success. For more information, see cast.org.
14. For example, we recently invited both the new chair and another teacher from mathematics as we knew that we would need a critical mass of academics to effect changes needed in a department whose curriculum affects many majors. We also invited law school academics because we had little presence in that school.

References

Ambrose, S., Bridges, M., Lovett, M., DiPietro, M. and Norman, M. (2010), *How Learning Works: Seven Research-Based Principles for Smart Teaching*, San Francisco, CA: Jossey Bass.

Block, P. (2008), *Community: The Structure of Belonging*, San Francisco, CA: Berrett-Koehler.

Brownell, S., and Tanner, K. (2012), 'Barriers to faculty pedagogical change: Lack of training, time, incentives, and … tensions with professional identity?', *CBE—Life Sciences Education* 11 (4): 339–46.

Dennin, M., Schultz, Z., Feig, A., Finkelstein, N., Greenhoot, A., Hildreth, M., Leibovich, A., Martin, J., Moldwin, M., O'Dowd, D., Posey, L., Smith, T. and Miller, E. (2017), 'Aligning practice to policies: Changing the culture to recognize and reward teaching at research universities', *CBE—Life Sciences Education* 16 (4): es5.

Diamond, R. M. (2005), 'The institutional change agency: The expanding role of academic support centers', *To Improve the Academy: Resources for Faculty, Instructional and Organizational Development* 23: 24–37.

Gaff, Jerry G., Pruitt-Logan, A. S., Sims, L. B., and Denecke, D. D. (2003), *Preparing Future Faculty in the Humanities and Social Sciences: A Guide for Change*, Washington, DC: Council of Graduate Schools & Association of American Colleges and Universities.

McManus, D. (2005*), Leaving the Lectern: Cooperative Learning and the Critical First Days of Students Working in Groups*, San Francisco, CA: Jossey-Bass.

MLA (2014), *Report of the MLA Task Force on Doctoral Study in Modern Language and Literature.* https://apps.mla.org/pdf/taskforcedocstudy2014.pdf(accessed 26 September 2020).

Schmier, L. (2007), 'Joyful Time', *The Random Thoughts of Louis Schmier* [Blog], 6 January. https://therandomthoughts.edublogs.org/2007/01/(accessed 8 September 2020).

Shadlow, L. (2013), *What Our Stories Teach Us: A Guide to Critical Reflection for College Faculty*, San Francisco, CA: Jossey-Bass.

Shulman, L. (1993), 'Forum: Teaching as community property – Putting an end to pedagogical solitude', *Change* 25 (6): 6–7. http://www.jstor.org/stable/40165011 (accessed 8 September 2020).

Wenger, E., McDermott, R., and Snyder, W. (2002), *Cultivating Communities of Practice: A Guide to Managing Knowledge*, Boston, MA: Harvard Business School Press.

8

The Need for Time and Space for Leadership Development in Learning and Teaching

Hannah-Louise Holmes

Introduction

As an academic and senior leader in higher education (HE), I am driven to achieve inclusivity in the student and staff experience. My approach to teaching and learning aligns with the theory of social interaction as put forward by Lev Vygotsky (1962). My interpretation of this theory is that a teacher should collaborate with his or her students in order to help facilitate meaningful construction in students. In academia, I observe a close correlation between the teaching strategy of lecturers and the style they adopt in leadership. I find that the leadership style I have is a mirror of the approaches which have been successful in supporting students. Both seek to bring out the best in individuals and empower them to achieve goals; in the case of students both personal and academic, and in the academic team both personal and collective goals.

I have been fortunate in my career to progress to a senior role within a UK post-92 HE Institution. I work in a large Faculty of Business and Law with about 10,000 students, which allows for significant impact within leadership positions. Whilst my role requires me to support academics in all aspects of their roles, this chapter will focus on my journey as a successful leader of learning and teaching. As is common in the field of education (European Commission, 2010), my career development, career stages and transition have been supported by mentors. Mentoring has been the tool through which I have sought refuge and guidance, a private space separate and protected from my front-facing roles and responsibilities. My use of mentoring can be seen through the lens of Goffman's *Presentation of Self* (1959), where I use mentoring to both manage the front self I portray in my workspaces, and as a private outlet for a presentation of self that is less confident and clear as I work through issues both professional and personal before stepping back into my front self.

In this sense, mentoring has been crucial in giving me both the space (defined as separation from those directly involved in my teaching and/or leadership roles) and time (interpreted as time away from the action or doing part of the role) that I needed to share and shape ideas. Mentoring has allowed me both time and space to focus on my personal development and confront insecurities and to develop coherent plans and approaches. This separate space and time have allowed me to present publicly as a calm, organized and self-assured leader.

Central to my leadership journey have been various forms of vulnerabilities. These have arisen due to me being young, being a female and being a leader in teaching and learning who has developed from the ranks within my subject area. My journey and reflection examine how I have fought to present a confident front self even when in my private self I have not shared the same feeling. Central to my journey of leadership in teaching and learning has been the role of mentors, my inclusive leadership approach and my organizational skills and attention to detail.

Leadership in Higher Education

Leite (2015) examined democratic leadership in higher education and, drawing on work by Lewin, Lippitt and White (1939), identified three main groups of leadership styles: authoritarian, democratic and laissez-faire. Reflecting on the work of Leite (2015), we can identify why these styles are effective and any problems which may occur when using these styles on a daily basis in the workplace. 'Authoritarian leaders determined the policies, expectations, and details about the processes. They tended not to share future steps but would keep that information to themselves until it was time to share the information so that tasks could be completed. This leadership style hindered creativity in problem solving and seemed impersonal' (Leite, 2015). In comparison, Gemeda and Lee (2020) identify laissez-faire leadership as being 'characterized by non-involvement, showing indifference, being absent when needed, overlooking achievements and problems as well. It is a style of leadership in which leaders offer very little direction and allow group members to make decisions on their own' (Gemeda and Lee, 2020, p. 3). These findings seemed to indicate that laissez-faire leadership may work in situations where the followers were highly skilled and required little supervision.

Turning the discussion to followers, Belbin (1996) identified five different styles of followers: receptive, self-reliant, collaborative, informative and reciprocating. With different followers within organizations, there will be times when there is a leadership style that does not work effectively because of the follower style. Therefore, a leader might be unsuccessful in one situation, but successful in another. Effective leaders should be able to change their leadership style to fit different situations.

I do not believe there is one single approach to leadership that can be consistently applied and result in success in every circumstance. To me, leadership comprises a multiplicity of approaches determined by the situation and/or individual(s) that form part of that. Overall, I adopt a democratic approach driven by the positive outcomes of such an approach described by Ogunola, Kalejaiye and Abrifor (2013). However, when the situation demands it, for example, time is short and the decision must be taken immediately to avoid any form of harm arising, I switch quickly to a more autocratic and directive form of leadership. However, in keeping with my overarching belief in open and transparent leadership, I ensure that when the immediacy of a situation has passed, I explain to stakeholders the reasons for the decision and lack of appropriate consultation. In my experience, leadership sometimes requires quick decisions and action; confidence to do this is essential. At other times, slow and meticulous planning – drawing in different stakeholders and seeking to identify where influence is required – is essential to building long-term strategic vision and transformational change in institutions. My personal approach to leadership has always been to prioritize kindness and empathy, attempting to treat people as individuals rather than as a collective. Further, I have a strong sense of duty and responsibility for my team's well-being and personal development. I have a belief that being authentic, honest, calm and organized is a foundation of forming trust as a leader, being someone who the team feels they can rely on, who is resilient to support or direct the team. This approach to leadership is however not sustainable in the long run without support. Therefore, to achieve this, I find spaces to share any worries or concerns in order to build my strength and resilience so I can maintain energy with the team. Creating time and space for me to gather the emotional skills or knowledge I need to perform my leadership roles has been key throughout my career.

However, leading throughout the Covid-19 crisis (UNDP, 2021), the separation between my work and home spaces has blurred. My experience is reflective of colleagues in the sector (Jandrić et al., 2020). For example, the requirement to work from home meant that I no longer had a daily commute, blurring my work and family personas. I could no longer use the space on the commute to transition from being mum and wife to being a professional and worker.

Through the disruption of Covid-19 and difficulties of maintaining separate spaces between work, home and personal struggles, I have understood leadership in a broader way than before. I have recognized that it is not a weakness to remove some of the gloss from the front self I present and that this is welcomed and supported by the team. Indeed, I have, in discussion with colleagues, understood that a glossy image can be intimidating or demoralizing as team members believe the 'front self' presentation. They feel I cannot relate to their situation as I appear so in control or that they are somehow weak or ineffective when looking at the apparent ease with which I seem to cope with challenging situations. Leadership can be shown through honesty about struggles and not completely retreating to private spaces to gain composure for a 'front self' representation. This has been an important lesson to me as, through the crisis, I have learned to share more of myself and some aspects of my family life, including the difficulties of managing both childcare and mental health challenges of continuous lockdowns (McMullan et al., 2021). Notwithstanding, I have done this in a manner that allowed me to remain in control of what I shared, that is not through uncontrolled emotional responses but through retrospective openness about difficulties I have faced. This has added a layer to my leadership that has publicly revealed a more fragile side, enabling people to see that, although I seek to remain reliable and supportive of the team, I share and deeply relate to the challenges they also encounter. As a leader in teaching and learning, I feel that I have grown throughout my time in HE to be comfortable presenting a more raw, fragile and arguably more authentic persona to the teams I support. In many respects, this has released unnecessary pressure that I placed on myself and has allowed me to build stronger relationships with people through showing a vulnerability that is more relatable to colleagues.

Overview of My Career in Academia

My career in academia started in 2005 as an associate lecturer. This commenced immediately after completing the postgraduate certificate in business education (PGCE). I was therefore very young when entering academia and one of the youngest in the university when being promoted. I was also a 'first-generation' student and had no family history or background in higher education, which added to the 'imposter syndrome' I had. I was also conscious that both initially in economics and then latterly in accounting, finance and banking (AFB), it was predominately male environments.

As I have grown professionally, and personally, the use of mentors and coaches has been invaluable in creating both time and space for me in which to breathe, take stock and provide my own safe space.

It is interesting for me to reflect at the current point in my career about how much of my leadership is shaped by experiences from my early career. It is during these periods that I developed the confidence to utilize different streams of information to enhance the learning environment and to lead change across programmes. The learning I did at these stages is fundamental to my ability to steer the department. My leadership encourages others to find time and space for personal and professional development, reflection and innovation. This may be through mentoring, coaching or academic networks. Without space and time, innovation is restricted. I feel privileged to be able to undertake my current leadership roles, but, even as my confidence grows, I continue to draw on my peers, including mentors and close colleagues, for support.

I will use interconnected periods in time that correspond to leadership roles I have held to examine my experiences and learning as a professional. These time periods track my career progression from early career academic to my current role as head of department (HoD).

In 2012, I became undergraduate coordinator (UGC) in economics, which extended my involvement and reach in terms of responsibility for teaching and learning as I assumed the role of leading these areas for the programme. The UGC role in my faculty is broadly equivalent to programme leader or subject leader in other institutions. This was my first experience of leadership; I was able to have some influence in the overall planning and delivery of the programme and bring my teaching and leadership philosophy into the department. Prior to taking on the role, relationships between academics in the department were strained due to historic disagreements over the direction and shape of the programme resulting in fractious relations between the prior leadership and the wider team. Taking on this role, I championed collaboration and teamwork, introducing a transparent and inclusive approach to decision-making. I shaped this around a collective ambition to achieve the programme Key Performance Indicators (KPIs). I knew from being part of the department for a number of years that some groups felt excluded and undervalued; this drove me to develop a culture where all voices and opinions were of equal value. During my time in HE, and through different roles, I closely observed other leaders and, drawing on my own values and beliefs, understood that in most scenarios an inclusive approach was the most effective and positive approach. I took time to speak individually with people and to bring people together in open forums for discussion around agreeing on a collective vision and sought to demonstrate the value of each colleague as an individual within the team. As academics, I knew we all shared a common belief in the power and importance of high-quality education and research, but that emphasis needed to be spread evenly across these, sometimes perceived to be competing, perspectives.

An important aspect of responsibility was my role in the programme review for economics in 2014. I led this and I wanted to ensure that the programme was reviewed to reflect the changing needs of students, for example, embedded essential graduate skills through an appropriate assessment strategy and adapted curriculum to ensure student success, such as progression and retention, and student experience. The strong overarching value of inclusive practice that drives my behaviours informed my vision for the programme. From observational experience of peers, and from my own values, I believe that developing programmes and structures that support a feeling of belonging and value in students and staff will result in better outcomes for both. For students, I see this being reflected in their satisfaction with, and performance on, the programme. For academics, this results in a more positive attitude towards work. To make the programme review process a success, I needed to ensure that the academic staff were supportive of changes and contributed to the planning discussions. This was important to me as I saw the programme review as an opportunity to change the long-standing division in the department and to bring the team together around a common objective. I knew that to build a strong and united department, everyone needed to feel that they were seen and heard. Whilst I had a strong vision for the department and understanding of what was needed to achieve it, I had concerns around my age and perceived legitimacy from colleagues who, prior to my promotion, I had worked with at the same or lower grade. To achieve my vision of using the programme review as a tool for uniting the team through strong and inclusive leadership, I approached the university coaching community and was matched to an academic who supported me as I progressed through my journey of leadership in learning and teaching.

Drawing on the Chartered Institute of Professional Development (CIPD) framework (CIPD, 2021), the coaching community comprised staff from the institution who have completed coaching development programmes equipping them with the skills needed to support colleagues. As my coach was from a different faculty, I was able to be my private self in the space and to talk openly and honestly about what I wanted to achieve, the barriers that would cause difficulties and how to overcome them. The support I received from this relationship, and having a space where I could be honest about my concerns and vulnerabilities, was transformational. By planning and talking through approaches and scenarios in advance of implementing them, I was able to appear calm, self-assured and organized to the programme team. This was important to me as I wanted to instil confidence in the team. I felt conscious about carefully managing the front self that I presented to the department and that displaying emotional responses or lack of organization and planning in front of my peers would be seen as weakness and attributed to my age and gender, undermining my leadership, and perceived suitability to be in the role. Briscoll (2016) discusses how gendered stereotypes can lead to biased evaluations of female leaders, and I have always been conscious about remaining in control of my own emotions to try and mitigate this sort of bias. To the academics, I did not appear affected by challenging behaviours and attempts to undermine my authority through being deliberately argumentative and obtuse. However, privately, and supported by my coach, there were tears as I navigated the complexities of managing academic colleagues and achieving consensus and collaboration. The journey in the department was difficult; I was moving the culture from highly fractious to collegiate and collaborative, but managing that transition was difficult as I had to put a lot of time and effort into building the team's trust in me and in each other. I held a lot of individual conversations with members of the department and often felt that if I made an error in my use of language, or took the wrong approach to discussions and meetings, the walls around people would be rebuilt. I felt every interaction, every email, every meeting posed a risk, particularly in the early stages as long-standing feelings of hurt and division were still dominating interactions within the department. The anxiety of getting something wrong, being under or wrongly prepared, or inadvertently making someone feel they were not equally valued often left me feeling exhausted and sometimes overwhelmed. The private spaces and opportunities to discuss and refine communications and approach provided me with an opportunity to let down my guard and share my anxieties and vulnerabilities. During this stage of my teaching and learning leadership journey, I started to understand the importance of continually aligning my behaviours to my values and using the private spaces to build resilience. At times, it was draining to manage negative and unsupportive reactions towards me, but over time, and continuing to demonstrate a consistent approach and leadership style, team members started to become more cooperative, and trust was slowly established alongside respect.

Without the support of a coach to allow an outlet for frustrations, these could have bubbled over into my front self, undermining the efforts to build relations with the team.

One specific example I recall was the organizing and execution of a meeting that I had planned with my coach. The objective was to bring the academic team together and, through a workshop approach, identify in four areas (research, teaching, assessment and student support) what we were doing well, what we should change and how we would change. The meeting was designed to allow the team an opportunity to shape the four areas and concluded with each attendee agreeing to take an action away and assume ownership and accountability for delivering it. The structure, agenda and format of the meeting were planned over a number of weeks. My coach had repeatedly advised me that not all of the team would attend but to focus on those that do, ensuring clear changes arose from the meeting, meaning those who chose not to attend would feel that they had missed out on something important. On the day of the meeting, at the time the meeting was due to begin, I stood in the room surrounded by flip chart paper and all my plans for the day, and no department colleagues arrived. It was the first time that I thought I was going to cry outside of a private space. As I waited and tried to remind myself that this was a journey and I had to be patient, a few colleagues arrived. After ten minutes, we had two-thirds of the team in attendance, and the meeting started. That meeting was the first of a number I led. Each time, as predicted by my coach, more colleagues attended until it became more unusual not to attend. The guidance of being patient as a leader and bringing my team along with me by gradually winning their confidence has been at the heart of every role I have moved into since.

During the period of time leading the programme, the National Student Survey (NSS) improved from 68 per cent to 92 per cent (National Student Survey, 2021), and progression improved from 75 per cent to 90 per cent, exceeding department KPIs. I believe that this was due to a student-centred pedagogic approach and the collaboration and collegiality created in the department.

Growing Confidence in the Private and Front Self

At the start of my role as HoD in accounting, finance and banking, I moved from leading a team of sixteen academics and 300 students to over forty academics and about 1,500 students. Furthermore, as a female aged thirty-seven, with an (at the time) eleven-month-old daughter, leading in a predominantly male subject area (King, Ortenblad and Ladge, 2018), I was not the stereotypical image of a HoD. To help overcome my imposter syndrome, transition into the role and management of my private and front self, I was supported by a coach, but in a change from my previous experience, they were external to the institution.

Focusing firstly on the first year as HoD, in the same way that I was able to extend my impact as a leader when moving from lecturer to UGC, I was now able to do this across the full department. Furthermore, I had a faculty-level role in addressing award and progression gaps. In this regard, I had influence over activity across the faculty through the implementation of approaches to different learning environments. Unlike when I was new to previous leadership roles, at the time of this promotion, I had a young child, and this added another layer to how I managed my time and spaces since both were compressed to include and balance parenting responsibilities. When I was promoted to HoD, I had been back at work for six months after taking four months of maternity leave due to family reasons. I am fortunate in that I have always been well supported in my career by my husband and parents.

With their support, the first year of my role as HoD was not significantly impacted by having a young child. I felt confident that I was balancing things and was able to maintain a clear separation between my personal and work lives, often using the commuting time to transition from one persona to another, that is Mummy to HoD and back to Mummy. However, this changed significantly in the second year of my HoD tenure with the Covid-19 pandemic.

Since becoming the HoD, the department has undergone a periodic review, and I have overseen this process for all programmes in the department. Within this role, I have oversight of ten programmes across undergraduate and taught postgraduate levels and of associated programme leaders. This has been very interesting as I have been able draw on my previous experiences to support the department and have used this as an opportunity to reshape the learning and teaching environment. Very few of the academics, including those in the Senior Leadership Team (SLT), had been involved in a previous periodic review. This lack of experience meant that I adopted both a leader and mentor role throughout the process. The lessons that I took from the previous review were that it was essential to be organized, open to student and staff contributions and clear on the overall objectives.

I was keen to use this programme review as an opportunity to work closely with the academic staff to ensure that the programme review reflected their values, having seen how powerful this approach was in my role as UGC. As a leader in learning and teaching, this programme review afforded me an early opportunity to work on a project with every member of the academic team and to 'walk the talk' on the values that I wanted to bring into the team. On my first day as HoD, I ran a facilitated workshop to determine the values and beliefs that were important to staff. The rationale for holding this meeting was drawn directly from the coaching I received as a UGC, providing an opportunity for teams to voice their views, shape the objectives of the department and create a culture of shared accountability. I wanted to continue my journey as a HE leader that demonstrated inclusive practice and to demonstrate that this could result in transformational change at department level. In October 2018, we launched the programme review planning process with a departmental meeting. Prior to the first meeting, I had worked with the SLT to agree a set of principles that we would apply, for example, examinations could only be applied in exemption-based units, digital skills and personal development would run across all three years and we would create a non-exemption route for students. These principles were underpinned by feedback from various stakeholders and split metric data.

The first meeting asked staff to keep in mind the values they had agreed in September and the principles from the SLT but to then shape a new programme to launch in 2020. The approach that I took in this second programme review was to ensure a clear timeline, schedule and assigned roles and responsibilities. I outlined this timeline at the first meeting with commitments from the SLT in terms of information that would be provided to support the department planning, for example, current and prospective student, alumni and employer feedback. The timeline and process worked really well. Over three meetings, we were able to completely redesign the programme and reach full consensus. Part of the learning from my first programme review was to plan the process in advance and outline parameters that the staff had to work within. This worked very well as we did not have endless discussions about small details but kept focused on the bigger picture in a clear and managed set of discussions.

I feel that I approached this second programme review with a more mature and clear approach because of the confidence I was able to draw on from earlier stages in my leadership journey. This allowed me more time to think about the outcomes we wanted to achieve and to listen carefully to all parties. I was also able to make better use of research to inform the programme changes. Whilst I felt that the economics programme review changes were particularly good and dramatically improved the programme, I feel that learning the process did detract from my ability to make truly innovative changes to the delivery and assessment. In this most recent review, we have been bolder and that is because I have been able to spend less time on the process and more time on leading and shaping the teaching and assessment strategy. The resulting impact on my leadership was that I could spend more time on the softer aspects of the role, providing more individualized support and time for discussion around innovation in curriculum development.

Similar to the first months in my role as UGC, externally I presented as an HoD who was confident, organized and in control of the situation. Privately, I was drawing on the support of a coach to manage imposter syndrome and uncertainty over how to best manage situations. The private spaces for reflection and openness around my areas of weakness provided an opportunity for me to develop as an individual and leader, particularly developing the confidence to recognize and value my own strengths. Moving from a leadership position with sixteen academics to over forty meant finding different ways to achieve the same sense of collaboration, transparency and co-creation that I value so highly and that I believe underpin the successful outcomes in previous roles.

I sought ways to embed more inclusive and transparent approaches into the department practices. I introduced a bi-weekly conference call that all department staff are invited to call into. Further to this, I changed the approach taken to SLT meetings by running a five-weekly cycle with invites extended to academics across the department in key roles to enable focused and supportive discussions on their areas of responsibility. This has been crucial in creating a collegiate approach to adapting the teaching and learning environment. One of the key challenges I want to address is ensuring that staff still feel comfortable to share their issues and critical reflections on the department operations and management so that I can ensure I respond and adapt.

Additional means of ensuring that colleagues are engaged has been achieved through the introduction of one-to-one meetings between line managers and those who they manage and the adoption of a coaching approach to meetings with staff. To support a high-quality teaching and learning environment, they function as a safe space for conversations about department or individual performance. The discussions seek to encourage staff to reflect on their own practice and development. They encourage staff to identify ways they can improve their practice and to improve the outcomes for students. To help with this process, staff are encouraged to undertake mentoring and/or coaching to support their development.

External to my own institution, the coaching helped me to develop the confidence to present myself as the HoD and to assure existing and potential partners and stakeholders that I am a competent HoD. I recall one example, early in my role as HoD, where I attended an external event and, in a networking discussion, presented myself as the HoD. The other person took several attempts to clarify what I meant, clearly not immediately able to see that I could be the head for a whole department. The questions, as they sought clarification, ranged from 'Head of a year group or undergraduates?', 'Head of a programme area?', followed by an awkward silence as I quietly responded, 'I am just the Head of Department, the whole department, all of the programmes.' Similar to the reflections of Wilkinson (2020), the awkward silence and the look of disbelief on the face of the other person will always stay with me; sometimes it can still tap me on the shoulder and shatter my confidence, forcing me to return to the coaching conversations and techniques I developed afterwards. That conversation was the moment that I knew I had to present externally as unapologetic for holding the position and own the title, or there would be a detrimental impact on the department's external positioning, creating barriers to opportunities for both staff and students. Without a coach at that time, I am unsure how I would have been able to achieve the self-belief I needed. As described by Sherman (2013), initially I played a role, I acted the part, I prepared myself tirelessly for external meetings to know who would be there and to ensure I had conversational topics that presented the department and university favourably. Eventually, my network started to expand, and spaces that had previously been filled with unfamiliar faces started to include people I had formed relationships with in previous interactions. Over time, I realized I was no longer consciously playing a part; I was genuinely feeling assured in the spaces I was inhabiting and even enjoying these events and spaces. This transformation has enabled me to find and exploit opportunities for my department, the wider faculty, and for our students.

The main crisis I have encountered in the role, eighteen months into it, was Covid-19; this resulted in me guiding the department and students through a very challenging situation. In a fortunate series of events, when Covid-19 impacted, I was receiving mentorship, from a highly experienced professor in the sector, in support of several departmental strategies I was seeking to develop. In similarity to the discussion by Watermeyer et al. (2020), Covid-19 resulted in university campus closures and an immediate move to online working, teaching and assessment from our homes. The various responsibilities, strategies, decisions and actions that took place during this period are too numerous to outline. Fundamental changes to our practice that would ordinarily have taken months of planning and consultation were brought in instantly, operationalized within hours or days. In my role, I was part of the Faculty Executive Group working to respond quickly and strategically to protect the operations of the institution. In my role as HoD, I was supporting the department to make significant wholesale changes to our practice whilst also offering individualized support to colleagues balancing an unprecedented sudden increase in workload whilst homeschooling their children. Indeed, I myself was balancing the responsibility whilst sharing the childcare of my two-year-old daughter. As previously discussed, this reconfigured how I presented my front self as I found my work and home lives blurring and I shared, retrospectively, the personal challenges I was facing with balancing childcare, work and the mental health impacts of being locked down.

I had, prior to the lockdown, planned to start working with a highly experienced professor who was supporting me with some strategic developments I planned for the department. The mentoring continued during the lockdown period and, whilst I did also continue to focus on the primary purpose of the mentoring relationship, I was also fortunate enough to have someone to support and advise me throughout. As with the previous mentoring and coaching I had received, I found a space to confide my anxieties, think through options and plan an approach. Having that space to privately share meant that, to the department, faculty and university, I appeared calm and in control, which consequently reassured the department. Privately, I did have periods where I felt overwhelmed by the pace of work, the pressure to take and implement decisions without time for consultation, and looking after my daughter full time alongside intense demands at work.

During the lockdown period, the university transitioned to a 'block and blend' approach that necessitated all academics to rewrite their materials into a blended learning model and into a six-week format from the previous twenty-four-week model we had in place. I was acutely aware of my role as the leader in the department and that, regardless of how I might feel about situations, I had to remain strong to maintain confidence in my leadership to drive the engagement required to implement the changes. The department responded incredibly. The collaboration that had grown through the team since the first meeting in September 2018 strengthened. We established buddy groups, platforms to share best practice, regular communications to teams and one-to-one meetings.

As the lockdown continued, the culture of collaboration and support became ever more important to each member of the team. I worked weekly with my mentor to continue strategic plans for the long-term future of the department, which I communicated as appropriate to instil a sense of normality amidst the unpredictability, but also planned continuously for the short term to prepare for the next stage of the crisis response. It was during this relatively calmer period that I started to recognize the importance of sharing my experiences with the department and openly acknowledging how difficult it had been at times. I can now see the value of navigating a line between being confident and reliable to the team but not hiding everything and showing a human side. This approach has resulted in a greater openness between the team and me as we've shared similar emotions and challenges. In addition, revealing a less polished version of me has taken the pressure off some of the team, who have told me they felt they were failing watching me appearing to manage the situation so easily. This second outcome and receiving this feedback has affected me profoundly as I saw my leadership through a different lens, whereby the confidence, organization and calmness could result in negative rather than positive outcomes for some members of the team. I have also been surprised by the reciprocal support and empathy I have received from the team who, rather than seeing this as a weakness and losing faith in me, have offered kindness and support to me. I feel that this sharing has enhanced my leadership and our team rather than undermining it.

As we initially returned to the campus, and the intensity of the training and material development response phase ended, I reflected on how we have responded as a department and can see that it has brought us all closer. The shared effort to respond, and clear framework and communications I was able to provide, have resulted in our team being even more collaborative and integrated than before.

As my career has progressed, I have increasingly adopted the role of mentor supporting colleagues across the sector in their academic journeys. I am aware of how beneficial mentoring relationships have been to my development and am keen to support others to have the same space to develop and reflect on their learning and future actions. Consistent with previous phases in my career, these relationships, which have emerged naturally rather than through formal agreement, can sometimes feel strange to me as I struggle to see myself as a role model to others. However, I do gain a significant amount of pride from being able to support colleagues through their academic journey and to see them succeed and overcome their own doubts. Increasingly, I can see that this part of my role and responsibility will expand, and I am keen to ensure that I have the necessary skills to provide the best possible mentoring. To this end, I have completed a qualification in leadership and management and engage in leadership development programmes that enhance my understanding of coaching and mentoring.

Conclusion

I have been in the HoD role for two and a half years and feel that in that time I have developed and evolved as a leader. I hope to continue to steer the department through the difficult external HE landscape and to put in place measures to protect the teaching and learning environment that has been developed through the programme review, working groups and other department initiatives. My leadership style has overall remained democratic, but I am comfortable to adopt different styles when the situation requires and would encourage others to see leadership as fluid.

Leadership in HE is challenging. We constantly juggle several competing priorities and support teams of academics who each have career aspirations and interests that, whilst overall have commonality, are incredibly individualized. As leaders, we must be able to provide the support that our team members need from us, but to achieve that, we need the time to reflect on our own journey and the space to manage our own internal conflicts, and I would encourage future leaders to create the space for personal reflection. In my career, mentoring has at every stage been pivotal, and I believe it would be a valuable source of support for other emerging and established leaders. I have grown as an individual and as a leader in HE; the space and time that has been granted to me through coaching and mentoring has been fundamental to my achievements. This will continue to play a central role in my future journey as I embed mentoring into the spaces I lead and cascade support to the future leaders in HE. The relationship between 'front' and 'private' self has been a dominant part of my leadership journey. As my confidence has grown, I have better understood the positive role vulnerability can play and would recommend that a controlled lowering of the 'front self' guard, supported by mentors, is helpful for leaders to be seen as authentic and to get people on board and help be part of the team and build relationships.

References

Barnett, R., and Hallam, S. (1999), 'Teaching for supercomplexity: A pedagogy for higher education', in P. Mortimore (ed.), *Understanding Pedagogy and Its Impact on Learning*, 137–55, London: Paul Chapman.

Belbin, R. M. (1996), *The Coming Shape of Organization*, Oxford: Butterworth Heinemann.

Biggs, J. (2019), *Aligning Teaching for Constructing Learning*, HEA Academy. https://www.heacademy.ac.uk/sites/default/files/resources/id477_aligning_teaching_for_constructing_learning.pdf (accessed 12 September 2020).

Bovill, C., Cook-Sather, A., Felten, P., Millard, L. and Moore-Cherry, N. (2016), 'Addressing potential challenges in co-creating learning and teaching: Overcoming resistance, navigating institutional norms and ensuring inclusivity in student–staff partnerships', *Higher Education* 71 (2): 195–208.

Briscoll, V. L. (2016), 'Leading with their hearts? How gender stereotypes of emotions lead to biased evaluations of female leaders', *Leadership Quarterly* 27: 415–28.

CIPD (2021), 'Coaching and mentoring: Identify ways to apply coaching and mentoring principles as part of an overall learning and development strategy'. https://www.cipd.co.uk/knowledge/fundamentals/people/development/coaching-mentoring-factsheet#7002 (accessed 7 February 2021).

Cook-Sather, A., Bovill, C. and Felten, P. (2014), *Engaging Students as Partners in Learning and Teaching: A Guide for Faculty*, San Francisco, CA: Jossey-Bass.

Daniels, H. (ed.) (2017), *An Introduction to Vygotsky*, 3rd edn, London: Routledge.

Eun, B. (2019), 'The zone of proximal development as an overarching concept: A framework for synthesizing Vygotsky's theories', *Educational Philosophy and Theory* 51 (1): 18–30.

European Commission (2010), *Developing Coherent and System-Wide Induction Programmes for Beginning Teachers – A Handbook for Policymakers*, Commission Staff Working Document SEC 538, Brussels: European Commission.

Gemeda, H. K., and Lee, J. (2020), 'Leadership styles, work engagement and outcomes among information and communications technology professionals: A cross-national study', *Heliyon* 6 (4): 1–10.

Goffman, E. (1959), *The Presentation of Self in Everyday Life*, Garden City, NY: Doubleday.

Jandrić, P., Hayes, D., Truelove, I., et al. (2020), 'Teaching in the age of Covid-19', *Postdigital Science and Education* 2: 1069–230. https://doi.org/10.1007/s42438-020-00169-6.

Jarvis, J., Dickerson, C. and Stockwell, L. (2013), 'Staff–student partnership in practice in higher education: The impact on learning and teaching', 6th International Conference on University Learning and Teaching (InCULT 2012), *Procedia—Social and Behavioral Sciences* 90: 220–25.

King, M., Ortenblad, M. and Ladge, J. J. (2018), 'What will it take to make finance more gender balanced?', *Harvard Business Review*, 10 December. https://hbr.org/2018/12/what-will-it-take-to-make-finance-more-gender-balanced (accessed 23 January 2021).

Leite, S. (2015), 'Democratic leadership in higher education', *Educating Internationally*. https://educatinginternationally.wordpress.com/2015/04/09/democratic-leadership-in-higher-education/ (accessed 13 February 2021).

Lewin, K., Lippitt, R. and White, R. K. (1939), Patterns of aggressive behavior in experimentally created social climates, *Journal of Social Psychology* 10 (2): 271–99.

McMullan, L., Duncan, P., Blight, G., Gutiérrez, P. and Hulley-Jones, F. (2021), 'Covid chaos: How the UK handled the coronavirus crisis', *The Guardian*, 3 February. https://www.theguardian.com/world/ng-interactive/2020/dec/16/

covid-chaos-a-timeline-of-the-uks-handling-of-the-coronavirus-crisis (accessed 6 February 2021).

National Student Survey (2021), *Why Take the NSS*. https://www.thestudentsurvey.com/ (accessed 14 February 2021).

Ogunola, A. A., Kalejaiye, P. O. and Abrifor, C. A. (2013), 'Management style as a correlate of job performance of employees of selected Nigerian brewing industries', *African Journal Of Business Management* 7 (36): 3714–22.

Sherman, R. O. (2013), 'Imposter syndrome: When you feel like you're faking it', *American Nurse Today* 8 (5): 57–8.

UNDP (2021), *COVID-19 Pandemic. Humanity Needs Leadership and Solidarity to Deafest the Coronavirus*. https://www1.undp.org/content/brussels/en/home/coronavirus.html (accessed 13 February).

Watermeyer, R., Crick, T., Knight, C. and Janet Goodall (2020), 'COVID-19 and digital disruption in UK universities: Afflictions and affordances of emergency online migration', *Higher Education* 81: 623–41. https://doi.org/10.1007/s10734-020-00561-y (accessed 13 February 2021).

Wilkinson, C. (2020), 'Imposter syndrome and the accidental academic: An autoethnographic account', *International Journal for Academic Development* 25 (4): 363–74.

An Accidental Journey towards Educational Leadership

Leopold Bayerlein

Introduction

I am an accounting education researcher, accounting teacher and (emerging) educational leader in an Australian business school. In my workplace, leadership is typically equated with leadership in research, or the uptake of administrative responsibilities. Pathways to formal or informal educational leadership are opaque, and a focus on educational excellence and leadership is implicitly discouraged by institutional promotion structures.

This environmental setting is neither unique to my institution (e.g. see Parker, 2008), nor is it a deliberate attempt by the institution to show preference to one form of academic activity over another. Instead, the setting in which my story unfolds is reflective of the regulatory and competitive pressures in contemporary higher education. Within this environment, research-focused indicators are highly important to determine individual academic as well as institutional success (Vernon, Balas and Momani, 2018), and leadership is provided through managerial top-down processes (Deem, Hillyard and Reed, 2007; Shepherd, 2018).

My personal beliefs about leadership also influence my story, as well as the descriptions and analyses in this chapter. Throughout my life, I have admired individuals that support those around them to become the best possible version of themselves. As a result, I strongly believe that leadership manifests itself in activities that enable others to positively impact communities of practice, while also supporting the attainment of each individual's goals and aspirations. Implicit in my personal beliefs about leadership are a series of key assumptions:

1. That the identity of a leader must be earned;
2. That leadership arises out of action;
3. That a leader is required to 'invest' before achieving a 'return'.

The remainder of this chapter describes my own accidental path to (emerging) leadership, identifies key decision points and draws conclusions that are transferable to other contexts and career trajectories. This chapter utilizes an autoethnographic framework (Chang, 2008) to report and analyse the actions through which I have interacted with others, as well as my workplace environment, systematically. However, it is important to note that my past actions were not in any way informed by formal leadership literature. I have only become aware of these connections and their importance through active post-experience reflection. Indeed, for substantial periods of time, my career progression has been aided strongly by the accidental, rather than planned, occurrence of events.

The Making of a Leader?

Over the years, I have listened to numerous keynote speakers at conferences and senior staff in my institution telling 'their story' about pathways to leadership. Inevitably, these stories represent inspirational tales of plans being made, plans being achieved, and rewards being attained. This chapter aims to provide a contrast to such tidy narratives by highlighting the often unsystematic, and initially unplanned, nature through which my story unfolds.

Humble Beginnings

The beginning of my story is one familiar to many new entrants to higher education, one of extensive personal commitments to high-quality student learning, bounded by institutional pressures, expressed through probation and promotion criteria (see also Parker, 2008; Smith, 2010), to establish a record of excellence in a given field of research. While my academic qualifications and training had prepared me to be a subject matter expert and specialist discipline researcher, I had not received any grounding in educational concepts, processes or strategies. At the time of commencing my academic career, my only teaching experience had been a series of sessional and fixed-term teaching contracts under the guidance of experienced colleagues, without systematic learning or development in education.

Facing the challenge of suddenly being responsible for students' learning outcomes, I focused all of my efforts on identifying suitable teaching strategies, as well as the improvement of the curriculum that now fell into my area of responsibility. Initially, much of my work to understand and improve teaching and learning for my students was driven by the fear of negative student feedback and the potential (but unknown) consequences of failing to meet what I perceived to be institutional expectations. In fact, during the first few years of my career, I thought that excellent teaching was an institutional requirement, and I felt ill-prepared to achieve this outcome.

Within twelve months of commencing my career, my student evaluation feedback was on a par with that of my colleagues. At that time, I was advised by colleagues and my supervisor to stop investing time to further improve my teaching and to focus my energy on research. This culminated in a university-wide training programme for 'future academic leaders', in which one of the most highly regarded academics in my institution stated: 'You will never become a successful academic if you worry about how your learning management system [a central feature of all teacher/students interactions in my institution] is set up.' As an emerging higher education teacher, I was shocked by the stereotyped concept of academic success that underpins this comment.

Several years later, and with benefit of hindsight, I now appreciate that my colleagues and supervisor aimed to align my work-focus with the incentive structures in my own institution and higher education more generally (Parker, 2008). However, I did not recognize this at the time, and resisted the advice provided because (1) I did not think I adequately understood teaching and learning in higher education, and (2) I was dissatisfied with the level of learning my students achieved. Following this decision, I spent several years developing my skills as a higher education teacher. This largely unreflective decision, which I made within twelve months of commencing my career, has had a substantial long-term impact on my work, as well as the way I am perceived by my colleagues and the institution. In effect, I unknowingly chose to adopt the identity of a higher education teacher, rather than any of the other career pathways available to me, and although academia is highly flexible in principle (Archer, 2008), only a series of unplanned events outside my own sphere of influence enabled me to transition away from this identity during the later stages of my career.

Becoming a Teacher

In the early years of my career, I focused my energy on the systematic development of my teaching and learning skills and knowledge, and on applying my learning for the benefits of students. I invested large amounts of time – my supervisor would have called it excessive amounts of time – on improving teaching and learning activities, while maintaining an adequate, but modest, publications profile in my discipline.

Over time, my skills, knowledge and confidence as a teacher grew, and I utilized increasingly sophisticated teaching strategies, whose development and implementation required increasing amounts of time. Looking back, I now realize that I was trapped in a positive reinforcement cycle, where the main reason for developing my teaching was the pursuit of external validation of my work through student evaluations. I was able to allocate large amounts of time to the development of my teaching because I never asked for permission to undertake this work – my thinking being that nobody would fault my activities if they were successful and, more importantly, if my activities were seen to be successful. In order to substantiate the success and impact of my teaching, I turned towards departmental/institutional/national and international education award schemes to gain recognition for my work. In addition, I commenced the systematic collection of empirical data about my work as a teacher, with a view to publishing a small number of peer-reviewed articles in the scholarship of teaching and learning (SoTL) literature.

A key consideration in both decisions was to gain additional recognition for work that I had already undertaken. At the time, I viewed the attainment of education awards as well as the publication of a small number of SoTL articles as the terminal outcomes of this process. I did not consider them to be defining aspects of my future career trajectory. As the level of my recognition as a teacher grew from school/institutional recognition to national/international recognition, criticisms about my work ceased. Looking back, I simply reached a level of recognition that could no longer be criticized by my colleagues or the institution. However, the attainment of teaching awards also cemented the view within my institution that I was first and foremost a teacher and that I was not interested in, or capable of, being a researcher or administrative leader. Although I had not made the conscious choice to become a teacher – and nothing but a teacher – I did not resist being classified as such by my colleagues. Accepting the label, in combination with my external recognition and my emerging SoTL publication profile, enabled me to share my strategies with others. Colleagues who had previously been critical of my work suddenly asked for feedback and advice. For the first time in my academic career, I was recognized for something that also mattered to me.

Transitioning from Teacher to Education Expert

Following an initial departmental and institutional wave of interest in my externally recognized teaching, my colleagues shifted their attention to an amalgamation of academic departments to form a new school, and my work was soon forgotten. Within my institution, I was again treated ambivalently, and my colleagues now regarded me as an outstanding teacher, but not as an education expert, researcher or leader. At this point in time (approximately four years after becoming an academic), I also started to engage with my institution's incentive structures for career progression by applying for academic promotion. While I was successful in my application for promotion, the process opened my eyes to the career limitations of being labelled a teacher, rather than a researcher, and it highlighted a need for change in my behaviour. Consequently, I made the first deliberate and well-considered decision about my future career. I decided to become a business education expert.

A review of what would be necessary to achieve 'expert status' within this space highlighted the following deficiencies in my record:

1. My existing 'education' research track record focused on discipline-based SoTL, rather than conceptual education questions;
2. I was viewed as an innovator in my own teaching, but the transferability of my work remained unclear; and
3. I had no real record of accomplishment or impact beyond my own teaching.

In order to address these deficiencies, I developed a research plan – akin to a post-doctoral research fellowship plan – that aimed to establish a business education research profile, while completely discontinuing my discipline-based research projects. In addition, I actively pursued networking opportunities through national and international education research communities within my discipline and beyond. At the beginning, much of my research, networking and impact work leveraged my personal teaching successes and awards. This was a necessary stepping stone to (1) form collaborations and relationships in the national and international community of higher education experts and (2) bridge the time until my more education-focused research became ready for publication. This strategy was highly successful outside my institution, leading to engagement, leadership, consulting and later education research activities for other institutions in Australia, New Zealand and internationally. Within my own institution, success was limited, and my colleagues, supervisor and the institution more generally continued to label me as a teacher, rather than the education expert persona I was trying to establish.

Over time, the disparity between my institutional persona as a teacher and my external persona as an education expert became substantial. I also grew frustrated because my colleagues and the institution failed to recognize my external impact and standing. At the time, I assumed that one can simply not be a prophet in one's own land. Years later, I realized that my institutional persona remained static because (1) I did not pursue one of the established paths to leadership at my institution, and (2) I failed to clearly communicate my personal aims to my colleagues and the institution at large (see also Schechter, 2020). Instead of stating my goals openly, and thus making my actions visible to others, I pursued my goals quietly until I had demonstrably become an education expert.

To this day, I have no sound explanation why I did not make my intentions more visible. I recognize that many misunderstandings and personal frustrations could have been avoided, and colleagues may have offered their support and advice if I had been more open. Given the absence of information about my personal aims, colleagues made their own, entirely appropriate, judgements based on my continued commitment to student learning.

Developing Leadership Skills

Approximately two years after my decision to become a business education expert, opportunities for leadership began to emerge. Initially, these opportunities related to the management of relationships with external partners, such as work-placement programmes, externally funded merit award schemes for students and the like. Although none of these activities where formally identified as leadership, I pursued them because they fitted well within my – internally held, rather than externally communicated – narrative of an education expert, where teaching, research and service to the institution were interconnected. Given that many of these activities included external partners, the communication of outcomes and impact, both inside and outside my institution, became critical parts of my work. The communication strategies I employed during this time focused on the impact of projects. However, my name became associated with these projects, and through this association, my colleagues and the institution started to form a broader view of my professional persona. In essence, my work as a successful facilitator of external engagement opportunities extended my existing persona as a teacher. While I did not recognize this at the time, the internal communication of these small successes was critically important for my future career, because it created a demonstrable record of accomplishment beyond teaching and allowed me to establish my next persona – the business education expert.

It took a complete reorganization of my institution (the creation of a new faculty structure) to further develop my leadership. At that time, I had become confident in my ability and considered it my personal responsibility to influence the standing and recognition of education in my institution. Accidental good fortune also played a part! As soon as the leadership team for my new faculty was appointed, I started a concentrated 'campaign' (a sustained and multipronged 'attack' on the status quo) to convince my faculty and institutional executives to implement a range of programmes that would support and recognize largely unacknowledged education activities across the institution. I was able to make these arguments because I had successfully transitioned from a teacher to an educational expert and emerging leader. In addition, I had also started to communicate the personal aims underpinning my persona as a business education expert clearly.

When campaigning for educational change, my extensive external engagement work – and more importantly the communication of outcomes and impact associated with this work – as well as my publication record in business education were critical to convince decision-makers of my expert status (Gunderson, 2018). When introducing my campaign to the new faculty executive team, I adopted my business education expert persona, rather than the teacher-based personas I had adopted previously. I was able to make this change because (1) I now had an established teaching, research and service to the institution record in this area, and (2) my newly established reporting line was unburdened by any knowledge about my previous personas. For many of my colleagues, the speed with which my public persona changed seemed to come as a surprise. Personally, I felt more comfortable as an education expert than I did as a teacher, because this new persona had now been in development for approximately four years, and I was confident that I had achieved expert status within this field.

My colleagues recognized the successful development and implementation of a teaching awards programme for my new faculty as my first step towards leadership, and several colleagues commented that they saw my 'long-held plans' come to fruition. Unfortunately, I cannot claim such long-term planning or foresight. Instead, the opportunity to lead a project with substantial impact arose due to contextual factors wholly outside of my control. My campaign to improve the recognition of educational excellence across my institution was possible because (1) the university's executive had lost sight of this objective, (2) the new institutional structure provided low-level leadership opportunities that were previously unavailable and (3) the new faculty executive wanted to demonstrate their commitment to teaching and learning. Although I did not foresee any of these factors, my persona as an education expert was, without active planning on my part, sufficiently well developed to make use of these circumstances.

Emerging as a Leader (in the Eyes of my Institution)

As my informal faculty leadership activities continued, I was still not widely recognized as a leader, chiefly because I held no identifiable role or title. I grew frustrated with this lack of recognition for my work and resolved it by inventing an innocuous title – 'Coordinator Education Awards Faculty of Science, Agriculture, Business and Law' – for my work, and adding it to my institutional email signature. This simple step of 'claiming ground' transformed how colleagues reacted to my work, presumably because they now had access to the appropriate language to describe, evaluate and support my leadership narrative (see also Bowles, 2012). In the last two years of my academic career, I have also tried to apply the learning of my earlier experiences to develop as an emerging leader. Specifically, I aimed to:

- utilize my emerging persona – the educational leader – when engaging with others both inside and outside my institution;
- actively pursue opportunities where my previous business education expert persona can be extended into leadership;
- communicate widely the personal aims that underpin my work, as well as the impact of that work, to make my intentions transparent to others.

In the current development of my leadership persona, I am also guided by my personal assumptions about good leadership. In combination, these guiding principles and lessons learned have enabled me to grow my impact from the faculty to the institution, while adding a supportive and compassionate aspect to my emerging leadership persona.

My emergence as an official leader (in the eyes of the institution) required another external event outside of my control. Approximately five years after starting to develop my leadership persona, the long-term chair of teaching and learning in my department contacted me to discuss succession planning for their position. As part of this succession plan, I was invited to apply for a position of deputy chair, with the opportunity to eventually apply for the role of chair of teaching and learning. These roles represented the first officially identified leadership roles for which I was approached by the institution and the first identified leadership roles for which I applied.

When considering applying for these roles, I was very concerned about my lack of experience in formal administrative roles – which is how my institution generally defines leadership. To put my concerns to rest, the then chair of teaching and learning told me that 'to fill this role you first and foremost need credibility as an education expert, and you have got that in spades'.

I have now transitioned to the role of chair of teaching and learning, and my past personas as teacher and business education expert have become a prerequisite for success in this role. In particular, the clear communications of my personal aims that underpin my business education expert persona have become critical because this persona allows me to influence others. While I did not appreciate this connection at the time, all of the personas I developed during my career were prerequisites for further steps, both planned and unplanned, down my personal path towards emerging leadership.

Joining the Threads

I confess to a personal motivation to maximize my professional influence and impact over time. However, I have never made a long-term plan to attain particular positions within my institution. Instead, my path to leadership is defined by a series of small steps, aimed at addressing skill, knowledge and work focus deficiencies as I became aware of them.

Personal Intentions as Developmental Guides

At the beginning of my academic career, my work activities focused on attaining external validation through student evaluations, supervisors' performance reviews and peer feedback from colleagues. This pursuit of external validation manifested in a strong focus on attaining positive student evaluation feedback through an extensive commitment of time and effort, and ultimately I became known as an outstanding teacher.

What was lacking at this point in my career was a clear intrinsic long-term aim that could serve as the narrative glue of my career. I first recognized the risk of being driven by the pursuit of external validation when I was asked to connect my various work activities into a coherent narrative to apply for promotion. I found this exercise extremely difficult due to the lack of connectedness between my various teaching and research activities. Following my promotion, which also provided my first exposure to the institution's incentive structures, I set myself one personal aim: to enable future graduates to make meaningful contributions to global societal challenges.

My path to leadership has been influenced substantially by the identification of this overarching personal aim. While I do not think that I will ever attain this aim, stating it allowed me to make systematic decisions about the development of my business education expert and emerging leader personas by assessing if particular projects and activities supported future-focused graduate outcomes. It also allowed me to emancipate my activities from short-term external validation-seeking behaviour, because I could now self-assess the relevance of my work against a long-term aim.

Personas as Artefacts of Personal Intentions

My career has developed over time through the personas of (1) teacher, (2) education expert and (3) emerging leader. The use of personas has been highly beneficial in the later stages of my path to leadership because it allowed me to develop my professional activities holistically while advancing towards my overarching personal aim. At the same time, different personas were highly useful at specific points in my career. Each persona is associated with a particular set of strength, weaknesses, opportunities and threats (SWOT) (Table 9.1). My first persona – the teacher – developed without thought or planning, and I only recognized the existence of this persona once I became aware of its weaknesses and threats to my professional future.

My other personas – the education expert and the emerging leader – are the result of a deliberate attempt to conceptualize the intentions underpinning my work, and to communicate these intentions to others. However, attaining my second and third personas would not have been possible without first achieving the status of teacher and education expert.

The persona of business education expert played a particularly important role in my path to leadership. Pursuing recognition as a business education expert allowed me to justify particular projects to colleagues and supervisors, and this provided a narrative focal point for my communication with institutional and external stakeholders. Establishing this loosely defined persona enabled me to

Table 9.1 Personal SWOT Analysis

	Personas		
	Teacher	**Education Expert**	**Emerging Leader**
Strength	Achievable entry point at start of career Meeting personal commitments to teaching	Connection of teacher persona with research and service work Aligns with institutional incentive structures	Pursue self-selected impact opportunities
Weaknesses	Does not align with institutional incentive structures	Prior discipline-based research record abandoned Education not viewed as a 'real' research area by colleagues and the institution	Gradual transition away from students Formal roles impact on personally constructed narratives
Opportunities	Formal recognition for excellence available Providing foundation for impact on others	Engagement with national communities of practice to develop research and impact Opportunities for formal and informal leadership arise	Affecting large-scale change Personal growth through leadership skills and impact opportunities
Threats	Long-term focus on teaching persona limits future opportunities	Time commitment to achieve impact is substantial and impacts on other activities	Negative impact on credibility through activities outside area of expertise

transition out of the role as teacher, while also allowing the integration of a wide range of activities in teaching, research and service to the institution.

A final benefit of using personas to conceptualize and communicate professional identities is their encapsulation of previous personas. In my case, the education expert encapsulates the teacher, and the emerging leader encapsulates both teacher and business education expert. This stacking of personas over time is critically important because it allows for a reversion to a pervious persona to meet specific situational circumstances. For example, as an emerging leader, I am able to revert to my business education expert persona to influence others in educational contexts. In addition, the existence of previous personas also provides a level of credibility, which literature has identified as being highly important for higher education leaders (Bryman, 2007).

Communicating Personal Intensions and Impact Attained

Academia is a field that allows individuals to pursue a wide variety of career choices (Smith, 2010). Given this flexibility, a clear intrinsic understanding of my personal long-term aims, and the personas through which these aims are operationalized, has been important in my path to emerging leadership. As I have transitioned through my various personas, I have become better in communicating my intentions, how my activities align with these intentions, and the real-world impact that is achieved through these activities.

At the beginning of my career, I failed to communicate this information, and as a result I was assigned a persona – that of teacher – by my colleagues and my institution. There are substantial risks associated with not making personal intentions clear. For me, these risks have included (1) not being made aware of opportunities, (2) being asked to undertake projects that were unaligned with my intentions, and (3) being asked to justify a long-term career trajectory in which I was not actually interested. Once I had established my personal aims and started to communicate these aims clearly, the perception my colleagues, supervisor and the institution held about my work started to change.

The communication of clear personal intentions also allowed a more authentic and targeted communication of impact. Specifically, the communication of personal intentions allowed me to connect small individual impact activities into a larger impact mosaic, without having to explain the fit and relevance of each piece. A positive side effect of the creation of such an impact mosaic is that its total impact exceeds the sum of its parts, because individual pieces of impact evidence become mere examples of the overall impact achieved.

Acknowledging Why Personally Decisions Are Made

In order to develop leadership through the guiding principles of personal intentions, it is critically important to understand why personal decisions are made. Throughout my career, I have made decisions for a variety of reasons: systematic, impulsive, and for every reason in-between. For many years, I thought that I made decisions for sound reasons, after extensive consideration.

However, I was unable to judge the quality of my decisions effectively, assuming that in hindsight some decisions were simply better than others.

A research project with a colleague (Bayerlein and McGrath, 2018) represented a major turning point in my ability to evaluate decisions. This project was based on the observation that an education development colleague from my department and I had formed a successful collaboration, when we saw many other attempts at such collaborations fail. Through analysis of our working relationship, previously opaque decision points – including factors that influenced our decisions in this relationship – became visible. For me, this project highlighted the extent to which others influenced my decision-making through their own perceptions, actions and statements, and it allowed me to reassess how I engage with personal and professional decision-making processes.

Understanding my own limitations in decision-making did not necessarily result in better subsequent decisions. However, it has allowed me to evaluate why I make particular decisions more honestly and effectively. Attaining this self-evaluation skill has assisted me in managing the development of my personas and supported my decision-making as an emerging leader.

Conclusion

This chapter describes my ongoing transition from personal teaching successes to emerging educational leadership. Important actions that have supported this transition are (1) the identification of personal intentions that underpin my work, (2) the use of personas as conceptual vehicles that incorporate all my activities and develop my identity holistically and (3) the clear communication of my personal intentions and personas to others. While the importance of these actions became apparent in my own story sequentially, it is highly likely that many of the challenges and frustrations I faced in the early years of my career could have been avoided if I had applied these actions earlier. In particular, the identification of a personal intention that could have bounded and contextualized my professional work would have helped me shape my own professional narrative. The potential benefits stemming from the identification of an overarching personal intention in the early years of an academic career are clear. However, it is important to recognize that I do not know if it would have been possible to identify such an intention without the trials, errors and false starts that I experienced in the early years of my career. At a minimum, I would have found the activity challenging.

The use of personas to conceptualize academic activity and development holistically during the early stages of an academic career appears to be less problematic. This is the case because personas are by definition temporary and suited to short-term career planning and development. Within my story, identifying the benefits that arise out of conceptualizing the various components of academic work in a holistic fashion, centred on personal development and impact, would have been highly beneficial. Potential benefits for my transition from personal teaching successes to emerging leadership would have included a regaining of control over the externally imposed narrative that dominated the formation of my teacher persona. In addition to regaining control over the narrative of my career trajectory, aiming to develop a particular persona in the early stages of my career may have assisted in justifying and communicating particular actions systematically. Finally, the conceptualization of holistic personas also played a crucial part in maximizing the impact of the various unplanned events that occurred during my career. While the occurrence of these events was purely accidental, I was also lucky enough to be able to utilize these events to my advantage.

Improving communication of my personal intentions, as well as the well-contextualized communication of activities and impact, played a significant role during the later years of my transition to emerging leadership. The extent to which this action translates to other contexts is unclear. As a life-long introvert, recognizing the transformational impact of communicating my personal aims and impact to colleagues and the institution provided a reason to persist. Others, and particularly those with more extrovert personalities, may not benefit greatly from this activity. However, increased awareness of the potential impact of this action is likely to be beneficial regardless of circumstances.

Unrelated to the three outlined actions, gaining a more detailed understanding about how and why I make decisions has been highly beneficial. Gaining this knowledge, and becoming more aware of the benefits of self-reflection generally, has helped me to identify situations in which I make decisions for unsystematic reasons. While I continue to make decisions for a variety of reasons, knowing what motivates, or triggers, a particular decision is highly useful both from a career planning perspective as well as a leadership perspective.

Throughout this chapter, I have tried to describe and analyse my transition from personal teaching successes to emerging leadership. I hope that the three actions and one core skill I have identified provide useful guidance for others aiming to navigate the less travelled paths to higher education leadership.

References

Archer, L. (2008), 'Younger academics' constructions of "authenticity", "success" and professional identity', *Studies in Higher Education* 33 (4): 385–403.

Bayerlein, L., and McGrath, N. (2018), 'Collaborating for success: An analysis of the working relationship between academics and educational development professionals', *Studies in Higher Education* 43 (3): 1089–106.

Bowles, H. R. (2012), 'Claiming authority: How women explain their ascent to top business leadership positions', *Research in Organizational Behaviour* 32: 189–212.

Bryman, A. (2007), 'Effective leadership in higher education: A literature review', *Studies in Higher Education* 32 (6): 693–710.

Chang, H. (2008), *Autoethnography as Method*, Walnut Creek: Left Coast Press.

Deem, R., Hillyard, S. and Reed, M. (2007), *Knowledge, Higher Education and the New Managerialism: The Changing Management of UK Universities*, Oxford: Oxford University Press.

Gunderson, T. (2018), 'Scientists as experts: A distinct role?', *Studies in History and Philosophy of Science* 69: 52–9.

Parker, J. (2008), 'Comparing research and teaching in university promotion', *Higher Education Quarterly* 62 (3): 237–51.

Schechter, D. J. (2020), 'Career transitions in the digital age: Mastering the art of communicating career direction clarity', Executive Doctorate in Business, Georgia State University.

Shepherd, S. (2018), 'Managerialism: An ideal type', *Studies in Higher Education* 43 (9): 1668–78.

Smith, J. (2010), 'Forging identities: The experience of probationary lecturers in the UK', *Studies in Higher Education* 35 (5): 577–91.

Vernon, M. M., Balas, E. A. and Momani, S. (2018), 'Are university rankings useful to improve research? A systematic review', *PLOS One* 13 (3): e0193762.

10

Valuing Collaboration in the Leadership of Learning and Teaching

Sandra Jones

Introduction

My journey through higher education has seen me advance in my career from an entry-level academic in one of the largest universities in Australia, through to professor and, in retirement, to professor emerita. Along my voyage I have engaged with a broad range of students, colleagues and external stakeholders (business, community and government) from diverse cultures, in ten countries across Australia, Asia, Europe, the United States and Canada. The pathways I traversed led me to integrate my original discipline of industrial/employment relations with the emergent field of knowledge management (from a human-centred perspective), and thence to leadership. Along the way, my discipline research journey was complemented by my deepening interest and expertise in the scholarship of teaching and learning (SoTL).

When I started my journey, leadership was not a term used in higher education; rather, the focus was on teaching and research. While there were positions labelled 'head of department', these roles were administrative, usually undertaken (somewhat reluctantly) by professors as part of their 'service' contribution to the university, and on a three- to four-year rotational basis. In this context, my leadership in learning and teaching developed more by accident than design.

My approach to leadership in learning and teaching has been influenced by my value commitment to collaboration. This has been the default philosophy that has guided my life, initially, in my practice and discipline-based research in industrial (employment) relations (Jones, 2000), and thereafter in my academic career. My commitment to collaboration resulted in my adopting a distributed, activity-based (Gronn, 2002), rather than the formal position-based, style of leadership. A distributed leadership approach is one of the more collective theories of leadership, alongside shared leadership (Pearce and Conger, 2003), relational leadership (Uhl Bien, 2006) and collective leadership (Ospina et al., 2020), rather than a single (heroic) leader approach (Fletcher, 2004).

My leadership style has focused on how to engage the many experts that contribute to effective leadership for learning and teaching. This placed my leadership identity at odds with the more individualistic, administrative management style that has increasingly intruded into the sector (Bolden et al., 2012; Deem, 1998). To create synergy between the two approaches, I focused on establishing collaborative internal processes to implement externally set standards (Jones, 2003). In so doing, I resisted the move towards treating academics as 'the new process workers employed to do and not to think' (Jones, 2004, p. 944), but rather engaged with academic and professionals to continuously develop learning innovations (Davis and Jones, 2014). The outcome for me was that my leadership identity became increasingly encapsulated in a contested space that required me to both take advantage of serendipity as it emerged and to build my resilience to face opposition to my leadership style.

Background

My leadership journey into, and through, learning and teaching in higher education commenced in the higher education sector over thirty-five years ago, when discipline-based research expertise underpinned a teacher-centred approach to education. Unlike teaching in the primary and secondary school levels, academics in higher education have been primarily employed for their discipline-based research knowledge, with little (or no) requirement for formal training in pedagogy or andragogy. When I became an academic in the business (management) field in a university, my appointment was based on my research expertise in employment relations. My theoretical knowledge, training and experience as a teacher in the Australian secondary school system[1] had minor (if any) importance. This placed me, from the beginning of my academic career in the business field, as a member of a small (often contested) minority of academics with teaching expertise, in an environment in which discipline-based research was valued over SoTL. Paradoxically, when the university introduced a systematized quality assurance approach for learning and teaching, my expertise in pedagogy and andragogy led to my being appointed to formal positional leadership roles in learning and teaching.

My initial leadership contribution to learning and teaching was based on my personal experience of designing and developing innovative learning activities in which students are actively engaged. This included the design of real-world, situated and experiential learning environments and scenarios aimed at developing student skills through role-play and problem-solving (Jones and McCann, 2004). These simulated learning environments are applicable for both face-to-face and online learning spaces, and they had the added advantage of avoiding the potentially adverse impact of undermining employment levels and conditions, of which I, as an employment relations expert, was apprehensive (Jones, 2019). To test the effectiveness of these simulated learning environments, I developed purpose-built student feedback mechanisms.

Applying SoTL to my innovations resulted in a mix of individual and collaborative research and publications that increased my influence on, and ability to collaborate with, colleagues (Creese and Jones, 2001; Jones, 2001, 2005, 2007, 2009, 2017; Jones and McCann, 2005; Jones and Richardson, 2002; Jones and Watty, 2010; Parrott and Jones, 2018). As my experience and contributions to SoTL grew, I was recognized with teaching awards at the national (2006) and university level (2009), further adding to my leadership influence. My appointment as a national assessor of national teaching awards and grants and my acknowledgement as a Principal Fellow of the internationally recognized UK Advance HE UK Professional Standards (Advance HE, 2019) consolidated my leadership in learning and teaching.

Based on my expanding leadership influence, I was appointed to formal leadership positions: as the deputy head (learning and teaching) for the School (Department) of Management, as the director of teaching quality for the Business College (Faculty) and as the university director of Learning and Teaching Unit. Complementing my leadership in teaching practice, my appointment as the inaugural director of the Centre for Business Education Research (CBER) consolidated my leadership in scholarship for the business context.

In summary, my leadership in learning and teaching began with my recognition as a leader in learning and teaching practice innovations and, combined with my contributions to SoTL, advanced as I was appointed to formal positional leadership roles in learning and teaching.

Leadership in Higher Education: A Personal or Collaborative Collective Endeavour

Serendipity and Resilience

A serendipitous opportunity for me to champion my commitment to a more collective, collaborative style of leadership in learning and teaching occurred when I was appointed as the university director of Learning and Teaching Unit. My appointment coincided with external (Australian government) financing of a grant to undertake an empirical project across the university to build leadership capacity to enhance learning and teaching and improve student feedback, using a distributed leadership approach. This grant was part of a then Australian federal government project to explore appropriate leadership for learning and teaching. One group of projects were designed to utilize a distributed leadership approach, based on the assumption that leadership in higher education involves the 'practical and everyday process of supporting, managing, developing and inspiring academic colleagues ... [L]eadership in universities should be by everyone from the Vice Chancellor to the casual car parking attendant, leadership is to do with how people relate to each other' (Ramsden, 1998, p. 4).

While a second group of projects explored a more single-leader-focused positional/structural approach, my commitment to collaboration attracted me to the distributed leadership approach that had been described by Marshall (2006) as an activity that recognizes 'complex multifaceted process[es] that focus on the development of individuals as well as the organisational contexts in which they are called to operate' (p. 5).

The single university project I led was one of five projects funded to use a distributed leadership approach to build leadership capacity for learning and teaching. As the project leader, I established a university-wide, multi-tiered research project that included experts from all levels and functions in learning and teaching, academic work, student support and services including technology, library and the like (Jones, 2014a). This inclusive research process developed trust and respect across the levels and functions of the university and built leadership capacity for learning and teaching (with some participants subsequently being appointed to formal positional leadership roles in teaching and learning); at the same time, it led to the establishment of a Learning Space Advisory Committee to monitor learning spaces (Jones and Novak, 2009).

Based on the positive impact of this single university project, I was successful in establishing a multi-university project team and obtaining further government funding for three multi-university projects that further explored a distributed leadership approach for learning and teaching. The first multi-university project explored synergies between the experience of five single university-distributed leadership projects. This resulted in a concise description and an action framework for a distributed leadership approach to build leadership capacity in learning and teaching (Jones et al., 2012a). The second multi-university project undertook a national survey of higher education institutions and, based on the findings, developed a conceptual framework and benchmarks for a distributed leadership approach (Jones et al., 2014). The third multi-university project identified national empirical case studies of distributed leadership approaches used to build leadership capacity in learning and teaching.

The research from these projects led to further proliferation of a distributed leadership approach to learning and teaching across the higher education sector in Australia. This was demonstrated by the publication of a range of case studies of empirical projects that used a distributed leadership approach to integrate the work of academics and professional learning designers (Jones, 2018; Jones et al., 2012b; Jones, Harvey and Lefoe, 2014), underpin social learning design (Jones and Harvey, 2017a), implement pedagogy (Jones, 2017b), improve quality of learning design and delivery (Jones et al., 2017), establish a network of academics in science (Sharma et al., 2017), underpin a professional recognition scheme for university educators (Beckman, 2017), improve learning and teaching quality (Carbone et al., 2017); identify the link between leadership capacity building and action research (Harvey and Jones, 2020a) and engage sessional staff in leading educational transformation (Harvey and Jones, 2020b). This plethora of research culminated in the development of a distributed leadership process model for learning and teaching (Jones and Harvey, 2017b).

My recognition as a leader and champion of a distributed leadership approach for higher education was consolidated with the Higher Education Research and Development Society of Australasia publication of a *Distributed Leadership in Higher Education* (Jones, 2017a). My influence was further confirmed through a collaborative research partnership I developed with academic colleagues in the UK with expertise in a shared leadership approach for higher education in the UK. This collaboration resulted in a collaborative *Stimulus Paper* on shared leadership published jointly by the (then) UK Leadership Foundation for Higher Education and the Australian L. H. Martin Institute (Bolden et al., 2015). More recently, I prepared a definition of a distributed leadership approach for the *SAGE Encyclopedia of Higher Education* (Jones, 2020).

Staying Committed to a Distributed Leadership Approach to Learning and Teaching

Despite the advances in my national and international reputation for leadership in learning and teaching, I remained within a 'contested space' as the Australian higher education sector, spurred on by the cessation of national funding in 2012 for projects on leadership in higher education, moved to a more single-leader, hierarchical, administrative management approach to leadership. My response was to continue to champion a collaborative, distributed leadership approach by focusing actions designed to synergize the need to implement regulated standards for learning and teaching, with implementation processes that relied on a distributed leadership approach. I used the six tenets that we had developed from our research into a distributed leadership approach to underpin my planning of these collaborative approaches. The six tenets are (1) *Engage*, (2) *Enable*, (3) *Enact*, (4) *Encourage*, (5) *Evaluate*, (6) *Emergence*. The next section presents exemplars of the action I championed to implement the six tenets.

Tenet 1: Engage

The first tenet of a distributed leadership approach identifies the importance of engaging with a broad range of experts, as well as positional leaders, who contribute to learning and teaching. In championing this tenet, I encouraged a collaborative approach between academics (full-time and contracted staff), professional staff with learning and teaching design expertise, external stakeholders, students, and national and international agencies and associations responsible for learning and teaching. One of the interesting findings we had made in our first multi-institutional research into a distributed leadership approach to learning and teaching was how, despite their role in graduating students as future leaders, academics did not self-identify as leaders. This changed after they actively participated in learning and teaching improvement projects that use a distributed leadership approach. This was exampled in one (typical) feedback response: 'I thought of myself as not being a leader ... [but after the project I realized] ... You can be a leader doing some of the everyday stuff that you do ... [it was] ... organised in the way we worked' (Jones et al., 2012a, p. 42).

Similarly, for students, despite their more active engagement in their own learning through a student-centred approach, few students saw themselves as leading their own learning. In engaging students more actively in accepting their personal leadership, I designed learning contracts through which students were encouraged to self-identify the skills they developed. Current discourse on what constitutes 'student leadership' is a welcome example of development of this concept (Skalicky et al., 2020). Likewise, while external stakeholders have traditionally acknowledged their leading role in identifying the work-related knowledge and skills required of graduates, they are not traditionally actively engaged as partners in learning design. By establishing partnerships with individual business and community stakeholders that more actively engaged them in learning activity design and in working with students to explore complex issues, stakeholders became more actively engaged in leading students for learning (Jones, 2014b). Together these actions were successful in developing more collaborative leadership in the practice of learning and teaching.

Tenet 2. Enable

The second tenet of a distributed leadership approach is to enable collaborative engagement by developing a context of trust and culture of respect. I committed to establish project teams and consultative committees underpinned by formal agreements to actively collaborate. The importance of this was evidenced in multidisciplinary projects designed to explore learning and teaching innovation (Jones et al., 2008), multifunctional collaborations between academics and professional staff to design opportunities for students to globally engage (Collins et al., 2015) and in partnership between academics and external professionals (Jones, 2014b).

Tenet 3. Enact

The third tenet of a distributed leadership approach is to enact processes and systems to support the involvement of a range of experts. I established workload agreements that acknowledged the time spent in collaboration as a work activity and established communication systems to support collaboration. These actions encouraged team-based approaches to design and develop learning and teaching innovations (Jones et al., 2008), and to engage external stakeholders (Jones, 2014b). Collaboration was further encouraged by establishing multi-tiered communication systems for formally structured committees.

Tenet 4. Encourage

The fourth tenet of a distributed leadership approach is to provide a range of support to encourage learning and teaching improvement. I implemented a formal university-wide innovation project that provided funding and time-release to encourage multidiscipline and cross-functional engagement in learning and teaching innovations. Engagement was supported by professional development sessions in collaboration and a distributed leadership approach. To encourage student engagement in innovative learning activities, I developed Certificates of Participation and Skills Acquisition that they could call on as evidence of skills they had developed. As the director of CBER, to encourage external stakeholder engagement, I established an Industry Engagement Committee made up of equal numbers of internal and external experts, chaired by a government minister. The committee was supported by, and in turn supported, multi-tiered and multidisciplinary research clusters that included academics for the five business disciplines (accounting, business information technology, economics, finance, management and marketing).

Tenet 5: Evaluate

The fifth tenet identifies the need to design evidence-based approaches that link aims and objectives. While I have earlier demonstrated in this chapter that collaborative projects and committees had been successful in achieving improvements to learning and teaching, it was less easy to identify evidence-based measurement of a growth in collaboration. I did propose several measures, such as the transfer of innovations across and between universities, fellowship and speaker invitations for individual and group experts, and number and sustainability of stakeholder partnerships. However, to date, these forms of measurement are yet to be included in standard measures of academic performance.

Tenet 6: Emergence

The sixth tenet recognizes the properties of a system (such as new knowledge or intelligence) that 'arise from the interactions and relationships among the parts' (Capra, 1996, p. 29). As the director of CBER, I developed a new co-partnership approach that I termed a living learning laboratory (Jones, 2019). As an emergent concept, the Living Learning Laboratory combined the concept of Living Laboratories (that bring together a variety of disciplinary experts to address complex issues) and Learning Labs (that utilize the virtual learning space to advance innovations and engage students online with technologies and enhance social and community collaboration in learning). While there have been some examples of Living Learning Labs in the sciences disciplines designed to develop sustainability across curriculum and to provide applied, real-world sustainability experiences for students (Zen, 2017), the concept has not been systematically adopted into learning and teaching. I designed the conceptual Living Learning Laboratory to develop student skills for future work. My aim was to achieve this by working collaboratively in partnership with external stakeholders. To achieve this, I employed the tenets of a distributed leadership approach to produce an ecology of a distributed leadership approach to university-community partnerships (Jones, 2017c). This was adopted by the university as the platform for an Industry Innovation Research Incubator.

Discussion: An Ecosystem of Collaborative *Leadship* for Learning and Teaching

My narrative has identified how my commitment to collaboration led me to adopt a distributed leadership approach to learning and teaching. There was some support for my approach, as indicated by the federal government project grants, which enabled me to attract multi-university collaborations. I have also demonstrated that, given the gradual move of the higher education sector towards single-leader-focused, hierarchical leadership approaches, my collaborative leadership identity placed me in a contested space. In my more recent, more indirect, leadership of learning and teaching, I remain in this contested space. My explanation above of my emergent role as an expert advisor on university-stakeholder collaborations continues to see me placed in a contested space. Ecosystems are attracting growing interest beyond their original biological and environmental origins, initially in human ecology theory exploration of the interactions between biological organisms, social being and the environment to create energy transformations (Bubolz and Sontag, 2009). More recently, business ecosystems are emerging alongside advances in start-up, mobility and technology as platform-based (McKinsey, 2020).

However, they have not yet figured significantly in leadership discourse beyond a recent publication of a radical ecosystem view of collective leadership from an indigenous Māori perspective (Spiller, Wolfgramm and Pouwhare, 2020). This presents me with the opportunity to suggest a conceptual collaborative leadership ecosystem for learning and teaching. Indeed, I go further and propose the need to term this a 'collaborative ecosystem of *leadship* for learning and teaching'. While I acknowledge that this change in nomenclature will be fiercely contested, particularly among scholars and practitioners of leadership, I argue it is necessary in acknowledgement of the 'strong and problematic colonizing effects of leadership vocabulary' (Alvesson and Spicer, 2012, p. 383).

The conceptual 'collaborative ecosystem of *leadship* for learning and teaching' acknowledges

1. The importance of identifying and actively *engaging* all parties whose expertise can contribute to learning and teaching, including academics and professional staff with expertise in learning and teaching, students, practitioners, government agencies establishing standards for quality learning and teaching, and professional associations;
2. The importance of all those engaged in designing formal agreements to *enable* collaboration;
3. The need to ensure that appropriate processes and systems are established to *enact* collaboration;
4. The provision of appropriate training, finance and time to *encourage* participation;
5. The significance of developing new approaches to *evaluate* the success of actions taken in support of the collaborative leadership ecosystem for learning and teaching;
6. The importance of focusing on continual *emergence* as new knowledge is identified.

In addition, there is a need to focus on the dynamic interactions between the actions taken to implement each tenet to explore how to encourage, identify and demonstrate the energy transformation that occurs and how it improves learning and teaching. The conceptual collaborative ecosystem of leadership for learning and teaching is illustrated in Figure 10.1. The hexagonal shapes, and their configuration around a central value proposition, are used to indicate that each of the tenets interact in multiple, and changing, ways with each other as energy is transformed.

Conclusion (and Postscript)

Writing a narrative is challenging. It requires the narrator to locate a balance between simply telling 'their' story, to identifying its purpose. This chapter had many iterations as I swung between these spectrums. I was assisted by the decision of the editorial team to locate my narrative in the section devoted to engaging values, resilience and serendipity. In this final iteration I have opted

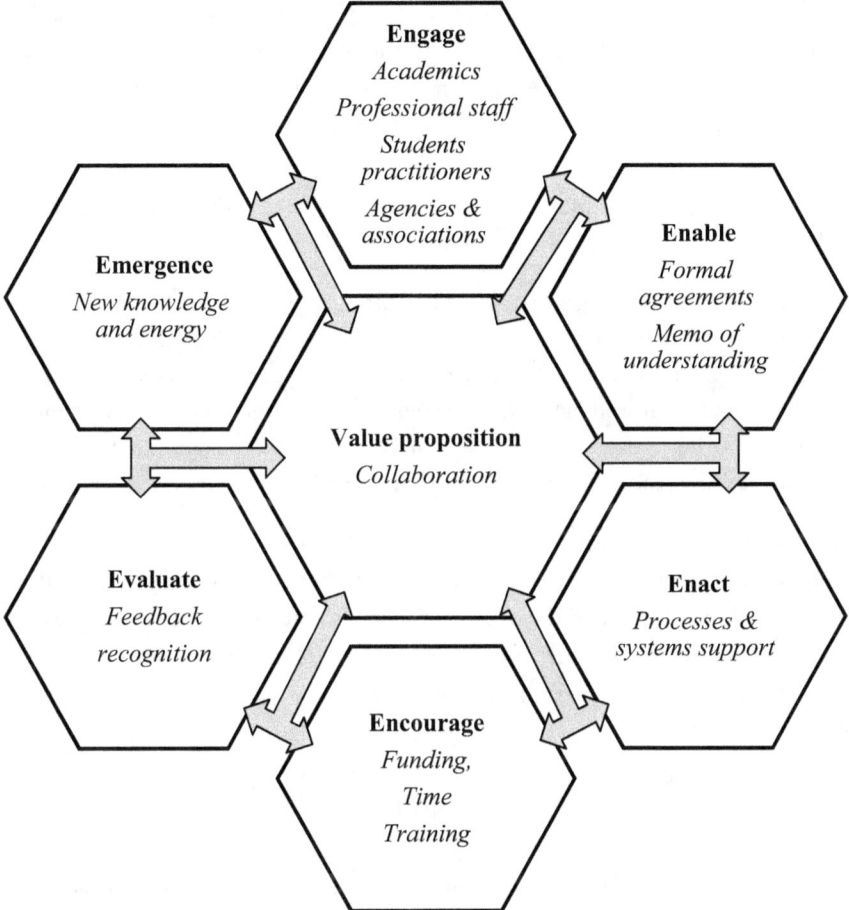

Figure 10.1 Conceptual collaborative *leadship* ecosystem for learning and teaching.

for a brief introduction and background to explain how I came to synergize my value commitment to collaboration with my leadership in learning and teaching by highlighting how I combined my practice and scholarship in learning and teaching to lead through influence. In this I was assisted by serendipity that enabled me to lead research projects into a distributed leadership approach to build leadership capacity for learning and teaching. This enabled me to implement change as a formal, positional leader in learning and teaching, in a collaborative manner. I have provided several exemplars of how I took action in accordance with the six tenets of a distributed leadership approach to illustrate my journey. Finally, calling on my recent experience from a more indirect leadership position, I proposed a conceptual collaborative ecosystem of *leadship* for learning and teaching.

In closing this chapter, I propose that given the challenges for higher education of 'living with Covid-19', and the world experience of the need for more collaboration between people, there is a need for more discourse upon the conceptual collaborative ecosystem of *leadship* for learning and teaching. I trust I have provided a sufficient outline narrative to assist this.

In finalizing this chapter, I refer back to an initial iteration of this chapter in which I referred to the Māori description of wayfaring leadership:

> After diligently reading the signs and adjusting yourself as the waka- needle, conceiving yourself as still and becoming calibrated to a moving world, an island appears on the horizon ahead. You keep the island in your mind's eye, but do not try to aim for it in a straight line; rather you continue to adjust to signs, with the world moving past you … Eventually the island comes closer and closer to you and the waka. And then it arrives. (Spiller, Barclay-Kerr and Panoho, 2015, p. 36)

In my case, my 'island' was my commitment to collaborative leadership, the moving world was the changing contexts and culture of the higher education sector within which I had the opportunity to explore leadership, and my waka-needle was the mix of serendipity and actions I took to implement a distributed leadership approach to learning and teaching.

Note

1 In exchange for government financing of my higher education undergraduate degree.

References

Advance HE (2019), *UK Professional Standards Framework*. https://www.advance-he.ac.uk/knowledge-hub/uk-professional-standards-framework-ukpsf (accessed 19 January 2021).

Alvesson, M., and Spicer, A. (2012), 'Critical leadership studies: The case for critical performativity', *Human Relations* 65 (3): 367–90.

Beckmann, B. (2017), 'Leadership through fellowship: Distributed leadership in a professional recognition scheme for university educators', *Journal of Higher Education Policy and Management* 39 (2): 155–68.

Bolden, R., Jones, S., Davis, H. and Gentle, P. (2015), *Developing and Sustaining Shared Leadership in Higher Education*, Stimulus Paper, London: Leadership Foundation for Higher Education and L. H. Martin Institute. Available online: https://melbourne-cshe.unimelb.edu.au/__data/assets/pdf_file/0010/2564263/Developing-and-Sustaining-Shared-Leadership-in-Higher-Education.pdf (accessed 28 July 2020).

Bolden, R., Gosling, J., O'Brien, A., Peters, K., Ryan, M. and Haslam, A. (2012), *Academic Leadership: Changing Conceptions, Identities and Experiences in UK Higher Education*, London: Leadership Foundation for Higher Education.https://www.advance-he.ac.uk/knowledge-hub/tags/dr-richard-bolden-professor-jonathan-gosling-dr-anne-obrien-dr-kim-peters (accessed 6 August 2020).

Bubolz, M. M., and Sontag, M. S. (2009), 'Human Ecology Theory', in P. Boss, W. J. Doherty, R. LaRossa, W. R. Schumm and S. K. Steinmetz (eds), *Sourcebook of Family Theories and Methods*, 419–50, Boston, MA: Springer.

Capra, F. (1996), *The Web of Life*, New York: Anchor Books.

Carbone, A., Evans, J., Ross, B., Drew, S., Phelan, L., Lindsay, K., Cottman, C., Stoney, S. and Jing, Y. (2017), 'Assessing distributed leadership for learning and teaching quality: A multi-institutional study', *Journal of Higher Education Policy and Management* 39 (2): 183–96.

Collins, N., Pimpa, N., Jones, S. and Scown, A. (2015), 'Co-designing peer learning experiences for students in multiple transnational locations', in ISSOTL 2015 Secretariat, *ISSOTL 2015 Program and Book of Abstracts, 12th Annual Conference of ISSOTL*, Melbourne, Australia, 27–30 October, 82–3. https://eprints.usq.edu.au/28746/7/ISSOTL%202015%20Program%20Book%20WEB.pdf (accessed 8 January 2021).

Creese, L. E., and Jones, S. (2001), 'E-education: Creating partnerships for learning'. UltiBASE. Available at: http://ultibase.rmit.edu.au/Articles/aug01/jones1.htm.htmGoogle Scholar (accessed 8 January 2021).

Davis, H., and Jones, S. (2014), 'The work of leadership in higher education management', *Journal of Higher Education Policy and Management* 36 (4): 367–70. https://doi.org/10.1080/1360080X.2014.916463.

Deem, R. (1998), 'New managerialism in higher education: The management of performance and cultures in universities', *International Studies in Sociology of Education* 8 (1): 47–70.

Fletcher, J. K. (2004), 'The paradox of postheroic leadership: An essay on gender, power and transformational change', *Leadership Quarterly* 15 (5): 647–61.

Gronn, P. (2002), 'Distributed leadership as a unit of analysis', *Leadership Quarterly* 13 (4): 423–51.

Harvey, M., and Jones, S. (2020a), 'Enabling leadership capacity for higher education (SoTL) through action research', *Educational Action Research* 19 (2): 173–90. https://doi.org/10.1080/09650792.2020.1803941.

Harvey, M., and Jones, S. (2020b), 'Leading educational transformation with sessional staff', in J. Potter, and C. Devecchi (eds), *Delivering Educational Change in Higher Education*, SEDA Series, 104–15, Abingdon: Routledge.

Jones, S. (2000), 'The relationship between workplace reform and workforce participation', PhD Thesis, Deakin University, Hawthorn, Victoria.

Jones, S. (2001), 'Information technology – partner or predator in teaching employment relations', *International Employment Relations Review* 7 (2): 75–87.

Jones, S. (2003), 'Measuring the quality of higher education: Linking teaching quality measures at the delivery level to administrative measures at the university level', *Journal Quality in Higher Education* 9 (3): 223–9. https://doi.org/10.1080/1353832032000151094.

Jones, S. (2004), 'Developing intellectual capital', *International Journal of Knowledge, Culture and Change Management* 4: article MC04-0099-2004, 943–51.

Jones, S. (2005), 'Using IT to augment authentic learning environments', in A. Herrington and J. Herrington (eds), *Authentic Learning Environments in Higher Education*, 172–81, Hershey, PA: Idea Group.

Jones, S. (2007), 'Adding value to online role-plays; virtual situated learning environments', in *ICT: Providing Choices for Learners and Learning; Proceedings 24th Annual Ascilite Conference*, Singapore, 2–5 December. https://www.ascilite.org/conferences/singapore07/procs/jones-s.pdf.

Jones, S. (2009), 'Virtual situated learning environments: Developing inter-professional skills for human services', in J. Martin and J. Hawkins (eds), *Interactive Computer Technology for Human Service Education and Delivery; Concepts and Cases*, 72–86, Hershey, PA: IGI Global.

Jones, S. (2014a), 'Distributed leadership: A critical analysis', *Leadership* 10 (2): 129–41.

Jones, S. (2014b), 'IPT developing managerial skills for the complex inter-disciplinary interface: Management education as an experiential learning laboratory', in *Final Report to Australian Government Department of Industry*, 33–44, Canberra: AGPS.

Jones, S. (2017a), *Leading the Academy: Distributed Leadership in Higher Education, HERDSA Guide*, Hammondville, NSW: HERDSA.

Jones, S. (2017b), 'Academic leadership', in I. Kinchin and N. Winstone (eds), *Pedagogic Frailty and Resilience in the University*, 163–78, Rotterdam: Sense Publishers.

Jones, S. (2017c), 'Distributed leadership: Implementing collaborative partnerships between universities and community groups', Paper presented at Leadership in Turbulent Times: ILA 19th Annual Conference International Leadership Association, Brussels, 12–15 October. Abstract available online: http://ila-net.org/Conferences/2017/2017-Brussels-Program-Book/index.html#110/z.

Jones, S. (2018), 'Blended leadership: From conceptualization to practice', in C. Bossu and N. Brown (eds), *Professional and Support Staff in Higher Education*, University Development and Administration series, 229–42, Singapore: Springer Nature.

Jones, S. (2019), 'Supporting workforce wellbeing: Institutions for education as living learning laboratories', *ILO Decent Work Conference*, Geneva.

Jones, S. (2020), 'Distributed leadership', in M. E. David and M. J. Amey (eds), *SAGE Encyclopedia of Higher Education*, 378–81, Thousand Oaks: SAGE Publications.

Jones, S., and Harvey, M. (2017a), 'Revealing the nexus between distributed leadership and communities of practice', in J. McDonald and A. Cater-Steel (eds), *Communities of Practice: Facilitating social learning in higher education*, 313–27, Singapore: Springer.

Jones, S., and Harvey, M. (2017b), 'A distributed leadership change process model for higher education', *Journal of Higher Education Policy and Management* 39 (2): 126–39.

Jones, S., Harvey, M., and Lefoe, G. (2014), 'A conceptual approach for blended leadership for tertiary education institutions', *Journal of Higher Education Policy and Management* 36 (4): 418–29.

Jones, S., and McCann, J. (2004), 'Virtually situated learning environments – the business educational model for developing countries in a knowledge era', in I. Alon and J. R. McIntyre (eds), *Business Education in Emerging Market Economies: Perspectives and Best Practices*, 201–16, Boston, MA: Kluwer.

Jones, S., and McCann, J. (2005), 'Virtual learning environments for time-stressed and peripatetic managers', *Journal of Workplace Learning: Special Issue E-Learning @ the Workplace* 17 (5/6): 359–69.

Jones, S., and Novak, B. (2009), *Developing Multi-Level Leadership in the Use of Student Feedback to Enhance Student Learning and Teaching Practice: Final Report Le6-7*, Australian Learning and Teaching Council. https://ltr.edu.au/resources/LE6-7%20Developing%20multi-level%20leadership%20in%20the%20use%20of%20student%20feedback%20Final%20Report%20RMIT%202009_0.pdf.

Jones, S., and Richardson, J. (2002), 'Designing an IT-augmented student-centred learning environment', in T. Herrington (ed.), *Research and Development in Higher Education: Quality Conversations 25*, HERDSA Conference Proceedings, 376–83, Hammondville, NSW: HERDSA. https://www.herdsa.org.au/publications/conference-proceedings/research-and-development-higher-education-quality-46.

Jones, S., and Watty, K. (2010), 'Pluridisciplinary learning and assessment: Reflections on practice', in M. Devlin, M. Davies and M. Tight (eds), *Interdisciplinary Higher Education: Perspectives and Practicalities*, 195–208, Bingley: Emerald.

Jones, S., Jones, M., Engels, B., Montague, A., De Silva, S. and Crist, G. (2008), 'Evaluating a multi-disciplinary virtual WIL project', *Work Integrated Learning (WIL): Transforming Futures: ACEN-WACE Asia Pacific Conference 2008 E-Proceedings*, Sydney, 30 September–3 October, 261–68. https://researchoutput.csu.edu.au/ws/portalfiles/portal/9686845/13523_Jennett.pdf (accessed 12 July 2020).

Jones, S., Harvey, M., Lefoe, G. and Ryland, K. (2012a), *Lessons Learnt: Identifying Synergies in Distributed Leadership Projects: Final Report*.https://ltr.edu.au/resources/LE9_1222_Jones_Report_2012.pdf (accessed 12 July 2020).

Jones, S., Lefoe, G., Harvey, M. and Ryland, K. (2012b), 'Distributed leadership: A collaborative framework for academics, executive and professionals in higher education', *Journal of Higher Education Policy and Management* 34 (1): 67–78.

Jones, S., Hadgraft, R., Harvey, M., Lefoe, G. and Ryland, K. (2014), *Evidence-Based Benchmarking Framework for a Distributed Leadership Approach to Capacity Building* in *Learning and Teaching: Final Report*. https://ltr.edu.au/resources/LE11_2000_Jones_Report_2014_0.pdf (accessed 12 July 2020).

Jones, S., Harvey, M., Hamilton, J., Bevacqua, J., Egea, K. and McKenzie, J. (2017), 'Demonstrating the impact of a distributed leadership approach in higher education', *Journal of Higher Education Policy and Management* 39 (2): 197–211.

Marshall, S. (2006), 'Issues in the development of leadership for learning and teaching in higher education: Occasional paper', Chippendale, NSW: Carrick Institute for Learning and Teaching in Higher Education. Available online: https://ltr.edu.au/resources/grants_leadership_occasionalpaper_stephenmarshall_nov06.pdf (accessed 12 July 2020).

McKinsey Digital (2020), 'Ecosystem 2.0: Climbing to the next level', *McKinsey Quarterly*, 11 September. https://www.mckinsey.com/business-functions/mckinsey-digital/our-insights/ecosystem-2-point-0-climbing-to-the-next-level (accessed 24 April 2021).

Ospina, S., Foldy, E., Fairhurst, G. and Jackson, B. (2020), 'Collective dimensions of leadership: Connecting theory and method', *Human Relations* 73 (4): 441–63.

Parrott, S., and Jones. S. (2018), 'Virtual mobility: Flipping the global classroom through a blended learning opportunity', in T. Hall., T. Gray, G. Downey and M. Singh (eds), *The Globalisation of Higher Education – Developing Internationalised Education in Research and Practice*, 167–81, Cham: Palgrave Macmillan. https://doi.org/10.1007/978-3-319-74579-4_10.

Pearce, C., and Conger, J. (2003), *Shared Leadership: Reframing the Hows and Whys of Leadership*, London: Sage.

Ramsden, P. (1998), *Learning to Lead in Higher Education*, London: Routledge.

Sharma, M., Rifkin, W., Tzioumis, V., Hill, M., Johnson, E., Varsavsky, C., Jones, S., Beames, S., Crampton, A., Zadnik, M. and Pyke, S. (2017), 'Implementing and investigating in a national university network-SAMNET', *Journal of Higher Education Policy and Management* 39 (2): 169–82.

Skalicky, J., Warr Pedersen, K., van der Meer, J., Fuglsang, S., Dawson, P. and Stewart, S. (2020), 'A framework for developing and supporting student leadership in higher education', *Studies in Higher Education* 45 (1): 100–16. doi: 10.1080/03075079.2018.1522624.

Spiller, C., Kerr, H. and Panoho, J. (2015), *Wayfinding and Leadership: Ground-Breaking Wisdom for Developing Leaders*, Wellington: Huia Publishers.

Spiller, C., Wolfgram, R. and Pouwhare, R. (2020), 'Paradigm warriors: Advancing a radical ecosystems view of collective leadership from an indigenous Maori perspective', *Human Relations* 73 (4): 516–43.

Uhl-Bien, M. (2006), 'Relational leadership theory: Exploring the social processes of leadership and organizing', *Leadership Quarterly* 17 (6): 654–76.

Zen, I. (2017), 'Exploring the living learning laboratory: An approach to strengthen campus sustainability initiatives by using sustainability science approach', *International Journal of Sustainability in Higher Education* 18 (6): 1–15.

11

Our Journeys through the Scholarship of Leading: What Matters and What Counts?

Wu Siew Mei and Chng Huang Hoon

Introduction

Many people's academic journey begins with an intense PhD programme in a chosen discipline, which inducts them to become a fully-fledged faculty member in a university, where they will further entrench their identities as academics who teach and conduct research in relevant disciplines. Any departure from this norm can result in a career path that is fraught with uncertainties and risks to career advancement. In the context of the tensions between the focus on individuals and the call for communities of practice where collegiality reigns (Green et al., 2017), the struggles Scholarship of Teaching and Learning (SoTL) scholars have faced in explaining what SoTL is, in justifying their SoTL involvement and in reconciling their SoTL work with their disciplinary identity are by now fairly well documented (Fremstad et al., 2020; and Scott, Coates and Anderson, 2008; Simmons et al., 2013). This chapter examines a struggle over identity negotiation on a different front – the identity of academics who chose to develop themselves as administrative/academic leaders of institution.

The struggles some academics face in reconciling their disciplinary identity with their work in academic administration, often classified as *service*, are particularly intense in research-intensive universities (RIUs), where value is pre-defined by disciplinary scholarship outcomes. Any deviation from the well-scripted value system defined by the established practices of *academic tribes* (Becher, 1989) poses immense risks to one's future as a scholar. We focus on an area of (service/leadership) work that many institutional leaders would readily agree is crucial, but are as yet hesitant to fully accept as a legitimate basis for career advancement. The immersion in change management, culture building and (SoTL, or any other type of) leadership work often translates into work that matters, but that often does not yet count in the institution. Given the personal slants of specific cases in point, we deploy narrative inquiry and reflection as an approach to frame our leadership narratives, because key defining elements of the construction and evolution of individual and collective identities (Green et al. 2017, p.178) can be found in the stories that academic leaders tell of their personal and professional journeys, which can inform us about the nature of institutional priorities and value system.

Our leadership journeys, operating at different levels of institution, provide a basis for reflecting on the value, meaning and risks of undertaking this work. The notion of liminal space (Meyer and Land, 2005; Gravett, 2021) captures well the in-between space where our identities as scholars and as academic leaders at the local (Siew Mei) and global (Huang Hoon) levels are regularly contested and negotiated. In our journeys, we traverse an uncomfortable but deeply reflective third space where value and meaning are interrogated, which necessarily leads to a constant evolution and reconstitution of our academic identities. As Simmons et al. (2013) have observed in relation to SoTL work, 'Academic identity in SoTL may certainly be troublesome, but the reward for continuing to wrestle with it can be transformative' (p. 18). We argue, too, that risk-filled as it is, what makes academic leadership work worth doing is our commitment to the deeply meaningful work of institutional culture building and collegial transformation, and the important task of paving the way for the advancement of future colleagues. We work towards a time when what matters to the institution will also count more explicitly within institutional performance outcomes rubrics that have traditionally privileged disciplinary scholarship output.

A Tale from Two Perspectives

The View from the Ground: Building Culture Locally at the Level of Department

The university's senior management appointed me (Siew Mei) as director in 2009 after a search amongst international and local candidates for the post. My main role at the Centre for English Language Communication (CELC) is to manage fifty-five staff and steer the centre to become an international leader in the teaching of English language and communication skills and develop research that informs scholarly teaching. As a teaching unit, our role was devoted to providing quality programmes and courses that support the development of students' English communication skills. The role appealed to me as I saw it as an opportunity to contribute to the Centre's development and profile, although I could literally feel the weight of the responsibility of bringing together fifty-five colleagues with differing personalities to fulfil the centre's mission. There were also opportunities to engage in pedagogical research in English-language teaching and learning and to continue developing my professional interests.

From the start, my leadership role involved the administration and facilitation of quality academic programmes for about 40,000 students (undergraduates and postgraduates) and staff. Policies, initiatives and events were conceptualized and implemented as a service to the university community. About 25 per cent of my time and attention was spent in leading pedagogical projects and projects which investigate the impact of our curriculum.

At the point of appointment, I only had limited leadership experience, having served as the curriculum and testing head at CELC and a short stint as the deputy director at the Centre for the Development of Teaching and Learning. There were no clear answers to questions that came to my mind at that time: Are colleagues comfortable with Senior Management's choice of a new leader who has surfaced from amongst them? To what extent do colleagues recognize my disciplinary expertise and research competencies to guide their academic and professional growth? What are the main challenges at CELC which need immediate resolution, more than others? What leadership style, approach or strategies is best to lead my fifty-five colleagues?

With the guidance and strong support of the then-vice provost who oversaw the centre, and other experienced colleagues in senior management, I learnt leadership roles and styles on the job. One concrete form of support was the mentoring guidance provided towards my promotion to associate professorship. Ultimately, the success in the promotion provided validation of the academic grounds on which my appointment as director rested, as it was the first application for associate professorship awarded to the department.

I learnt the importance of communication with staff as we navigated the path ahead and to ensure that they had a path of communication to me and the management team too. Importantly, the setting of strategic directions for the centre was a crucial area that I engaged staff on, through staff meetings and smaller communication sessions. Effective leadership necessitates that my colleagues' perspectives are heard and that they have a voice in conceptualizing the direction and mission of the centre.

Leadership in pedagogical research also grew in importance as the university developed the Educator Track (ET) Policy for the career advancement of education-focused academic staff. The institutional-level ET policy development is a significant, transparent milestone that clearly articulates the place of pedagogical research, the role scholarship plays in our professional development and the rewards that accompanied good reflective teaching.

As the director, I was actively involved in the university's development of the ET policy. As scholarly teaching and learning (i.e. SoTL) became the main nomenclature for describing the type of desired research for ET staff, it also became clearer how I would lead the centre from pedagogical research towards SoTL-type inquiry into classroom practice and student learning. There were many similarities between SoTL inquiry and the way pedagogical research was conducted at the centre. As such, the transition to a seemingly different type of research and its leadership was not so daunting.

While the leadership work I do at CELC has sufficient clarity for myself both as an educator and a director, my own professional career advancement towards full professorship has been less clear until quite recently with the formalization of the ET Policy at my university in 2016/17. Academic leadership had not figured in the established promotion rubrics for at least the greater half of the time I have been immersed in directing CELC. On the other hand, there seem to be indications that the leadership work done has enhanced the professional career paths of colleagues who have been willing to be guided and developed in coming on board the ET and riding on its tracks to promotion. It has also effected the development of the centre's community interest in pedagogical research projects and initiatives concerning the teaching of English-language writing and communication. Most importantly, there seems to have been a shift in colleagues' mindsets where there is more clarity and guidance provided in terms of what their professional path might be and how these can be negotiated.

The View from above: Building Culture Globally at the Level of Institution

When I (Huang Hoon) was called to serve in university administration in 2012, I had already crossed to *the dark side* of academic administration for eight years, having served as an institutional leader in two other appointments. A change in university leadership resulted in a gap that needed to be urgently filled, which launched me on a journey through the undergraduate curriculum, providing leadership for curriculum chairs, and assisting senior management on all education-related initiatives.

I stepped into the role because I felt it was a job worth doing, and I am motivated by good people to work with. Teaching, though a primary mission in many institutions, has been a second cousin to research in RIUs, at least in terms of funding priorities and career prospects for the faculty (Cashmore, Cane and Cane, 2013). For individuals who are committed to bettering education in our institutions, we are largely intrinsically motivated. In this light, academics like my co-author and me have to make tough choices to look beyond the reward system and to be prepared to embrace a different value system, with little/no realistic expectation that the well-entrenched academic culture that reveres disciplinary scholarship will change in our lifetime. Our belief is that making visible the good work of like-minded colleagues, who devote their life's work to education and/or leadership, is itself a journey worth the distance and sacrifice.

I was only the second woman to join the provost's team in my institution's history, which in itself also spurred me to accept the appointment because I am deeply conscious of the need for women to step up when opportunity is available. Though I had no formal curriculum leadership experience, I have always been one who has less fear of the unknown than most. In fact, change and new learning opportunities drive me, and the journey was also made easier by the strong support from relevant administrative staff teams, who are deeply experienced in this work.

As someone who actively creates meaning and makes specific leadership roles work for myself, it has not been an entirely bad way to carve out a career, even if my career path turned out more unconventional and riskier than most. What attracted me to the roles I have assumed was the opportunities provided for a platform to *advocate* for those I work with and for me to learn new things.

My stated job scope included everything to do with the undergraduate curriculum and other initiatives. I have also regularly taken on other endeavours, including creating informal educational networks devoted to enriching teaching practice through the scholarship of teaching and learning (or SoTL, such as my Asia- and NUS-SoTL groups) to help colleagues gain visibility within and outside Singapore. Though neither Siew Mei nor I were asked to do additional work of this kind, this self-defined work has proven to be extra meaningful, perhaps because it is aligned with our broader vision relating to culture change, and offers targeted ways in which we can advocate for our colleagues and, in the process, enhance the collegial culture.

Siew Mei and I see ourselves as advocates and are motivated by the simple fact that being a leader is to enable growth in others and, in doing so, facilitate the growth and reputation of the organization both internally and externally, as Bernstein has argued. Mighty (2013) provides a simple definition of leadership as 'the capacity to influence others to work towards a set of shared goals' (p. 114). This *capacity to influence* allows us to view our leadership journeys as something we undertake to promote collegial welfare, and in this sense, we journey with others as a community of academic leaders rather than alone.

In short, Siew Mei and I followed a leadership pathway, not to seek material rewards but because we were focused on the intangible, longer-term value that can result, whether it is in the empowerment of colleagues or in creating value for the community as a whole. While material rewards are not as crucial, we think institutional *recognition* of the work is essential, because recognition is a form of endorsement and an empowerment of the self. We feel empowered and to some extent valued, at least by those we have immediately impacted. We know our leadership work matters to colleagues, and to some extent to the institution. This feeling of recognition and empowerment serves as further motivation for both personal and professional investments in such work.

The misalignment between being appreciated and being explicitly rewarded has much to do with how and what the institution formally defines as *value*. In a research-intensive institution, research output counts much more concretely than teaching output. It is often explained that this is owed to research impact having measurable, *objective* and established benchmarks. Both of us do not personally agree with this view, even though we understand it. Apart from being a lesser cousin to research, educational achievements are not always understood by institutions that privilege research accomplishments. This problematic state of affairs, however, is what further motivates us to make visible the intellectual work that educators do, precisely because their work counts for less even when the institution regularly maintains that such work matters.

Our narratives about leading at unit and institutional levels, respectively, detail the journeys we have traversed from our formal appointments as institutional leaders, through our own development and lived experiences in the respective roles. While our journeys are not particularly unique (cf. the struggles of SoTL scholars and academic developers establishing themselves vis-à-vis disciplinary identity), these stories illustrate in real terms what it means to navigate ill-defined identities as academic leaders against the backdrop of an entrenched academic culture. In the next section, we contextualize our experiences within the concepts of liminality and identity negotiation.

Liminality and the Negotiation of Identity

Just recently, a colleague from elsewhere joyfully proclaimed that he has recently stepped down from his administrative leadership role and is now enjoying his life as a *pure professor*, devoting his time to teaching. It fascinates us that he equated the state of purity with being *home* in his disciplinary space. The implication is that those who stayed within the leadership (or any non-mainstream) space continue to occupy a tainted, troublesome space, lost in an ill-defined hybrid identity that remains problematic in the eyes of *pure* academics. Such a stated position reinforces and reproduces the traditional culture in academia that values different contributions unequally.

The concept of the liminal space as applied to the transitional stage in student learning appears to be an excellent frame that can be usefully applied to the oscillatory state of being betwixt and between experienced by academic leaders, as may be discerned from our two narratives (Meyer and Land, 2005, p. 376). Beginning from a formal appointment to a role that marks the entrance into a new space, to a gradual entrenchment in the practices of (SoTL) leadership, including the leader equipping herself with the new domain expertise of both SoTL and academic leadership, which further evolves into a fuller identity of *academic/SoTL leaders*, this journey is marked by the rituals that move an individual from one end of the identity spectrum, through a state of flux involving multiple identities, to the other extreme of an altered, transformed state. This is, however, not a linear path but a movement through a 'liquid' and evolving space (Meyer and Land, 2005, p. 380), where individuals dynamically carve out an identity even as the space itself and the rituals and practices within that space exert a transformative effect on them. Like the student who is transformed by a threshold concept in the relevant discipline, our academic identities are now embedded in liminality, and we are irreversibly changed within that liminal landscape. Our new *home* as leaders is increasingly distant from our disciplinary home the longer we partake in and negotiate the new rituals of academic administration.

While challenging and uncomfortable, our own negotiation of identity within liminality is made easier by the support of like-minded colleagues. We recall fondly the words of a senior colleague who said that administration, when done well, facilitates the work our colleagues do in pursuing their research and/ or teaching. There is a sense of a shared community bond, among leaders who outwardly moaned about the thankless tasks they have been saddled with and who nevertheless persevered to carry them through. The shared vision, goals and activities regularly and actively undertaken define a community of practice and an identity that makes meaning out of thankless tasks and provides the mutual support that fuels the work and enriches the new space and identity. After all, as Lave and Wenger (1991) have observed, identity construction happens within communities, and not in a vacuum, and in what Roxå and Mårtensson (2009) have called small significant networks. It is however important to note that negotiating a new identity within liminality demands active redefinition through at least a partial if not full abandonment of safe, well-defined disciplinary identities. For established SoTL scholars, with SoTL serving as a new disciplinary site for identity integration (Simmons et al., 2013, p. 16), some degree of comfort may have settled in for them in their new third space after decades of struggles (Simmons et al., 2013, p.16). No such affordances are as yet readily available to leaders like us who perform leadership work as the negotiation of identity for academic leaders is, relatively speaking, new terrain.

In the next section, we contextualize our narratives within these ideas of liminality and identity negotiation, to frame our journeys within the broader experience of academic leadership.

Elements of Academic Leadership: Challenges in Transforming Culture

We began our respective leadership journey in similar ways: we were called by our institution to serve. Formal appointment is the conventional way that puts most academics along this path as academics seldom consider academic leadership as a deliberate part of their career plans. Writing about the struggles in promoting SoTL scholarship in the institution, Mighty (2013) alluded to 'the kinds of stories and legends that are often passed on to new or junior faculty members about what they need to do to succeed in our institution's promotion and tenure process'. Chief among such stories is the age-old adage to 'publish or perish' (p. 115; cf. Heron, Gravett and Yakovchuk, 2021, on publishing and flourishing). Similarly, academic leadership is usually spoken of as a journey to *the dark side* (Bengtsen and Barnett, 2017), as a role that consumes time and energy without tangible recognition in a research-based performance culture that overwhelmingly privileges scholarly/disciplinary output over other contributions. The risks academic leaders have to bear were, and continue, to be clear to both of us as we actively invest time in identifying the *opportunities* for collegial engagement and advocacy that come with our formal leadership positions. The value, purpose and meaning, if not the outcome (Simmons et al., 2013) of these roles motivated us intrinsically, and this shared outlook is what allowed both of us to support each other professionally and on more personal levels.

Why then do work that does not align well with the institutional reward system? Because for us, that is what advocacy is about – to change the institutional mindset and value system, to align what matters with what counts. We think leadership is about changing the lives of the underserved. The important work that lies ahead is to find a way to resolve this tension, to ensure that work that matters will also count, so that those who undertake future leadership work are not forced to choose. Our belief is, when what matters also counts, individuals and institutions will be enriched because every individual in the community can bring good work to fruition without fear of risks that would often discourage capable leaders from doing the much-needed work of academic leadership.

Like many leaders, we are also sustained by an informal leaders' network (cf. communities of practice among SoTL practitioners, see Green et al., 2017, for instance). We have both been championed by other academic leaders who have served as our role models. In addition, we have built good relationships with colleagues and enjoy the ground-level support in our institution. These support structures and mentorship from other senior leaders are significant enablers of our growth, and such gestures of support are things we consciously emulate and pay forward in helping to nurture younger colleagues by advocating for them through our work.

Academic leadership has been variously defined. Mighty's definition of leadership, as 'the capacity to influence' (Mighty, 2013, p. 114), speaks to us directly. These *knowledge catalysts* or influencers have the requisite expertise to spread change through the institutional networks (Fields et al., 2019). This reference to networks calls to mind other definitions of leadership that privilege 'a practical and everyday process of supporting, managing, developing and inspiring academic colleagues' (Ramsden, 1998, p. 4), which we have adopted in our own approach to leading. For leaders like Siew Mei, the scope of influence is locally and discretely defined, as she is situated within her disciplinary home and leads her colleagues directly. For leaders like Huang Hoon, the scope of the transformational culture-building project is global, potentially impacting more colleagues from across the institution. We hasten to add, however, that whether local or global, the *collegial* culture of universities means that the preferred leadership approach is through consensus, not power (Scott et al., 2008). The work at both levels of academic administration is equally hard-going, because building culture and change management require fundamental mindset shifts from a critical mass of colleagues. In spite of the relatively smaller size of her department and the fewer number of *small significant networks* (Roxå and Mårtensson, 2009) that need to be cultivated and maintained, Siew Mei still faces the challenge of effecting a departmental shift (e.g. towards SoTL scholarship) among *already-good* teachers who nevertheless did not all see the need for systematic self-inquiry or scholarly work. In this challenging landscape, where some of her colleagues are attitudinally not as inclined to change, a formal institutional policy for career advancement (e.g. the university's promotion policy, which allowed for Siew Mei and Huang Hoon to work together) proves to be a good lever to shift the department culture.

According to Ramsden,

> Leadership is about 'doing the right thing'. Leadership foresees and enables, enabling people to adapt to change rather than to resist it. (1998, p. 108)

This 'contingent nature of leadership' requires us to be willing to respond to the situational needs as they come, and this means that our identity as academic leaders is itself in a constant state of constitution and reconstitution.

Unlike Siew Mei who interacts locally with her colleagues in her department, Huang Hoon faces the steeper challenge of the multivariate politics of a diverse group that cuts across all disciplines in a comprehensive university context. The need to not just promote local cultures but to *connect* them in a directed way, so that they are *not* siloed centres of activity, is an important goal for both of us doing local and global leadership work.

A big challenge to academic leadership is that such work has received somewhat mixed recognition from institutional decision-makers. Many colleagues in institutions around the globe who ascend to the level of a dean, a provost, or a president, are almost without exception full professors who have risen through the ranks by first attaining their disciplinary credentials and secondarily as leaders of institution. Having themselves been schooled in the traditional academic culture, many senior leaders have not actively seen the need to reconsider the entrenched institutional reward system. The result is that while many associate professors (due often to the paucity of (willing) full professors) are called to serve, these colleagues face the challenge of advancing their career because individuals are often not able to operate at full throttle to meet the promotion requirements of a full professorship based predominantly on disciplinary research output. In short, the call to service is not coupled with a reward system that values the service. The prevailing view is that full professorship requires international recognition by disciplinary peers (cf. Bernstein's (2013) counterargument for the great value cosmopolitans bring to their institutions), and service or leadership work is not part of those criteria. This institutional stance results in many individuals either making the strategic decision to resist these leadership appointments or to make an explicit sacrifice. What counts and what matters clearly are somewhat out of alignment in the political reality that still largely defines modern-day academia, though change is afoot in institutions like ours.

Prior to 2016, conversations within the authors' institution had already paved the way for a new reward system that counts scholarly teaching and leadership as promotional criteria. From 2016, the place of teaching and systematic inquiry into teaching have been given more weight in recruitment and promotion processes at our institution, especially for education-focused faculty. Evidence-based good teaching and the critical encapsulation of one's reflective practice in teaching portfolios are high on the list of priority criteria and enshrined by policy. A more rigorous review process for recruitment and promotion by an external review panel is now in place, especially for associate professor and above. These are positive indicators of change in practice that is endorsed by our senior management, who recognize that informed teaching practice and educational leadership *do matter and will count* in our institution.

The formation and sustenance of communities of practice that prioritize teaching development through institutional funding are further indicators of mindset shifts. These communities spur cultural change even as they are themselves the products of change, and they thrive on the coordinated actions of individuals working in linked social networks (Williams et al., 2013). The informal institutional-level NUS-SoTL network and the regional-level Asia-SoTL community are two examples of such communities that continually pursue pedagogical inquiries that will, with time, translate into better classroom practices. The NUS-SoTL group, which Siew Mei and Huang Hoon collaborate on, brings together staff across disciplines to engage in teaching and learning meetings and events (Chng et al., 2020). Annual events such as the Campus Teaching Day are also points of active engagement amongst the NUS-SoTL group members, which see the participation of many of Siew Mei's colleagues, for example.

The journey of growth of the *Asian Journal of the Scholarship of Teaching and Learning* (*AJSoTL*, est. 2015), a journal which Siew Mei, Huang Hoon and other colleagues help to direct, also constitutes another milestone in academic leadership outcomes. *AJSoTL* is an international, peer-reviewed, open-access, online journal that seeks to promote SoTL in and beyond classrooms in Asia, to develop practice in service of improved student learning outcomes. The increased number and quality of submissions since its inception testify to the positive outcome of the successful effort by academic leaders in NUS (and our regional partners) to provide a platform for a SoTL perspective that is informed by the Asian context. Additionally, on the SoTL world stage, our own SoTL profiles and that of some of our colleagues (e.g. serving as keynote speakers, reviewers, and office bearers in professional organizations like the International Society for the Scholarship of Teaching and Learning (ISSOTL)) have become more visible, and point to the cosmopolitan asset (Bernstein, 2013) that these leaders have accrued for the university within the culture change effected in the last five years.

Sub-communities of practice are further replicated at local levels in developing good teaching practices. These sub-communities of practice, whether organically formed or by design, are guided by network theory for the purposes of culture construction and maintenance (Roxå et al., 2010) and are engaged through activities organized over a period of time, such as CELC's teaching conferences and faculty teaching days, where discipline-based pedagogy is showcased. Intermittently, friendly peer reviews of classroom teaching have been arranged amongst members. Members have also collaborated in small groups to attain teaching grants to undertake systematic inquiries into teaching. Such activities are conducive for the support of weak links, which has been shown to be highly effective in culture-building and change. One example of such a community subset is found within Siew Mei's department, where the entire English-Language Teaching (ELT) faculty forms a disciplinary SoTL community. Besides an elaborate mentoring programme for new and mid-career staff, regular SoTL-in-ELT events are organized for Siew Mei's staff every semester.

The range of outcomes that has instantiated the values, purpose and meaning of both of our leadership work, amidst the challenges and risks, are now becoming more visible as the institutional culture evolves to recognize these contributions. In the closing section below, we address the implications of our effort for aligning what matters with what counts, and our vision for the future.

Implications for Making What Matters, Count

Like the SoTL scholar, the academic leader's journey is 'filled with doubt and insecurity, self-questioning, credibility issues' (Simmons et al., 2013, p. 12), and is one that requires the establishment of 'an alternative identity' (Simmons et al. 2013, p. 14). It is not an uncommon experience for staff who prioritize educational practices and who are in educational leadership positions in research-intensive institutions to face challenges in accounting for their output. The tensions and misalignments between what matters (good educational leadership) and what counts (disciplinary scholarship), and the experience of affectively struggling within the troublesome, liminal space, echo the difficulties faced in assuming identities as SoTL scholars or leaders in discipline-based departments. Simmons et al. (2013, p. 12) have proposed in relation to SoTL that there is need for us 'to develop the capacity to become comfortable being in a nexus of discomfort', created by an involvement outside accepted core disciplines. The suggestion of becoming comfortable would entail academics finding ways to redefine their misaligned identities as disciplinary and SoTL scholars, and/or as academic leaders. For change to happen, however, it is ultimately more important that institutional leaders develop an awareness of the need to narrow the gaps between what they asked of the professoriate and what matters to institutional growth and well-being. The idea of academics becoming comfortable necessitates that we 'learn to be comfortable in the discomforting spaces we currently inhabit … [by] adopting an integrative identity' (Simmons et al., 2013, p. 17). The adoption of a new, alternative identity suggests that the former identity stays but that an alternative identity is forged in new contexts and with the support of alternative academic communities that inspire further growth. Practically, it is necessary to engage deeply and imbibe the inherent values characterizing the new space for meaningful, situated transformation within communities of practice, both for the individual and for the entrenchment of this new identity (Green et al., 2017, p. 162). These new communities of practice also form sites for transformational leadership which is change-and-learning-focused (Ramsden, 1998). Influential effects evolve as learning the role is continuously co-constructed between community facilitator and members within the respective communities (Green et al., 2017, p. 173).

Becoming comfortable could further involve the agency of educational leaders (Fremstead et al., 2020) to influence the direction of institutional culture, to critically review misalignments by relooking at reward systems and/or the criteria for 'rewardable outcomes' in the institution. Fremstead et al. (2020, p. 109) term this as deliberative academic development, where educational leaders are both horizontal and vertical brokers who navigate the interconnected policies and commitments towards legitimate compromises.

In our journey as leaders, we recognize the challenges in crafting new identities and transforming culture, but we have also experienced degrees of success in advocating for the change in underlying mindsets and institutional culture. Change would not happen if we did not engage with these challenges, and change in even marginal degrees will pave the way for bigger shifts and clearer leadership visions in the years ahead.

References

Becher, T. (1989), *Academic Tribes and Territories: Intellectual Enquirer and the Cultures of Disciplines*, Buckingham, UK: Society for Research into Higher Education and the Open University Press.

Bengtsen, S., and Barnett, R. (2017), 'Confronting the dark side of higher education', *Journal of Philosophy of Education* 51 (1): 114–31.

Bernstein, D. (2013), 'How SoTL-active faculty members can be cosmopolitan assets to an institution', *Teaching and Learning Inquiry* 1 (1): 35–40.

Cashmore, A., Cane, C., and Cane, R. (2013). *Rebalancing Promotion in the HE Sector: Is Teaching Excellence Being Rewarded?* York: Higher Education Academy. https://s3.eu-west-2.amazonaws.com/assets.creode.advancehe-document-manager/documents/hea/private/hea_reward_publication_rebalancingpromotion_0_1568036858.pdf.

Chng, H. H., Leibowitz, B. and Mårtensson, K. (2020), 'Leading change from different shores: The challenges of contextualizing the scholarship of teaching and learning', *Teaching and Learning Inquiry* 8 (1): 24–41.

Fields, J., Kenny, N. A. and Mueller, R. A. (2019), 'Conceptualizing educational leadership in an academic development program', *International Journal for Academic Development* 24 (3): 218–31.

Fremstead, E., Bergh, A., Solbrekke, T. D. and Fossland, T. (2020), 'Deliberative academic development: The potential and challenge of agency', *International Journal for Academic Development* 25 (2): 107–20.

Gravett, K. (2021), 'Troubling transitions and celebrating becomings: From pathway to rhizome', *Studies in Higher Education* 46 (8): 1506–17.

Green, W., Ruutz, A., Houghton, L. and Hibbins, R. (2017), 'Enabling stories: Narrative, leadership, learning, and identity in a faculty-based teaching community of practice', in J. McDonald and A. Cater-Steel (eds), *Implementing Communities of Practice in Higher Education*, 159–81, Singapore: Springer Nature.

Heron, M., Gravett, K. and Yakovchuk, N. (2021), 'Publishing *and* flourishing: Writing for desire in higher education', *Higher Education Research & Development* 40 (3): 538–51. doi: 10.1080/07294360.2020.1773770.

Lave, J., and Wenger, E. (1991), *Situated Learning: Legitimate Peripheral Participation*, Cambridge: Cambridge University Press.

Meyer, J. H. F., and Land, R. (2005), 'Threshold concepts and troublesome knowledge (2): Epistemological considerations and a conceptual framework for teaching and learning', *Higher Education: The International Journal of Higher Education Research* 49: 373–88.

Mighty, J. (2013), 'One important lesson I've learned from my involvement with SoTL', *Teaching & Learning Inquiry* 1 (1): 113–16.

Ramsden, P. (1998), *Learning to Lead in Higher Education*, London: Routledge.

Roxå, T., Mårtensson, K. and Alvertag, M. (2010), 'Understanding and influencing teaching and learning cultures at university: A network approach', *Higher Education*, 62 (1): 99–111.

Roxå, T., and Mårtensson, K. (2009), 'Significant conversations and significant networks – Exploring the backstage of the teaching arena', *Studies in Higher Education* 34 (5): 547–59.

Scott, G., Coates, H. and Anderson, M. (2008), *Learning Leaders in Times of Change: Academic Leadership Capabilities for Australian Higher Education*, Sydney: University of Western Sydney and Australian Council for Educational Research. https://research.acer.edu.au/higher_education/3/.

Simmons, N., Abrahamson, E., Deshler, J. M., Kensington-Miller, B., Manarin, K., Morón-Garcia, S., Oliver, C. and Renc-Roe, J. (2013), 'Conflicts and configurations in a liminal space: SoTL scholars' identity development', *Teaching & Learning Inquiry* 1 (2): 9–21.

Williams, A. L., Verwoord, R., Beery, R. A., Dalton, H., McKinnon, J., Strickland, K., Pace, J. and Poole, G. (2013), 'The power of social networks: A model for weaving the scholarship of teaching and learning into institutional culture', *Teaching & Learning Inquiry* 1 (2): 49–62.

Part Three

The Future of Learning and Teaching Leadership

12

Towards an Ecological Perspective: Reflections on Leadership Journeys

Ian M. Kinchin

Introduction

It is evident from numerous comments in the preceding chapters that leadership journeys are often unplanned and painful experiences that can be the source of stress and discomfort. There is no clear linear trajectory that is evident for colleagues to follow if they want to specialize in teaching at university, and so academics often have to cut their own path towards leadership in teaching. Within the narratives that are offered in this book, colleagues emphasize the individualized nature of their journeys and offer detailed descriptions of their own personal and professional contexts. Interestingly, these stories rarely offer explicit alignment to any of the theoretical models of leadership that are discussed in the leadership literature – though they may inform thinking more implicitly. This leads one to question the utility of such models and whether the apparent disconnect between the theory and practice of leadership is something that should be a concern. There are numerous models of leadership that are discussed in the literature. Changes in emphasis placed on different models at different times reflects changes in the dominant discourses of higher education more broadly – particularly reflecting the increasing accountability of all aspects of university activity. The analysis offered by Gumus et al. (2018) shows that the relatively new concept of distributed leadership is currently the most studied model in the literature (see Chapter 10), followed by instructional leadership, teacher leadership and transformational leadership. Gumus et al. (2018, p. 30) suggest that 'a theory based on the distribution of leadership authority seemed inevitable', as commentators criticized the traditional hierarchical, command-and-control leadership approaches. This aligns with a move away from 'rational-technical systems' that presuppose a linear cause-and-effect arrangement towards a more nuanced approach to the key human relations and increased focus on the interactions within complex institutions (Spillane, 2005). The human relations are commonly commented on in passing by the chapter authors in this volume, often in the form of a critical incident that tipped the balance away from disciplinary research and towards a career that focusses on teaching. These elements of the personal story are often seen as part of a colleague's professional background, but perhaps these elements need to be more actively foregrounded as the negotiation and navigation of professional relationships form the essence of leadership and will inform leadership narratives and their contribution to the wider 'narrative ecology' (Gabriel, 2016).

In my own development, as an aspiring leader in academia, supportive interactions with colleagues have been key to my survival. This has sometimes been impeded by my conflicting role as a middle manager – squeezed by the conflicting discourses of the university, from the bottom-up and from the top-down. The distinction between leadership and management (Kotter, 2008) has been very important to me in my career, where I have found that I enjoy the former much more than the latter. The tensions between leadership and management have been helpfully described by Haddock-Fraser et al. (2018, p. 16):

> Management involves planning and budgeting, organizing and staffing, controlling and problem-solving. Leadership involves establishing direction, aligning people and motivating and inspiring others. This distinction is perhaps best summarized by Bennis and Nanus: 'Managers are people who do things right and leaders are people who do the right thing.' (1985, p. 221)

Towards an Ecological Perspective

Paradoxically, the de-centring of leadership as an activity (e.g. from a command-and-control model towards a more distributed model) and the complementary movement towards systems thinking (Capra and Luisi, 2014), in an ecological university (e.g. Barnett, 2017), pushes the concept of ecological leadership centre-stage as a community endeavour. The articulation of systemic leadership offered by Allen et al. (1999, p. 76) highlights this:

> Leadership processes and individual actions should create a community of reciprocal care and shared responsibility and promote harmony with nature thereby providing sustainability for future generations.

This comment also emphasizes the links that immediately present themselves to parallel issues of care and sustainability.

Within the viewpoint of the ecological university, a useful metaphor for change is provided by the adaptive cycle (Holling, 2001), which represents the stabilizing and destabilizing processes that maintain ecosystem health (Figure 12.1). The cycle includes a sequence of four stages: growth (r), conservation (K), release (Ω) and reorganization (α). The α-phase is a relatively rapid period of assembly of system components that occurs after a disturbance to the system and is an opportunity for novel recombination. It is this phase of the evolution of the university ecosystem where efforts made to innovate are likely to have most impact. In contrast, the K-phase is a relatively slow-moving phase of consolidation and accumulation of material that occurs during moments of environmental stability. During this phase, practices and habits within the university ecosystem will become re-established, and change will be more difficult to initiate as colleagues become sedimented into set ways of doing things. Overall, the adaptive cycle heuristic provides a fundamental unit of study that contributes to the understanding of the dynamics of complex systems.

The evaluation of a system's resilience is its performance in the release stage of the cycle, as it is here that the capacity for a system to survive an extreme disturbance (such as the impact of the Covid-19 pandemic on the functions of the university) is tested. A system must maintain vital functions throughout the crisis if it is to survive. In universities, it is often up to leadership, both assigned and assumed, to identify and prioritize what that means (Fath et al., 2015). It is evident that during the Covid-19 crisis many of the vital teaching functions of universities have been maintained even if there have been several emergency measures put into place (Watermeyer et al., 2021) that have

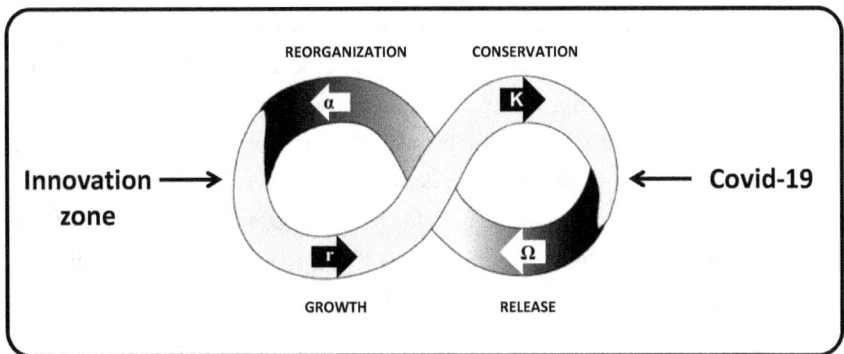

Figure 12.1 The adaptive cycle (redrawn and modified from Holling, 2001).

impacted greatly upon the teaching practices and well-being of those involved (Jandrić et al., 2020). But in the extraordinary context of the pandemic many teachers may have been forced to make decisions that were inconsistent with their espoused beliefs about teaching and learning (Sansom, 2020). In the short term we are all likely to have to endure periods of tension where we have to make compromises with available resources. However, in the long term this is not sustainable and is damaging to the well-being of those in the institution. Management teams need to plan ahead so that university pedagogy emerges from the pandemic in a new, improved and more sustainable form (Sandri, 2020) that will be ready for the next disturbance to the system – that has already been predicted (Morens and Fauci, 2020). This will require a refocusing on people (and leadership) rather than commodities (and managerialism) as discussed by Shankar et al. (2021). In short, 'It is a time for academic leaders courageous enough to disrupt longstanding patterns of behaviour, to challenge opinions and organizational norms, and disrupt the status quo' (Fernandez and Shaw, 2020, p. 41).

The university-as-ecosystem represents an assemblage of closely entangled concepts that need to be considered together in the context of ecological leadership to appreciate the wider standpoint of the ecosystemic perspective. The ecosystem functions as a unit of analysis and cannot be divided arbitrarily to focus on one element or other in isolation. However, within that unit there are contributing concepts that need to be considered – chief among these are sustainability, care and resilience.

Sustainability

The concept of sustainability leadership challenges traditional assumptions – for example, that a respected leader (or top management team) fulfils a designated role, stands somewhat above the people, and knows and determines the best course of action. In contrast, sustainability leadership does not require designation of a specialist role that sets the individual apart from other members of the community. Sustainability leadership is understood to be concerned with creating current and future benefits while improving the lives of those concerned. According to Leal Filho et al. (2020), it is based on the following assumptions:

1. Sustainability problems are complicated or even 'wicked'. That is, they are related to phenomena that cannot be reduced to easily manageable parts

or separated and isolated from the wider ecology of the institution. Blok et al. (2016) argue that:

> Wicked problems are highly complex because they concern global issues like climate change, desertification and poverty, and cannot be solved in traditional ways or by simple solutions; the complexity of sustainability consists in the fact that cause and effect relations are either unknown or uncertain, and that multiple stakeholders are involved with differing ideas about what the 'real' problem is and often having conflicting norms, value frames and beliefs regarding the subject. (p. 5)

Hence, purely rational and mechanistic approaches to problem-solving in this arena are expected to fail (Thomas, 2020).

2. Anyone can take responsibility to foster more sustainable conditions in university communities – anyone can become a leader. Leadership does not always have to be associated with positions of management, and indeed it is evident that many of the leaders within an institution do not necessarily sit at the top table, but rather influence practice from the middle.
3. The role of a leader involves co-generation and learning, instead of being a leader over, and of, other people. This requires the leader to see themselves as part of the system, and not operating externally to it. This co-generation requires an understanding of the terrain and so raises questions about whether the expertise required to manage is the same as the expertise required to lead (Kenedi and Mountford-Zimdars, 2018). The 'co-learning' element also implies an underpinning philosophy of *becoming* where leaders and leadership develops out of the network of connections rather than an external force that can be applied to the network. This is contrary to the notion of the 'hero' leader who holds all the answers once a problem has been identified.

In the pursuit of sustainability leadership it may be helpful to adopt a deeper shared understanding of sustainability that moves beyond the practical activities that we are all encouraged to undertake to reduce consumption. We need to have more nuanced ways of thinking about sustainability that embrace complexity and plurality. Loring (2020) has proposed five threshold concepts to help in our departure from industrial and neoliberal paradigms that have so far failed to address sustainability leadership in any meaningful way. These concepts are summarized in Table 12.1, and provide a guiding framework for the consideration of sustainability as it relates to leadership.

Table 12.1 Threshold Concepts in Leadership for Sustainability That Have Consequences for Leadership Roles (Modified from Loring, 2020)

Threshold Concept	Replaces	Summary
Complexity	An 'industrial model' of simple, mechanistic understandings of causality in which analysis is of isolated fragments – losing sight of the wider system	An 'ecological model' of the world as a collection of indivisible systems in which outcomes are greater than the sum of the parts
Collaboration	Atomistic, flawed understanding of human nature	People are collaborative (social) by nature and can develop shared systems of behaviour
Epistemological pluralism (different ways of knowing)	Positivism: A single, external reality that is knowable only through the scientific method	Multiple realities that are knowable through simultaneously valuable knowledge systems – post-abyssal thinking
No panaceas	Technological fixes exist that are scalable and widely deployable by applying a rigorous evidence base	Solutions to wicked problems must fit with local cultures and indigenous knowledges
Adaptability	Sustainability is a matter of seeking and managing for stability and equilibrium, where 'being expert' is an end state	Sustainability is a process of managing change and uncertainty in a state of non-equilibrium, recognizing the illusion of stability, and 'becoming' as an end state

Care

Closely related to the problems presented by sustainability are those that come from a consideration of the 'ethics of care' (Nicholson and Kurucz, 2019). Care has been explored extensively as an element of the discourse of higher education (Clouder, 2005; Noddings, 2012), and has recently taken a posthuman turn (Bozalek, Zembylas and Tronto, 2021) to focus 'specifically on how care ethics and posthuman ethics may be put into conversation with each other, and how these approaches might be used in higher education pedagogies' (p. 9). I will not review that literature here. Suffice to say that authors are starting to recognize the need to consider care and leadership as two interdependent facets of university life, where care for human and natural capital needs recognition as being at least as important as care for financial capital. Only then will sustainability and resilience have meaning that allows them to play a positive role within the university ecosystem. Nicholson and Kurucz (2019) propose that we should replace the fundamental assumption about effective leadership as an individual pursuit with the relational assumption of growth-in-connection, and in so doing take the 'heroic' leader that has dominated Western culture out of leadership (Clifton, 2017) to facilitate a more effective approach to leadership for sustainability. In so doing leadership may also adopt a more care-full stance to counter the narrative of care-less that is seen by some to permeate higher education (Lynch, 2010).

Resilience

With reference to the SARS crisis of 2003, which now has increased global resonance after the Covid-19 crisis of 2020–1, Teo et al. (2017) considered how leaders help to activate organizational resilience by exploiting relational resources (see Table 12.2). Their Relational Activation of Resilience (RAR) model is premised on three key pillars:

1. Organizations function as networked structures. This overlaps with ecological thinking that emphasizes links and connections (Guattari, 2014).
2. Leaders act as embedded actors with social influence within these networks. This overlaps with the idea of distributed leadership (Spillane, 2005).
3. Resilience is a process of developing relational networks (Branson and Marra, 2019) that allow the organization to adapt and restore function. The term 'restore' does not necessarily mean that things will go back to the way they were before the crisis. Essential functions may be restored under improved arrangements and employ novel process so that rather than 'bouncing back', the organization can 'bounce forward' to a new way of working.

One of the basic tasks of leaders in a crisis is to recognize early signs of that crisis, identify that a threshold has been crossed and usher in a new phase of

Table 12.2 Summary of the Themes and Subthemes Relating to How Healthcare Leaders Developed Organizational Resilience during the SARS Crisis in Singapore in 2003 (after Teo et al., 2017)

Theme	Description
1. Ushering liminality	A different modus operandi
Restructuring	New hierarchies and relational structures
New ways of doing things	New work procedures, work reassignments
2. Forming relational connections	Forming social connections during crisis
Those with a shared history	Personal knowledge leads to mutual trust
With new partners	Reliant on swift trust and mutual respect
3. Making meaning and sense out of the crisis	Actively managing overall narratives and communication updates to help staff make meaning and sense of the situation
Trusted relationships to make sense of things	Trusted individuals help collective sense-making
Influencing sense-making of others	Creating sense of order, control in the chaos to give confidence
4. Mindful communication to activate positive emotions	Noticing, feeling empathy and reaching out to staff

organizational development, where new routines and structural patterns need to be acquired (Teo et al., 2017). Or in other words, to identify the entry to the α-phase (reorganization) of the adaptive cycle (Figure 12.1). The activation of the RAR model requires a deep and constant engagement between individuals, and this cannot be established reactively when a crisis strikes (Longstaff and Yang, 2008). The existence of a healthy diversity of narrative structures (*sensu* Gabriel, 2016) may, therefore, be a prerequisite for effective implementation of the RAR model within the university context.

The consideration of resilience in a manner that will not be counterproductive requires leaders within an institution to have a clear image of what they mean by resilience – crucially, whether we are talking about 'ecological resilience' or 'engineering resilience' (Holling, 1996). Holling describes engineering resilience as being focused on characteristics such as efficiency, control, constancy and predictability – to promote 'sameness'. This is a feature of linear university managerialism, where the idea of sameness has been confused with issues of quality and professional standards. In contrast, ecological resilience is seen as focusing on persistence, adaptiveness, variability and unpredictability – to promote difference and complexity. These are characteristics of communities that thrive in an unpredictable environment. In the context of engineering resilience, managerial interventions are likely to attempt to damp down fluctuations in the system to try to maintain a steady state – an illusion that results from selective inattention to inconvenient data (Schön, 1971). This type of resilience can be seen as the 'enemy of adaptive change' (Holling and Gunderson, 2002, p. 32) and will actually inhibit ecological resilience. If different communities within the university ecosystem are using the same terminology (i.e. resilience), but this represents different concepts (i.e. engineering resilience or ecosystem resilience), then the conditions are set for the development of pedagogic frailty (Kinchin and Winstone, 2017), where tensions in the system impede the evolution of teaching. The ecological university needs to embrace ecological resilience in order to maintain some consistency in thinking and to promote the diversity of ideas that is required to overcome disturbances in the system. It should also be evident that the concept of ecological resilience is not synonymous with ideas such as individual 'grit' or 'tenacity' (Tewell, 2020). Ecological resilience is a characteristic of the system rather than of individuals, and as such cannot be 'fixed' with snappy workshops or online tutorials for individuals to complete – to 'enhance your resilience'.

From Network to Ecosystem

There may be a tendency (at least an aspiration) to move away from linear, command-and-control models of leadership (Figure 12.2A), that may appear to be more aligned to the manufacturing industries of the nineteenth-century rather than the twenty-first-century university, in which the underpinning philosophy may be perceived as 'divide and conquer'. This is displaced by a move towards more networked structures (Figure 12.2B) that are seen as a way of sharing responsibility across the institution while bringing the team closer together. However, the complaint among colleagues working within a networked set-up is often that they have responsibility without power. This is because the direction of the network is towards preordained goals using preferred processes of operations that are determined by centrally decided network management (Kinder et al., 2021). In contrast, ecosystems (Figure 12.2C) operate without central direction, even if a multiplicity of agents take a leading role for a certain time, after which roles may change as the context evolves. The self-organizing principles that govern ecosystem maintenance appear to be at odds with the idea

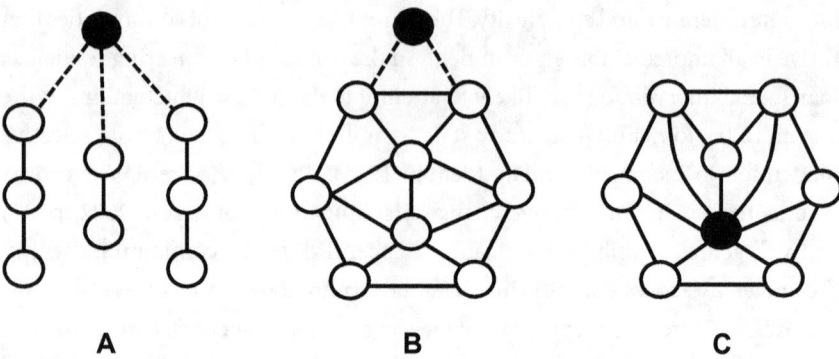

Figure 12.2 The relationship between leaders (●) and team members (○), conceptualized as linear (A), networked (B) and ecosystemic (C) arrangements. In some instances, the 'leader' is only partially integrated into the team, separated by managerial duties (dotted lines). This figure could be developed to indicate where leadership is distributed across the team by using an additional symbol to represent team members with leadership responsibilities (e.g.⊙). This has not been included here to maintain simplicity of the figure.

of leadership to direct the development of a team in a particular direction. As explained by Branson (2010, p. 98):

> In self-organising systems, order comes from the actions of interdependent agents who exchange information, take actions and continuously adapt to feedback about others' actions rather than from the imposition of an overall plan by a central authority. Thus, complex systems are characterised as non-linear because the components that comprise them are constantly interacting with each other through a web of feedback loops.

Kinder et al. (2021) describe how moving from a network to an ecosystem involves ideational leaders (not necessarily occupying formal management positions) leading by building an overall collective consciousness, by creating and encouraging relationships founded on learning from the logic of practice. This is informed by feedback, to help to synthesize a team discourse. Leaders provide potential conceptual frameworks for sense-making and new ideas legitimating new practices, reinforcing or altering collective consciousness. Only where high degrees of trust and empathy prevail are ideational leaders' ideas distributed.

Within ecosystems, roles will vary continuously (Branson and Marra, 2019) – unlike the traditional hierarchical structure where an individual's role may seem fixed at a certain point of the ladder (see Figure 12.2A). In addition, whereas the network strives for stability, the ecosystem is explicit in never reaching equilibrium – continually exploring diversity and difference. This is synonymous with the philosophy of becoming described by Deleuze and Guattari (1987), in which *becoming*, rather than *being*, is the final state. That is, it is a move from *rigidity* to *fluidity*. In distinguishing between being and becoming, Trifone (2019, p. 11) suggests that 'a state of being is static and unchanging, like a stagnant puddle; a state of becoming is dynamic and changing, like water flowing down a river toward an unknown point downstream'. For the benefits of an underpinning philosophy of becoming to be accrued by a team, it is important that it is shared (implicitly or explicitly) as the tension created by conflicting philosophies (being vs. becoming) is likely to promote pedagogic frailty (Kinchin and Gravett, 2022).

This ecosystemic view of becoming has been a foundational philosophy, underpinning my approach to leadership with my own academic team. I was the head of department for several years but have now relinquished the administrative and managerial demands of that role, so that I am now able to concentrate more on my continuing role as an academic leader. Providing a conceptual framework to encourage sense-making and the development of new ideas (*sensu* Kinder et al., 2021) has been a central element of my leadership approach to support my team members' professional development. To this end, we have coauthored a number of research papers that have drawn overtly on the empathy and trust within the team (Gravett et al., 2020; Kinchin et al., 2018, 2023), actively exploring the affective dimension of our shared development as well as the cognitive. That is not to say that this is 'the correct' or 'only' way to proceed, but it provides an approach for others to consider which accommodates key concepts to promote sustainable (Leal Filho et al., 2020) or ecological (Allen et al., 1999) leadership, that can promote an ethics of care (Nicholson and Kurucz, 2019), and can be seen to relate to the elements of organizational resilience given in Table 12.2, in terms of developing trust and mutual respect in a process of collective sense-making.

The collective consciousness (mentioned above) that I have tried to encourage within my department has been driven by a 'narrative buzz' within the team, where ideas are shared freely and frequently and are positively critiqued with interest and enthusiasm. Gabriel (2016) has argued that grand narratives and counter-narratives can be thought of as co-constructing elements of narrative ecologies and has proposed different types of narrative ecology that foster different narrative patterns (Figure 12.3). Within Gabriel's typology, the pattern within my own department may be viewed as a 'narrative garden' where, people grow their private narratives, carefully protecting them from hegemonic counter-claims and counter-narratives, and promoting harmonious relations between people, where individual stories and experiences are treated with great interest and respect (Gabriel, 2016). This exists within the wider neoliberal

Narrative type	Icon	Narrative characteristics	Institutional characteristics
Narrative temperate regions		Diversity, versatility and tolerance	Culturally and functionally diverse, complex and pluralistic
Narrative deserts		Few narratives	Traumatized
Narrative mono-cultures		Dominated by hegemonic narratives	Totalitarian
Narrative mountains		Devoid of passion and energy	Focus on doing business at the expense of developing community
Narrative marshlands		Heavy, 'wet' narratives	Exclusive communities of practice
Narrative jungles		Change, stress and uncertainty	Extreme anxiety promoting nostalgia
Narrative gardens		Private and protected	Harmonious sanctuaries of respect

Figure 12.3 A typology of narratives (based on Gabriel, 2016).

narrative monoculture which can obliterate other voices and demonize competing narratives. In such an impoverished environment, elements of the managerial monocultural narrative can be subject to 'sacralization' (Sabri, 2011) or 'fetishization' (Moore et al., 2017). Within Gabriel's typology, we also need to be aware that the constraints imposed by the emergency online migration of academic activities during the Covid-19 pandemic had the potential to degrade the richness of our narrative garden, tending towards a context described by Gabriel as a 'narrative mountain' that exhibits a pathology, of which the symptoms are anaemic narratives, stripped of passion and energy. This is because the limitations of online meetings result in a tendency to focus on doing business together rather than fostering any kind of community. Zoom meetings simply cannot replace those chance conversations by the water cooler.

Additionally, I see one of the roles of an academic leader is to support academics in developing a voice within the community, both internally (within my own institution) and externally (on the national or international stage). Within our ecological context, the multiplicity of voices can be shared (Lygo-Baker et al., 2019), as authorship is shared, where 'sharing authorship requires the sharing of much more than ownership. It also requires a shared perspective on the part of university-based teachers and researchers on how classroom-based teachers and researchers experience their work' (Smagorinsky et al., 2006, p. 100). This sharing does not require homogeneity in our perspective as our voices can express diversity within our narrative ecology (often driven by differences in our disciplinary heritage) that are underpinned by a shared set of professional values (Kinchin et al., 2018). Indeed, such difference (= diversity) is essential in a healthy ecosystem, where exploration of contested spaces can challenge monocultures of thought. Unless these contested spaces are given space to breathe, we are likely to reduce ecological resilience to external disturbances by reducing the range of resources that can be drawn upon to deal with a new threat.

Conclusion

In this chapter I have proposed a re-conceptualization of 'the leader' as a 'narrative ecologist', helping colleagues to navigate the patchwork of often contradictory narratives within the university. In particular, colleagues need support to survive the hegemonic, neoliberal narrative monoculture by identifying the liveable cracks in the system (described by Manathunga and Bottrell, 2019). This needs to be juggled with the need to provide space for the cultivation of 'narrative gardens' where counter-narratives can be nurtured (Gabriel, 2016). The relative status of the various narratives within the patchwork will vary as the university ecosystem navigates the adaptive cycle (Figure 12.1). During times of disruption, some narratives will be abruptly replaced by others, especially during the release (Ω) phase of the cycle, where the narrative monoculture may give way (if only temporarily) to a narrative jungle. As the ecosystem moves back towards the conservation phase (K), a new configuration of the narrative ecology will emerge. An appreciation of the adaptive cycle and the associated narrative ecology provides a framework against which leaders can evaluate their roles within the complexity of the university ecosystem and help their team members thrive. This needs to be viewed as a continuous process of becoming, where there will be no endpoint for leadership development, and no stable endpoint for the development of the ecosystem in which we work. The ecological leader needs to accept, and thrive in, an environment where change and dynamism are the normal condition.

References

Allen, K. E., Stelzner, S. P. and Wielkiewicz, R. M. (1999), 'The ecology of leadership: Adapting to the challenges of a changing world', *Journal of Leadership Studies* 5 (2): 62–82.

Barnett, R. (2017), *The Ecological University: A Feasible Utopia*, London: Routledge.

Bennis, W. G., and Nanus, B. (1985), *Leaders: The Strategies for Taking Charge*, New York: Harper & Row.

Blok, V., Gremmen, B. and Wesselink, R. (2016), 'Dealing with the wicked problem of sustainability', *Business and Professional Ethics Journal* 34 (3): 297–327. https://doi.org/10.5840/bpej201621737.

Bozalek, V., Zembylas, M. and Tronto, J. C. (2021), *Posthuman and Political Care Ethics for Reconfiguring Higher Education Pedagogies*, London: Routledge.

Branson, C. M. (2010), 'Free to become: The essence of learning and leading', in A. H. Normore (ed.), *Global Perspectives on Educational Leadership Reform: The Development and Preparation of Leaders of Learning and Learners of Leadership*, 85–104, Bingley, UK: Emerald.

Branson, C. M., and Marra, M. (2019), 'Leadership as a relational phenomenon: What this means in practice', *Research in Educational Administration & Leadership* 4 (1): 81–106.

Capra, F., and Luisi, L. (2014), *The Systems View of Life: A Unifying Vision*, Cambridge: Cambridge University Press.

Clifton, J. (2017), 'Taking the (heroic) leader out of leadership: The *in situ* practice of distributed leadership in decision-making talk', in C. Ilie and S. Schnurr, S. (eds), *Challenging Leadership Stereotypes through Discourse: Power, Management and Gender*, 45–68, Singapore: Springer.

Clouder, L. (2005), 'Caring as a "threshold concept": Transforming students in higher education into health (care) professionals', *Teaching in Higher Education* 10 (4): 505–17.

Deleuze, G., and Guattari, F. (1987), *A Thousand Plateaus*, trans. B. Massumi, London: Bloomsbury.

Fath, B. D., Dean, C. A., and Katzmair, H. (2015), 'Navigating the adaptive cycle: An approach to managing the resilience of social systems', *Ecology and Society* 20 (2): 24.

Fernandez, A. A., and Shaw, G. P. (2020), 'Academic leadership in a time of crisis: The coronavirus and Covid-19', *Journal of Leadership Studies* 14 (1): 39–45.

Gabriel, Y. (2016), 'Narrative ecologies and the role of counter-narratives: The case of nostalgic stories and conspiracy theories', in S. Frandsen, T. Kuhn and M. W. Lundholt (eds), *Counter-narratives and Organization*, 208–26, London: Routledge.

Gravett, K., Kinchin, I. M., Winstone, N. E., Balloo, K., Heron, M., Hosein, A., Lygo-Baker, S. and Medland, E. (2020), 'The development of academics' feedback literacy: Experiences of learning from critical feedback via scholarly peer review', *Assessment and Evaluation in Higher Education* 45 (5): 651–65.

Guattari, F. (2014), *The Three Ecologies*, trans. I. Pindar and P. Sutton, London: Bloomsbury.

Gumus, S., Bellibas, M. S., Esen, M. and Gumus, E. (2018), 'A systematic review of studies on leadership models in educational research from 1980–2014', *Educational Management Administration & Leadership* 46 (1): 25–48.

Haddock-Fraser, J., Rands, P., and Scoffham, S. (2018), *Leadership for Sustainability in Higher Education*, London: Bloomsbury.

Holling, C. S. (1996), 'Engineering resilience vs. ecological resilience', in P. C. Schultze (ed.), *Engineering within Ecological Constraints*, 31-43, Washington, DC: National Academy Press.

Holling, C. S. (2001), 'Understanding the complexity of economic, ecological, and social systems', *Ecosystems* 4: 39–405.

Holling, C. S., and Gunderson, L. H. (2002), 'Resilience and adaptive cycles', in L. H. Gunderson and C. S. Holling (eds), *Panarchy: Understanding Transformation in Human and Natural Systems*, 25-62, Washington, DC: Island Press.

Jameson, J. (2018), 'Critical corridor talk: Just gossip or stoic resistance? Unrecognised informal higher education leadership', *Higher Education Quarterly* 72: 375-89.

Jandrić, P., Hayes, D., Truelove, I., et al. (2020), 'Teaching in the age of Covid-19', *Postdigital Science and Education* 2 (3): 1069-230.

Kenedi, G., and Mountford-Zimdars, A. (2018), 'Does educational expertise matter for PVCs education? A UK study of PVCs' educational background and skills', *Journal of Higher Education Policy and Management* 40 (3): 193-207.

Kinchin, I. M., Balloo, K., Barnett, L., Gravett, K., Heron, M., Hosein, A.,Lygo-Baker, S., Medland, E., Winstone, N. E. and Yakovchuk, N. (2023), 'Poems and pedagogic frailty: Uncovering the affective within academic development through arts-based collective biography', *Arts & Humanities in Higher Education*, in press. Doi: 10.1177/14740222222114782.

Kinchin, I. M., and Gravett, K. (2022), *Dominant Discourses in Higher Education: Critical Perspectives, Cartographies and Practice*, London: Bloomsbury.

Kinchin, I. M., Heron, M., Hosein, A., Lygo-Baker, S., Medland, E., Morley, D. and Winstone, N. E. (2018), 'Researcher-led academic development', *International Journal for Academic Development* 23 (4), 339-54.

Kinchin, I. M., and Winstone, N. E. (eds) (2017), *Pedagogic Frailty and Resilience in the University*, Rotterdam: Sense.

Kinder, T., Stenvall, J., Six, F. and Memon, A. (2021), 'Relational leadership in collaborative governance ecosystems', *Public Management Review* 23 (11): 1612-39. https://doi.org/10.1080/14719037.2021.1879913.

Kotter, J. P. (2008), *Force for Change: How Leadership Differs from Management*, New York: Simon and Schuster.

Leal Filho, W., Eustachio, J. H. P. P., Caldana, A .C. F., Will, M., Salvia, A. L., Rampasso, I. S., Anholon, R., Platje, J. and Kovaleva, M. (2020), 'Sustainability leadership in higher education institutions: An overview of challenges', *Sustainability* 12: 3671.

Longstaff, P. H., and Yang, S. U. (2008), 'Communication management and trust: Their role in building resilience to "surprises" such as natural disasters, pandemic flu, and terrorism', *Ecology and Society* 13 (1): 3.

Loring, P. A. (2020), 'Threshold concepts and sustainability: Features of a contested paradigm', *Facets* 5: 182-99.

Lygo-Baker, S., Kinchin, I. M. and Winstone, N. E. (eds) (2019), *Engaging Student Voices in Higher Education: Diverse Perspectives and Expectations in Partnership*, Cham: Palgrave Macmillan.

Lynch, K. (2010), 'Carelessness: A Hidden Doxa of Higher Education', *Art & Humanities in Higher Education* 9 (1): 54–67.

Manathunga, C., and Bottrell, D. (eds) (2019), *Resisting Neoliberalism in Higher Education Volume 2: Prising Open the Cracks*, Cham: Palgrave Macmillan.

Moore, S., Neylon, C., Eve, M. P., O'Donnell, D. P. and Pattinson, D. (2017), '"Excellence R Us": University research and the fetishisation of excellence', *Palgrave Communications* 3 (1): 1–13.

Morens, D. M., and Fauci, A. S. (2020), 'Emerging pandemic diseases: How we got to COVID-19', *Cell* 182 (5): 1077–92.

Nicholson, J., and Kurucz, E. (2019), 'Relational leadership for sustainability: Building an ethical framework from the moral theory of "ethics of care"', *Journal of Business Ethics* 156 (1): 25–43.

Noddings, N. (2012), 'The caring relation in teaching', *Oxford Review of Education* 38 (6): 771–81.

Sabri, D. (2011), 'What's wrong with "the student experience"?', *Discourse: Studies in the Cultural Politics of Education* 32 (5): 657–67.

Sandri, O. (2020), 'What do we mean by "pedagogy" in sustainability education?', *Teaching in Higher Education*. https://doi.org/10.1080/13562517.2019.1699528.

Sansom, R. L. (2020), 'Pressure from the pandemic: Pedagogical dissatisfaction reveals faculty beliefs', *Journal of Chemical Education* 97: 2378–82.

Schön, D. A. (1971), *Beyond the Stable State: Public and Private Learning in a Changing Society*, London, Temple Smith.

Shankar, K., Phelan, D., Suri, V. R., Watermeyer, R., Knight, C. and Crick, T. (2021), '"The COVID-19 crisis is not the core problem": Experiences, challenges, and concerns of Irish academia during the pandemic', *Irish Educational Studies* 40 (2), 169–75. https://doi.org/10.1080/03323315.2021.1932550.

Smagorinsky, P., Augustine, S. M., and Gallas, K. (2006), 'Rethinking rhizomes in writing about research', *Teacher Educator* 42 (2): 87–105.

Spillane, J. P. (2005), 'Distributed leadership', *Educational Forum* 69 (2): 143–50.

Teo, W. L., Lee, M., and Lim, W.-S. (2017), 'The relational activation of resilience model: How leadership activates resilience in an organizational crisis', *Journal of Contingencies and Crisis Management* 25: 136–47.

Tewell, E. (2020), 'The problem with grit: Dismantling deficit thinking in library instruction', *Portal: Libraries and the Academy* 20 (1): 137–59.

Thomas, G. (2020), 'Experiment's persistent failure in education inquiry, and why it keeps failing', *British Educational Research Journal* 47 (3): 501–19. https://doi.org/10.1002/berj.3660.

Trifone, J. D. (2019), *From Being to Becoming: Living an Authentic and Meaningful Life*, Bethany, CT: Graduate Institute/James Trifone Books.

Watermeyer, R., Crick, T., Knight, C. and Goodall, J. (2021), 'COVID-19 and Digital Disruption in UK Universities: Afflictions and Affordances of Emergency Online Migration', *Higher Education* 81 (3): 623–41.

Index

academic career(s) 34, 150, 154, 155, 159, 164
academic identity; xii, 86, 92, 125
adaptive cycle 10, 199, 204, 209

barrier(s), 38, 92, 118, 126, 135, 140

career planning 160
collaboration(s) ix, xiii, 10, 25, 27, 58–9, 60–1, 133–6, 139–41, 151, 159, 163, 166–74, 202
colonization 2–4, 172
community x, xv, xvi, 9, 20–1, 24, 28, 51, 54, 102, 107, 108, 113, 117, 119–24, 134, 151, 163, 169–71, 181–91, 198–200, 208
contested identity/identities 2, 11
contested spaces 1, 2, 6–10, 18–20, 168
COVID-19 xv, 8, 35, 40–1, 44, 61–2, 69, 74–5, 82, 89–92, 100, 124, 132, 137, 140, 174, 199, 203, 208
critical pedagogy 21, 29
culture xi, xv–xvi, 9–10, 22, 43, 50–1, 54–9, 66–74, 91, 105, 114, 118–19, 123, 133, 135, 138, 141, 163, 169, 174, 179, 180–92, 202, 203
culture change xvi, 10, 183, 190

distributed leadership xi, xvi, 10, 68, 164, 166–74, 197, 203
diversity and inclusivity/inclusion x, 8, 22, 27–8

early career academic(s) xv, 2, 8, 9, 54, 81, 133
educational developer/development x, xi, xii, xiv, 7, 18–19, 33–44, 53, 102, 114–16, 119–25
equity xi, xiv, 7, 18–22, 27–30, 69, 71, 75
ethnicity and race 2, 6, 17–30

Finland xi, xiii, xiv, 5, 7–8, 49–58, 62

gender and gendered spaces, xiv, 2–4, 6, 11, 17, 19, 26, 38–43, 122, 130, 135–6

joy xv–xvi, 9, 115–18, 122, 124–5

leadership
  academic leadership xiii–xv, 2, 9, 10, 44, 81, 92, 95–6, 100, 102, 105, 149, 179–80, 184–8, 190, 200, 207
  ecological leadership xvi, 10, 11, 198, 200, 207
  leadership journey(s), xvi, 2, 6, 11, 106, 142, 179–80, 184,
  leadship ecosystem 10, 171–4
  luck 6, 56, 160
  participative leadership xv, 9, 81–82, 84–9
  pathways to leadership 10, 148
  playful leadership xii, 7, 40–3
  programme leader/leadership xv, 5, 9, 95–108, 133, 137
Lewin's model of change 66–7, 70, 130
liminality xvi, 10, 180, 184–6, 191, 204

marginalized and marginalization xiv, 1–3, 7, 11, 19, 21–2, 24–5
mentors and mentoring xv, 9, 37, 40, 43, 50, 76, 86, 102–3, 107, 113–14, 119, 129–30, 133, 137–8, 140–3, 181, 187, 190

New Zealand ix, xiii

pedagogical training 50–9

resilience xiii, xv, xvi, 7, 8, 10, 104, 131, 164, 166, 172, 199, 203–9
reward system 183, 187–91

serendipity xv–xvi, 6–7, 10, 164, 166, 172–4
sustainability ix, 10, 68, 170, 198–203

third space, xiv 7, 40–4, 180, 186

threshold concepts 185, 201–4

university teachers xi, 50–1, 56, 62

white privilege 3–4, 22, 24

www.ingramcontent.com/pod-product-compliance
Lightning Source LLC
Chambersburg PA
CBHW071834300426
44116CB00009B/1542